FIRE ALONG
THE FRONTIER

FIRE ALONG THE FRONTIER

GREAT BATTLES OF THE WAR OF 1812

ALASTAIR SWEENY

DUNDURN
TORONTO

Editor: Allister Thompson
Design: Jesse Hooper
Printer: Webcom

Library and Archives Canada Cataloguing in Publication

Sweeny, Alastair
    Fire along the frontier : great battles of the War of 1812 / Alastair Sweeny.

Includes index.
Issued also in electronic formats.
ISBN 978-1-4597-0433-6

    1. Canada--History--War of 1812--Economic aspects. 2. Canada--History--War of 1812--Social aspects. 3. Canada--History--War of 1812--Campaigns. 4. United States--History--War of 1812--Economic aspects. 5. United States--History--War of 1812--Social aspects. 6. United States--History--War of 1812--Campaigns. I. Title.

FC442.S95 2012   971.03'4   C2012-900085-X

1   2   3   4   5   16   15   14   13   12

We acknowledge the support of the **Canada Council for the Arts** and the **Ontario Arts Council** for our publishing program. We also acknowledge the financial support of the **Government of Canada** through the **Canada Book Fund** and **Livres Canada Books**, and the **Government of Ontario** through the **Ontario Book Publishing Tax Credit** and the **Ontario Media Development Corporation**.

Printed and bound in Canada.
www.dundurn.com

Dundurn	Gazelle Book Services Limited	Dundurn
3 Church Street, Suite 500	White Cross Mills	2250 Military Road
Toronto, Ontario, Canada	High Town, Lancaster, England	Tonawanda, NY
M5E 1M2	LA1 4XS	U.S.A. 14150

CONTENTS

ACKNOWLEDGEMENTS 7

INTRODUCTION 9

ONE: MISTER JEFFERSON'S WAR 27
    Unfinished Business, 1783–1798 29
    The Louisiana Purchase 42
    Madison Takes Command 48
    The View from Canada 54
    John Jacob Astor 60
    Isaac Brock 65
    Declaration 70

TWO: 1812 77
    War Plans 79
    Isaac Brock Takes Charge 84
    Detroit 88
    Queenston Heights 96
    Old Ironsides 105

THREE: 1813 111
    Battles in the Wilderness 113
    The Taking of York 119
    Paying for the War 126
    Attack on Sackets Harbor 131
    Stoney Creek and Beaver Dams 137
    Fire on Lake Erie 142
    Battle at the Thames 148
    Chateauguay and Crysler's Farm 153
    By Fire and Sword 169

Four: 1814 177
   The Empire Strikes Back 179
   Stalemate at Lundy's Lane 184
   The Battle of Washington 200
   Lake Champlain 217
   Ghent 223

Five: Birth of Two Nations 233
   New Orleans 235
   Waterloo and War Weariness 245
   Twin Destinies 248

Notes 257
Index 265

ACKNOWLEDGEMENTS

Fire Along the Frontier IS TO SOME EXTENT AN OUTSIDER'S VIEW OF the war, because there is an immense body of 1812 experts, from battle-field site programmers to professors to reenactor groups to private scholars, all intimately in tune with this war and its particular fascinations.

I have tried to take a somewhat different, at times radical, tack in my book, concentrating on the business of war, the campaigns and battles, and the lessons to be learned from them, and particularly why the Jeffersonians thought they could get away with armed robbery on an international scale against Britain's crack regulars and thousand-ship navy.

I have tried to build on the scholarly foundations of War of 1812 experts like Donald Graves, Michael Gnarowski, Wesley Turner, Rene Chartrand, Robert Henderson and many others, including some reenactment groups and living history experts. And in the U.S., scholars like J. Langguth and Donald Hickey have done fine work, and I am in their debt.

Reading their works, I sometimes feel like an outsider peeking through a lace curtain into a regency drawing room, or a crack in the logs of a barracks wall. Reading them is sometimes like taking a trip in a time machine.

Any mistakes in this book are my own, but I have added a corrigendum on the support website, and astute or cranky readers can contact me there with criticisms, comments, and suggestions.

Above all I would like to thank the capable publishing people at Dundurn Press for adding this book to their 1812 oeuvre, of almost forty books on the war. From Kirk Howard and Beth Bruder, to Margaret Bryant and Shannon Whibbs, to my editor Allister Thompson, designer Jesse Hooper, and the editorial and marketing crew, thanks guys.

April 2012

INTRODUCTION

A Window on the War

I have always been struck by the richness of the War of 1812. Like most fans of this conflict, I regard it as a fascinating parade of human glory and folly, with elements of sheer terror and shameful stupidity.

I also have some personal interest in the War. I have done research for Parks Canada on the Rifle Brigade at Fort Wellington, one of the British outposts on the St. Lawrence during the war, and wrote a biography of George-Étienne Cartier, Canada's first Minister of Militia, whose uncle served with de Salaberry. I recently discovered that one of my ancestors, George Keefer of Thorold, joined the 2nd Regiment of Lincoln Militia in 1812. In 1813, the Americans commandeered his house as a hospital and his wife died of army fever, probably typhus. His sixteen-year-old daughter, Elizabeth, performed nursing chores for the invaders (one of whom later returned to marry her). Keefer rose to the rank of captain early in 1814 and fought at Chippawa and Lundy's Lane. Another ancestor, a captain in the 62nd Foot, fought with his brothers and cousins alongside Wellington. According to the Army Lists, one of them, poor bastard, served as a surgeon at the Battle of New Orleans.

So, like many North Americans, my ancestors had a personal interest in the outcome of this conflict.

With the 200th Anniversary of the War of 1812, we Canadians and Americans have a thousand-day window to study and debate and understand this event that set such a pattern for our national characters, and I hope this book adds insight for the interested and fuel to the debate.

I have also set up an extensive book support site on the Web at *www. alastairsweeny.com/1812*. This portal contains chapter galleries and linked footnotes, but also a wide-ranging resource set for the public and for students of the war. In the endnotes or text of this book, where you see the symbol <*>, it indicates that a more extensive note exists on the site to provide further reading.

The images in this book can also be found on the site, along with many more that could not be included here. Image credits and sources are also on the site, where possible.

Twisting History

A little nostalgia. When I was in my early teens, my grade eight teacher, Mister Peace, packed the class into a big yellow school bus, and we rolled off on a tour of War of 1812 battlegrounds and historic sites of the Niagara Peninsula (the Canadian side of the river only). It was a spectacular May day, and I remember how we strolled through Niagara-on-the-Lake, put our hands over our ears as a big black cannon boomed at Fort George, and climbed all the way up to the top of Brock's monument at Queenston Heights. The town's houses and shops were elegant, the fort had a spiffy coat of grey paint, the gardens were well trimmed, the green lawns immaculate, and the view was out of this world.

Back on the bus, someone had a transistor radio, and on the way home we sang along to a great pop song called "The Battle of New Orleans," with Johnny Horton's raucous voice crowing about beating the bloody British in the town of New Orleans.[1]

When I was a decade older, I learned a bit more about the sights we saw that day:

- On a cold November morning in 1812, hundreds of terrified American militiamen piled into boats and crossed to Queenston under heavy fire. Some climbed a slippery path to the heights, where one young sharpshooter killed the British general himself. They were soon attacked by Mohawks and British regulars, and in their panicked retreat, many of them slid off the cliff and fell to their deaths.

- On May 25, 1813, Fort George was hit by a firestorm of cannon balls, heated red-hot in the ovens of Fort Niagara across the river. The fort burned to the ground, trapping the families of soldiers in the stone storerooms under the fort.

- On a freezing night in December 1813, a gang of lawless Canadian deserters galloped into the town of Niagara, bashed down the doors of private homes and took the men prisoner, threw women and children out into the snow, and burned over three hundred houses to the ground.

I have often wondered what we should make of such horrific events as we grow older. And should we learn about them when we are young? Certainly, with the blossoming of the Web and with so much material online, any attempt to spare younger readers the gory details about their history is probably doomed to failure.

The Internet changes a lot of things, including how we treat history. Many generations since 1815 have rediscovered and redefined the War of 1812 in their own light. At worst, they have puffed up events or ignored them, depending on their social, political, or patriotic prejudices.

Today, it's much harder to twist history and tamper with historical truth, although some people keep trying.

I'm afraid political correctness is still a factor in our schools and ministries of education, where some well-meaning souls would rather turn the war into a lesson in civics rather than a study of violence, greed, and glory in human nature. Some jurisdictions in Canada even ignore the war entirely. For example, Quebec was invaded by three U.S. Armies in 1812, 1813, and 1814, and French Canadian regulars, militiamen, and Aboriginal people played major roles in stopping the American conquest, in both Upper and Lower Canada. And yet the Ministry of Education's curriculum designers touch only on the French and American Revolutions and teach nothing about an equally formative period in Quebec history. In fact, the War of 1812 was a crucial factor in the survival of French Canada. As Henri Bourassa perceptively wrote in 1902, "If the Treaty of Paris had saved us for France, what would have become of us? Assuming we would have escaped the bloody Reign of Terror [in the French Revolution], it is more than probable that Napoleon would have sold us to the Americans without even consulting us, as he did with Louisiana."

American history likewise has felt the smothering effects of PC, but from different angles ranging from Marxist populism and guilty handwringing to raging boosterism. Reading some accounts or watching some video docudramas, you would think that not much happened in the War of 1812 after Old Ironsides, Baltimore, and New Orleans.

Most Americans are confused by the War of 1812 and why it was fought. There are several reasons for this. First, the partisan propaganda of the era hid the real motives for the war. Second, it seemed a small, isolated war sandwiched between the American Revolution and the Civil War, whereas it was a major front in the Napoleonic Wars. Third, Americans are rightly embarrassed by the first 900 days of "Mister Madison's War" — a string of painful political and military failures. Never mind that the last 100 days were marked by three glorious victories. And finally, the war of 1812 was an attempted land grab of today's good neighbour Canada, a baffling country that had abolished slavery, rejected the blessings of American democracy, and refused to be liberated.

Americans are also confused for another very good reason. The major driving force behind the war was not "Mister Madison," but their eloquent, maddening founding father Thomas Jefferson himself. Readers will note that I title one chapter "Mister Jefferson's War," because Jefferson's love of France (and toleration of Napoleon), combined with his everlasting hatred of the British, drove most of his foreign and even domestic relations.

My take on the man is that he and Napoleon needed each other, but in Napoleon's case, actions spoke louder than words. With Jefferson it was the opposite.

A glamorous but baffling man, Jefferson was capable of the most flowery language and the loftiest of sentiments, yet in his treatment of others was often either a hypocrite or a sociopath.

He was illiterate in economics. Even with his thousands of acres and hundreds of slaves, he was a virtual bankrupt who lived way beyond his means and desperately tried to escape his British creditors by political manipulation. He was a snob who glorified the simple American farmer yet looked down his nose at business and manufacturing. He brought in measures that favoured Napoleon while bankrupting thousands of American merchants and traders, leaving their ships rotting in the harbours. His protégé and friend, James Madison, who followed him as president, changed Jefferson's program very little, and was if anything a better listener and a smarter politician.

Jefferson's major impact rests in the fact he was an American expansionist. He had more than doubled his country's size with the purchase of Louisiana from Napoleon. And at Napoleon's urging, the capture of Canada was one of his major goals.

Another factor that has twisted the history of the war is the growth of history documentaries made by filmmakers who want to show that history needs to be dramatized because it is so boring. I suspect this attitude has more to do with selling a project to investors than with telling a true tale. Fair ball. History Television and the History Channel have to be focused as much, if not more, on eyeballs and ad dollars as on the quality of the production.

There are some happy exceptions; the recent PBS documentary *War of 1812* walks the line very well. By way of antidote, College Humor has produced a wonderful satire of video clichés about the war.[2]

Today, it's also much easier to browse through the War of 1812 online. Just Google "Lundy's Lane."

In some ways, the Web is a form of artificial memory-keeping, and that benefits our study of the war. In the past, historical memories have tended to fade or become clichés lodged in history books, but it is getting easier to keep these memories alive and for people to find original memoirs and texts.

To help this process along, I have added images, quotations, timeline data, and first-hand accounts to the book support site, so readers can go deeper inside the minds of the people who were there, and understand what they went through. The accounts are first-hand, but most of the images are not and should be regarded as impressions of the war from a particular place and time. Some are hilarious cartoons, some are decent schoolbook illustrations, but some are outright propaganda.

I have also tried to dig deeper into this war and its characters to identify and unlock some of its many puzzles.

This means getting behind the heavy-handed stage settings of the war, which tend to dim the vitality of the real events beneath. Some of the heroics, I suggest, were not so heroic after all. Much of the glory lavished on the victors was as much due to bumbling or foolishness or greed on the losing side. Or in the case of the Battle of Lake Erie, a probable love affair between the British commodore and a widow in distress. It was not, as one writer suggested, the mystical blessing of a bald eagle who wheeled screeching in the bright blue sky over Commodore Perry's flotilla as he prepared for battle.

Canadians and Americans today are mature enough that we don't have to soft-pedal memories of this war to keep feelings warm and fuzzy between our two nations. The War of 1812 hurt people on both sides of the border and from all walks of life very badly. The war was armed robbery writ large.

So how do we respect the events that really happened to our ancestors? While big sums are being spent today on public relations campaigns to win the War of 1812 tourist dollar, many of the old battlegrounds and sites are still endangered, and politicians seem to have lost the political will to act.[3]

The best way to remember the dead of the War of 1812 is to tell their story unblemished, and to protect their graves and battlegrounds so they can sleep in peace.

PUZZLES OF THE WAR

For those in this Facebook era whose critical faculties are still functioning, it's a challenge to dig deeper into this conflict and look at what we assume about it, what is taught in schools and colleges, how it is portrayed in videos and docudramas, and what it really was.

The war's "moments of sheer terror" are of course the most fascinating bits, but that also includes the events leading up to the battles, and what both sides brought to the fight. What role did planning play? Technology and arms? How was human stupidity a factor in whether a battle was won or lost? How important was luck? Who benefitted financially? Are there lessons to be a learned from the war?

The War of 1812 poses a number of puzzling problems that we usually see in these old assumptions:

1) U.S. President Madison's pretext for going to war was to get justice on the high seas and stop the British from taking American sailors to serve on British warships.

2) Henry Clay and the War Hawks in Congress were 100 percent behind Madison, and pushed him to declare war.

3) Madison failed to find out in time that the British had decided to stop impressing American sailors, because it took two months for a message to cross the Atlantic. Otherwise this unnecessary war would never have started.

4) At Detroit, William Hull went insane and handed the fort over to Isaac Brock.

5) Isaac Brock was the hero of Queenston Heights.

6) Henry Procter was a bad general who betrayed Tecumseh.

7) Brilliant seamanship and pluck won the naval battles of Lake Erie and Lake Champlain for the Americans.

8) Lieutenant FitzGibbon would have lost the Battle of Beaver Dams without the brave trek of Laura Secord to warn the British.

9) De Salaberry defeated an army of American invaders by blowing bugle horns in the woods to make the enemy think he was facing a much larger force.

10) The Battle of New Orleans was a useless victory for the Americans, because the war was already over.

11) The War of 1812 was the war that nobody won.

12) The War of 1812 was a war that both sides won.

13) The War of 1812 was a civil war between North American cousins.

14) The Native Americans were the real losers in the war. During the peace talks, the British went against their promises and shafted their allies.

In this book, I argue that most of these notions about the war are pretty half-baked. Not to debunk them, because they all contain grains of truth, but it's far more interesting to assemble a truer picture of the actual war and its authentic battles.

In truth, the realities of the War of 1812 are far more interesting than its stale old mythologies, which sometimes resemble, at best, cheap Victorian stage pieces, or at best, Gilbert and Sullivan operettas.

Eighteen Twelve as a Melodrama

In some respects, the War of 1812 is a pure three-act melodrama. Perhaps with a dash of *Pirates of Penzance* or *HMS Pinafore,* or a shot of pantomime or even Japanese Kabuki.

I like to think that, properly staged, it would go something like this:

In **Act One**, the curtain rises on the American president and his gang of Virginia squires sitting around a candlelit table. They argue about the best way to trump up the war, seize a beautiful damsel named Canada, and exterminate the whole race of bloodthirsty savages. Stage Right, their aged British parent doesn't notice their shenanigans, as he is occupied warring with an evil Corsican dictator named Bonaparte.

First off, the pygmy president (so called because he is only five feet tall) invites all his old friends to dinner at the White House and appoints them major generals. He gets his tailors to dress them up in the finest blue serge and gold braid uniforms. Then they head off into the wilderness, leading hastily planned attacks on an unseen enemy, lurking in the woods. The curtain falls.

First Intermission. The oldest of the major generals, William Hull, performs a deeply moving vignette right out of Greek tragedy. He leaves the stage and comes out into the audience to explain why he will never fight the Indian Sachem Tecumseh. He simply refuses to risk the life of his dear daughter and his grandchildren, helpless in Fort Detroit. The Red Men should be our friends, he declares. He then smashes his sword over his knee, and as the pieces clang on the floor, he strides off stage, never to fight again. Fade to black.

Act Two. The curtain rises to the clash of arms, the blare of bugles, the crack of muskets and the boom of cannons as the real battling begins. In fight after fight, the old generals get thoroughly thrashed, first by a young Byronic hero right out of central casting, the lovelorn Isaac Brock, who dies tragically. Then a plucky band of British regulars, Loyalist militia, their Mohawk scouts, and a woman with a cow appear on the scene. They fight on bravely, even though they are heavily outnumbered. Stage Right: their evil commander in faraway Montreal refuses to send them enough salt pork, whisky, ammunition, and money. He laughs like a madman as he plays with a pile of gold coins. The curtain falls.

Second Intermission. In a clever on-stage regatta, stagehands billow blue sheets to imitate waves, as two naval teams entertain the playgoers with an inconclusive series of yacht races on Lake Ontario.

Meantime, Stage Left: The pygmy president's officials are finally getting serious about fighting, but it's too late. Stage Right: across the Atlantic, the Iron Duke is chasing Bonaparte from the field. Shiploads of redcoats leave ports in France, racing against time to save the damsel Canada from the clutches of the pygmy president. It seems to be curtains for the Americans. Soon a bunch of hellfire British aristocrats are galloping up to Washington. They find nobody there, not even the president's wife, Dolley Madison. They lounge around the White House smoking cigars and drinking the president's brandy wondering where Dolley has gone. Then they get really annoyed and torch the place.

But wait, in **Act Three**, the whole frame is turned upside down. Up in the rafters, a turbaned Goddess of War, played by Dolley Madison herself, decrees that it is time the British bullies got thrashed instead. To do this noble work, she chooses a gallant young naval commander in his twenties, a mob of irate Baltimore merchants, and the meanest general in American history, Old Hickory, who most assuredly is not from Virginia.

All that's missing is the music. Oh, sorry. Cue Beethoven's 3rd "Eroica," Tchaikovsky's "1812 Overture," and "The Star-Spangled Banner."

MORALS OF THE STORY

Seriously, dear reader, behind the scenes, the War of 1812 was much more than a magnificent melodrama. It also had its share of real human tragedies, often from the actions of soldiers against civilians. But what I find most fascinating of all are the mistakes made by the players.

An old English proverb says,

> For want of a nail the shoe was lost.
> For want of a shoe the horse was lost.
> For want of a horse the rider was lost.
> For want of a rider the battle was lost.
> For want of a battle the kingdom was lost.
> And all for the want of a horseshoe nail.

Each War of 1812 battle has some pivotal moment, when victory hangs in the balance, and time seems to stop. Then suddenly the game tips away from one side or the other because some fool forgot to bring a horseshoe nail, or took a wrong turn, or had to meet a lady, or just gave up in disgust.

Sure, some 1812 battles feature quite brilliant individual efforts by commanders, whose smart actions or by-the-book tactics generate the momentum to win. But some battles, like Chateauguay, are simply farces, play fights.

To my mind, the most interesting and unique battles encapsulate a hard lesson about what to do or what not to do in order to win. They provide useful maxims for business and life, which I have added — bear with me, dear reader — as morals here and there in the narrative. For example:

- Queenston Heights: Have the depth to carry on regardless, even when your charismatic commander gets himself killed.
- Lake Erie: There are times when you DO give up the ship, especially if it is sinking.
- Lake Champlain: A dithering commander-in-chief can ruin everything.
- Washington: Why you should keep politicians away from the battlefield.

Then there are those baffling battles that simply turn on guest appearances by the Gods of War, who intervene when they feel like slapping down human pride. They sometimes appear on the scene just when you least expect them, or just for the hell of it.

THE BUSINESS OF WAR

As an historian interested in business and technology, I also wanted to look at the War of 1812 in business terms. Who profited, who paid?

Clausewitz called war "politics by other means," but it is also "business by other means."

War can happen when one country wants something badly enough to get violent with the other and resorts to armed robbery. So it was with the War of 1812.

War is a business, crueler than most, but still a business, with goals, investments of time and money, hope for returns, profits, and losses. In war as in business, finance, leadership, morale, and technology are all crucial elements of success.

In business we talk of campaigns — a term that comes to us from warfare.

We talk of leadership — and military leadership very often translates well into the civilian sphere. However business leaders with military training often lack some of the soft arts meant for marketing. Isaac Brock is an exception;

skilled at recruiting, he would have made a decent high tech entrepreneur, or perhaps a charismatic film director.

We talk about toxic bosses. Military leaders like Napoleon, who could inspire millions, are those. Such a man could also lead millions to their deaths, as in his insane quest to conquer Russia. Canada had its own toxic boss, Sir George Prevost, whose actions, I argue, were duplicitous if not traitorous. America had a whole slew of toxic politician-generals, all narcissists utterly incapable of empathy. Thomas Jefferson was a prime example. An economic illiterate, he had the audacity to nearly bankrupt his country by an embargo against all foreign trade, in the mistaken opinion he was helping France. Exceptions to the rule were perhaps William Henry Harrison on the American side and Sir James Yeo on the British.

Armies march on their stomachs, as do sales forces. Quartermasters win wars, and so do supply chains. Corrupt quartermasters, and there were several on the U.S. side, contributed to losing causes by supplying tainted water, rotten meat, and maggoty flour to the troops. More men died of corruption and typhus than died of courage in the face of the enemy.

We talk of arenas of conflict, as if battles were boxed-in venues for spectator sports. We are happy to watch superbly trained, testosterone-charged young athletes prove themselves and risk serious injury (and even death) for glory and plunder. Wars can be like that.

The ugly side of war can be mirrored in business. If companies are unrestrained by laws, they can sicken or devastate a population, which is normal practice in warfare. Rape and pillage are the stock-in-trade of a marauding army, and there are leaders who encourage these activities, and understand the pack behaviour of young animals, and young men. The War of 1812 was not immune from this type of warfare, A Scottish doctor, John Howison, who practiced for a time in Niagara, noted the continuing presence of venereal diseases five years after the war was over.[4]

The Laws of War are a genus all to themselves. All wars are preceded by politeness, but once declared they usually degenerate into brutality. At least businesses are restrained by laws. The Laws of War are not always respected, and the Golden Rule not always followed on the battlefield. There were exceptions in the War of 1812, and some commanders banned the looting of civilians on pain of death. But the end of the war, some frustrated commanders encouraged what was essentially armed robbery and rapine.

Civil wars are the worst kinds of wars, and some have called the War of 1812 a North American civil war. I disagree. As with conflict inside a corporation, civil wars happen between people who should be friends, but who cannot resist getting some short term advantage over their fellows. I think the American Revolutionary War was more of a civil war. The War of 1812 was an uncivil war.

The War of 1812 was a dirty business, a rowdy and cruel war by a people whose goals were to dominate a continent and eliminate a race of people.

For many Americans, especially those with their eyes on western property, 1812 was a war to seize and control vast tracts of land, and kick out the Indian inhabitants. As such it was a form of block busting. In this respect, the War of 1812 was astonishingly successful.

For many people, like John Jacob Astor, the war was business as usual, because he had protected himself with strong links on both sides of the conflict, and had politicians in his pocket, and bought war debt for pennies on the dollar. For him it was a decent war.

THE THOUSAND DAY WAR

This book is in four parts. The first part looks at the personalities and issues that drove men like Napoleon and Thomas Jefferson, the one a dictator, the other an aging revolutionary, to make common cause not just against Britain, but against humanity.

The second talks about why a young adolescent nation of seven million people went to war against a country with the strongest navy the world had ever seen.

The central part of the book shows why the U.S. tried and failed in three campaigns over three years to capture British North America, an under-populated land with only 700,000 inhabitants. And how in the last hundred days of the war the Americans suddenly woke up and beat back three simultaneous invasions that would have ended U.S. independence and brought the nation back into the British Empire.

In part four, I tally up what really took place and why, in this pivotal little war. What were its short- and long-term results and are we still feeling them today?

A Baptism of Fire

Those who know the history of the War of 1812 know that it was a war generated by ambition, greed, pride, and fear; and it was a war fuelled by fire.

For three peoples this conflict was their baptism of fire:

- Fire kindled by Native Americans, whose lands were being swallowed by settlers, who burned down their crops and cabins, and were themselves burned out by blue-coated soldiers.

- Fire on the sea and over the great lakes — murderous cannons roaring with flame, blasting out flash and grapeshot, that whistled sickeningly across decks and snuffed out the lives of sailors.

- Walls of fire blazing out from columns of regulars who with their paper powder cartridges could pump out three volleys a minute of heavy lead.

- Fires razing the villages and towns of Upper Canada and the Niagara frontier, homes and farms put to the torch by frustrated soldiers in Niagara, York, Buffalo, Long Point, Port Dover, and all along the road from Niagara to Detroit.

- Fire from the British blockaders, with their lust for booty, who sailed into American ports, took away the treasures and stores of the merchants and shopkeepers and farmers, and then set their warehouses and docks aflame.

- Campfires of thousands of troops on the march. Fire from the funeral pyre at Lundy's Lane, where the corpses of American soldiers were heaped on a bonfire fuelled by cedar fence rails, which burn hotter and faster than any other wood.

- And perhaps the biggest fires of all: the Senate and House of Representatives in Washington, D.C., fuelled by the books and shelves of the Library of Congress, and by two huge oil paintings of the King and Queen of France, given to George Washington by King Louis himself. And when these objects wouldn't burn hot enough, pyrotechnic fireworks from the Congreve rockets to finish the job.

- Flames that blackened the White House, fuelled by the curtains and sofas and linen and tables and chairs, and all the clothing and personal belongings of James and Dolley Madison and their staff, all burned to avenge the torching of towns in Upper Canada.

- Fire over Baltimore Bay, and the rockets' red glare from British fireships, their mortars spewing out fire bombs that burst in the air and rained down destruction on the defenders at Fort McHenry.

- And finally, a blaze of murderous rifle fire from the Kentucky militia at New Orleans, whose sharp aim mowed down 800 of Edward Packenham's redcoats. Fire that the general himself felt all through his dying body, shot at least six times as he led his men into the flames of hell.

And when it was over, the sick stench of smoke and cinder and ashes all along the frontier.

Beautiful Little Battles

> "All the business of war, and indeed all the business of life, is to endeavour to find out what you don't know by what you do; that's what I called "guessing what was at the other side of the hill."
>
> –*Arthur Wellesley, Duke of Wellington*

The horrors of war aside, one of the real delights about the War of 1812 is that it features a whole raft of fascinating little battles, to delight, amuse, educate, and engage.

To my mind, these conflicts serve as excellent case studies. They show how boldness can win against major odds, how supply is all-important, how training can beat valour, how stupidity is commonplace, how hubris or war weariness can lead to disaster, and how the Gods of War can ruin everything.

Some have argued that 1812 was the second American Revolutionary War. It was not. It was the first American Expansionary War. In the war of independence, France had to step in to save the colonists, a fact that severely rankled the

British. But in 1812 there was no rich Oncle Louis across the seas to send his navy and regiments of troops to Yorktown. There was a rapacious new emperor named Napoleon, whose only real interests were European. In exchange for cash, and for attacking the British in North America while he invaded Russia, Bonaparte donated Florida and Louisiana to his American friends, and gave them a western destiny.

This subsidy of Napoleon rankled the British, but they were in a much better position to do something about it, having mastery of the seas. America faced an estranged old parent who regarded it as a pain in the ass, but in the end, let it go its own way.

North American War of 1812 battles were small skirmishes compared to the monstrous battles of the Napoleonic War. At Leipzig, in the Battle of the Nations, 600,000 men sought to slaughter each other, and nearly succeeded. Or Waterloo, in Wellington's words "the nearest run thing you ever saw in your life," at which Napoleon would have won if Blücher had not arrived in time to rescue the British from the French cavalry.

Yet the War of 1812 battles are bijoux, precisely because they are small, and the actions and reactions of the major players are easy to grasp. Glittering individual actions, or one stupid decision, often made an immense difference.

You have to marvel at the cast of characters the war threw up.

At Detroit, Isaac Brock's boldness and Tecumseh's charisma reduced the American commander to a blubbering idiot. (At least that's how the story goes; Hull may have been the only sane person there).

At Queenston, two American armies were on site, but only Federalist general van Rensselaer decided to attack. Republican general Smyth sat petulantly in his tent in Buffalo, totally ignoring van Rensselaer's orders. But then, his real orders were not to fight, but rather to destroy van Rensselaer's political reputation, and his chances in the upcoming New York gubernatorial race.

At Bladensburg, President Madison and Secretary of State Monroe dropped by and actually gave interfering orders to the troops. Only one American, the privateer Joshua Barney, knew how to fight. He brought big naval guns up to guard the bridge and mowed down the British in waves. Badly wounded and unable to escape, he was saved by the British commanders, who congratulated him heartily for his valour and got him all stitched up by their best surgeons.

At Washington, the incomparable Dolley Madison, with her husband away playing soldier, calmly ordered the Declaration of Independence and Articles of Confederation and Peale's portrait of George Washington stuffed into flour bags before departing the White House in her carriage.

At New Orleans, often discounted as a useless battle because a peace treaty had just been signed, the Duke of Wellington's brother in law and his glorious Peninsular War veterans were beaten, and beaten really very badly, by the greed of a British naval commander and the sharp shooting of a ragged gang of Kentucky ruffians who had been deer hunting since they were young boys.

Other Battles

> "In war, the moral element and public opinion are half the battle."
>
> *–Napoleon*

Battles in the War of 1812 were not just fought in the field, but also in councils, offices, naval yards, drawing rooms, and print shops.

Examples are Tecumseh's battle to rally the tribes and instill them with pride and respect. Or U.S. Treasury Secretary Albert Gallatin's struggle to pay for a war when his cupboard was bare and his president didn't have a clue about finance. Or British Governor Sir George Prevost, whose main goal in the war was preventing his young Turks from stealing his glory, and, it would seem, preventing British victories on U.S. soil. Or Isaac Chauncey and his Boston shipbuilders, who showed how solid oak, capital training, and better guns could trump the biggest navy in the world, at least in one-on-one combat. Or Joshua Barney, privateer, who knew how to mint money in wartime. And John Jacob Astor, America's fabulous furrier, who traded with the enemy, financed the war and made everybody happy, including Mister Madison's wife, Dolley, who struggled to make a president out of a sour Virginia squire.

The war was also fought in banks and counting houses. For many, like quartermasters, road builders, and suppliers, the war was a chance to make fortunes. For British army officers like Isaac Brock, who had borrowed on family credit to purchase their commissions, the chance to seek booty and a share of the prizes was one of the goals that drove him to succeed. (The capture of Detroit eased his mind considerably.) For British Vice Admiral Alexander Cochrane, ninth son of the impoverished eighth Earl of Dundonald, prize money was uppermost on his mind, and his lust for booty blinded him to danger, leading to crushing British defeats at Baltimore and New Orleans.

For politicians loyal to Jefferson and Madison, the war was their party project. It was a bonanza of glory, with grants and sinecures and titles and uniforms and supply contracts for everybody from governors on down. Virtually all of the early commanders were old fogeys from Virginia or New York, and party stalwarts all. The Federalists who opposed the war were primarily from New England, and when war was declared, they draped themselves in black and rioted in the streets. Most of them wisely continued to trade with the British all through the war, partly to keep the Royal Navy from bombarding their ports. But many of them also made tidy fortunes, trading Russian hemp for British gold.

Now to the war. To find out why James Madison and his Jeffersonians finally resorted to violence in 1812, we first have to travel thirty years back in time, to the creation of the American republic, the revolution in France, and the warning words of George Washington as he left the presidency and retired to Mount Vernon.

ONE

MISTER JEFFERSON'S WAR

"The tree of liberty must be refreshed from time to time with the blood of patriots and tyrants. It is its natural manure."

– *Thomas Jefferson*

AT FIRST GLANCE, THE WAR OF 1812 SEEMS NOTHING MORE THAN A ridiculous spat that accomplished nothing, with a peace treaty that simply restored the status quo. But this thousand-day conflict did have major consequences, both on its own and as part of a wider world war.

The goals, the timing and the results of this war show that, behind a smokescreen of bombast and propaganda, 1812 was a special project of French Emperor Napoleon Bonaparte and his American allies, U.S. presidents Thomas Jefferson and James Madison. To look closely at their motivations is to truly understand why America went to war.

UNFINISHED BUSINESS, 1783–1799

O N SEPTEMBER 3, 1783, BRITAIN SIGNED THE TREATY OF PARIS, ENDING
the American War of Independence.

The British delegates were so furious, they refused to pose for Benjamin West's commemorative painting, and it was never completed

Most British leaders felt cheated by the peace. They saw the victory of the American patriots as a theft of a major part of the British Empire by France. They had a point. While General Cornwallis had foolishly concentrated his forces in an area where he could be trapped, it was French naval vessels that closed the trap. French regiments made sure of the defeat. In fact, there were more French soldiers at Yorktown than there were Americans.

This image shows "The American Commissioners." Front: John Jay, John Adams, Benjamin Franklin, and Henry Laurens.

Under the new treaty, the United States now owned the territory north and southwest of the Ohio River, but Montreal fur traders and their agents kept selling pots and axes and guns to the Indians. This seriously rankled the Americans.

For their part, the British were annoyed as well. Under the treaty, the Americans had agreed to indemnify the Loyalists for losses suffered during the Revolutionary War, but the money was proving devilishly hard to get, since many American and British merchants who had suffered losses were also clamouring to be reimbursed.

For the purpose of our story, we should note that one major debtor to British moneylenders was a forty-year-old Virginia squire named Thomas Jefferson.

Jefferson was born in 1743, the son of wealthy slave owner, planter, and surveyor Peter Jefferson, and Jane Randolph, daughter of a prominent Virginia family. Peter Jefferson was a member of the Loyal Company and surveyed and promoted land sales in Virginia and west of the Allegheny Mountains.

After his father's early death, young Thomas boarded with a Scotch tutor, the Reverend James Maury. He kept a literary book filled with Greek, Latin, and English literature. He then went to the College of William and Mary to study mathematics, philosophy and French, then turned to the study of law.

Jefferson was not always encumbered by debt. In his twenties, he came of age, inheriting 2,750 acres from his father's estate. He passed his bar examination and started building a new house, Monticello, at the top of a little mountain on his estate.

Jefferson's finances first suffered in the 1760s, when the Virginia courts shut down during the Stamp Act Crisis, as the American colonists started pushing for more independence from Britain. Turning from law to politics, he was elected to the Virginia House of Burgesses at age twenty-six, and soon got swept away by revolutionary fervor.

Another financial crisis hit in 1770, when his family estate at Shadwell burned to the ground, destroying most of his personal and family papers and books.

He earned some relief in January, 1772, when he married a twenty-three-year-old widow, Martha Skelton. Her dowry almost doubled his land and slaves. But these 11,000 acres and 135 additional slaves were heavily encumbered by £4,000 in sterling loans from British creditors. When his father-in-law died a year later, Jefferson inherited a debt that he never really escaped.

In 1774, he sold some of his land to settlers and planters who paid in installments, but when the American Revolution broke out, the state of Virginia let buyers pay with inflated paper money, which Jefferson was obliged to accept, even though, as he complained, the money was "worth less than oak leaves."

Jefferson's expensive tastes made matters worse. He always lived beyond his means and never denied himself anything. He adored French wines, fine furnishings and clothing, works of art, and especially expensive leather-bound books — "I cannot live without my books," he commented to frugal John Adams. During his diplomatic years in Paris alone, he bought two thousand books. The result was a personal debt that now reached almost £7,000.

Liquidating personal debts never seemed a priority to Jefferson the gentleman farmer. He waved off his obligations, always expecting that his rising government salary would cover them. A bit of an aristocratic snob, he regarded money-making as beneath his contempt. Jefferson professed to be appalled by the crass commerce of the New England states and New York. "As commercial avarice and corruption advance on us from the north and east," he wrote his friend Henry Middleton, "the principles of free government are to retire to the agricultural States of the south and west, as their government for her portion, agriculture may abandon contentedly to others the fruits of commerce and corruption."

And yet the man could put pen to paper and come up with arguments that appeared reasonable, if a touch radical. In July of 1774, he drafted instructions for the Virginia delegates to the first Continental Congress. In "A Summary View of the Rights of British America" he argued forcefully that the British Parliament had no governing rights over the colonies and asserted that the colonies had been independent since their founding.

A year later, at age thirty-two, he arrived in Philadelphia as the youngest Virginia delegate to the second Continental Congress, and was tasked to help Benjamin Franklin and John Adams craft a manifesto titled "The Declaration of Independence." John Adams's resolution charging the states to write constitutions and create new, independent state governments, was Congress's real substantive declaration of independence, but the Declaration became the real holy writ of the American republic.

This document, so identified with Thomas Jefferson the Legend, was in fact the work of a committee that included Adams, Franklin, Robert Livingston, and

Roger Sherman. After discussion, the committee asked Jefferson, the junior delegate, to prepare a rough draft. Leaning heavily on the English Bill of Rights of 1689, Jefferson wrote it up in two or three days and submitted it to Adams and then to Franklin, Livingston, and Sherman, who together made a total of forty-seven changes to the draft, including moderating several of Jefferson's more radical ideas, except perhaps "the pursuit of happiness." Adams in particular changed "we hold these truths to be *God-given*" to "self evident."

The Declaration was laid before Congress, and 39 further changes were made, including the deletion of Jefferson's arguments holding King George III responsible for continuing the slave trade in the colonies.[1]

On July 4, copies of the Declaration were printed, and on July 9, General George Washington read it to his troops in New York. On September 9, Congress designated "United States" as the new nation's official name.

That October, Jefferson declined an offer to represent the U.S. abroad with Benjamin Franklin and Silas Deane. He returned to Virginia to attend to his finances and serve in the House of Delegates. He and a talented young Virginia lawyer, James Madison, eight years younger, become fast friends and lifelong political partners.

On June 1, 1779, Jefferson was elected governor of Virginia and was reflected in 1780. In September of that year, he showed his warlike mettle by planning an expedition of Virginia militia, led by George Rogers Clark, against the British and their Indian allies at Detroit.

The war reached deep into Virginia in January of 1781, as General Benedict Arnold, now defected to the British, burned the capital at Richmond, forcing Jefferson and his officials to flee. British General Lord Cornwallis also attacked Charlottesville and nearby Monticello. Jefferson and his family barely escaped capture.

In 1782, with the British defeat at Yorktown, Congress again invited Jefferson to join John Adams, Benjamin Franklin, and Henry Laurens in France to negotiate a peace treaty with Great Britain. But with the death of his wife, he had to decline the appointment.

On June 6, 1783, Jefferson was elected a delegate to Congress from Virginia. He introduced in Congress the Ordinance of 1784, which put forth the principle that new states could be formed from the western territories and admitted to the Union on an equal basis with the original states. He also proposed that slavery be abolished in new states by 1800, but Congress rejected this idea, and Jefferson drew back from his position. His own attitudes to slavery were mixed, even hypo-critical. In general, he wanted to abolish the practice but not offer citizenship to blacks — rather send them back to Africa.[2]

In May of 1784, Jefferson finally accepted the position of minister to France, to join John Adams and Benjamin Franklin in negotiating treaties of amity and commerce with European nations.

In April and May of 1785, Adams and Jefferson successfully negotiated a very important loan from bankers George and Ferdinand Grand to consolidate U.S. revolutionary war debts to France, pay long-overdue salaries to French officer veterans of the American Revolution, and ransom American captives held by the Barbary pirates in the Mediterranean.

John Adams then took his position as first ambassador to the Court of St. James's in London, while Jefferson replaced Benjamin Franklin as minister to France, while at the same time inheriting Ferdinand Grand as his banker.

In March and April, 1876, Jefferson visited the Adamses in London. The visit did nothing to heal Jefferson's Anglophobia. In fact, when he and Adams were presented at court, they had the honour of being rudely snubbed by King George III himself.

JEFFERSON AND FRANCE

It was in France that Jefferson really blossomed and became a roman-tic Francophile of the first order. He served as ambassador in Paris from 1785–89, witnessing the glory days of the French Revolution on both sides of the fence: first as a friend of Madame de Stael, salon-keeper and daughter of Louis XVI's finance minister Jacques Necker, and then as one of the revolu-tion's philosopher kings.

As America's eyes in France during five crucial years, he became immersed in the last crisis of a bankrupt French monarchy. Ironically, the major cause of Louis XVI's downfall was his support of the American revolutionaries, which ruined royal credit and led to the breakdown of the national order.

Jefferson, crowned with prestige as one of the chief drafters of the American Declaration of Independence, gloried in nudging the French in far more radical directions. In 1789, he helped Lafayette draft the Declaration of the Rights of Man, the seventeen commandments of the French Revolution, while his friend Joel Barlow wrote pamphlets urging the French to overthrow the monarchy.

For Thomas Jefferson, it was all about burning down the house. A clue to his pyromaniacal motives can be found in his letters. In 1787, he learned of "Shay's Rebellion" in western Massachusetts, from an alarmed John and Abigail Adams. "I like a little rebellion now and then," he wrote Abigail. "It is like a storm in the atmosphere."

In Paris, he was in revolutionary heaven, writing to Madison: "The revolution of France has gone on with the most unexampled success." To Tom Paine, he crowed: "The National Assembly showed a coolness, wisdom, and resolution to set fire to the four corners of the kingdom and to perish with it themselves rather than to relinquish an iota from their plan of total change."

Jefferson in Paris.

He was in Paris for the opening of the Estates General (May 5, 1789) and for the fall of the Bastille (July 14). But he missed the real bloodletting that followed — the suspension of the Rights of Man, the mass guillotining of the Reign of Terror, the fall of Robespierre, and the rise of Napoleon.

Returning home in 1790, Jefferson served as first U.S. Secretary of State under George Washington, whom he increasingly regarded as a stodgy Anglophile.

Jefferson resigned in 1793, and he and his protégé James Madison soon started a war of pamphlets and polemics designed to undermine Washington and his successors: John Adams of Massachusetts and Alexander Hamilton of New York.

John Adams was exasperated with his old colleague and perceived that money problems were at the root of his politics. In a February 3 letter to his wife Abigail, he wrote, "I wish somebody would pay his debt of seven thousand pounds to Britain and the debts of all his countrymen, and then I believe his passions would subside, his reason return, and the whole man and his whole state become good friends of the Union and its government."

Over the years Adams had a maddening relationship with Jefferson. He saw, increasingly, "... evidence of a mind soured, yet seeking for popularity, and eaten to a honeycomb with ambition, yet weak, confused, uninformed, and ignorant."[3]

To his son John Quincy Adams, he wrote, "You can witness for me how loath I have been to give him up. It is with much reluctance that I am obliged to look upon him as a man whose mind is warped by prejudice and so blinded by ignorance as to be unfit for the office he holds. However wise and scientific as philosopher, as a politician he is a child and the dupe of party!"[4]

Yet Jefferson didn't care. He gloried in the romance. He was determined to go his own way and build a political party in his own image. As his chief go-to man, James Madison worked diligently in the background building the bases, pulling together state and local leaders, mainly from New York and the South, and founding the Republican Party. He and his chief propagandist, John Beckley, published pamphlets and newspapers criticizing "Hamiltonianism," praising the small American farmer while looking down on manufacturing, glorifying the French Revolution, and demonizing Great Britain. Jefferson argued that Jay's treaty with the British violated the French alliance of 1778 and betrayed a glorious ally.

They had their own behind the scenes, Edmond-Charles "Citizen" Genet, the new French ambassador, who worked to mobilize pro-French sentiment, and urged Americans to support France's First Coalition. But when Genet outfitted U.S. privateers under the French flag to attack British shipping, he went too far, and an embarrassed Jefferson had to disavow his actions.

In 1796, the Jeffersonians turned their paper cannons on the Father of the Country himself. Beckley, writing anonymously as "A Calm Observer," directly charged President Washington with stealing public funds.

A weary Washington was preparing to resign anyway, appalled by the party politics that were being spawned. In his 1796 Farewell Address, he warned the Jeffersonians against threatening the unity of the country, that the United States should:

> Observe good faith and justice towards all nations; cultivate peace and harmony with all. Religion and morality enjoin this conduct; and can it be, that good policy does not equally enjoin it — It will be worthy of a free, enlightened, and at no distant period, a great nation, to give to mankind the magnanimous and too novel example of a people always guided by an exalted justice and benevolence.

Speaking directly to the Jeffersonians, he warned about the dangers of going to war, since

> nothing is more essential than that permanent, inveterate antipathies against particular nations, and passionate attachments for others, should be excluded; and that, in place of them, just and amicable feelings towards all should be cultivated. The nation which indulges towards another a habitual hatred or a habitual fondness is in some degree a slave. It is a slave to its animosity or to its affection, either of which is sufficient to lead it astray from its duty and its interest.
>
> Antipathy in one nation against another disposes each more readily to offer insult and injury, to lay hold of slight causes of umbrage, and to be haughty and intractable, when accidental or trifling occasions of dispute occur. Hence, frequent collisions, obstinate, envenomed, and bloody contests. The nation, prompted by ill-will and resentment, sometimes impels to war the government, contrary to the best calculations of policy.

The government sometimes participates in the national pro-pensity, and adopts through passion what reason would reject; at other times it makes the animosity of the nation subservient to projects of hostility instigated by pride, ambition, and other sinister and pernicious motives. The peace often, sometimes perhaps the liberty, of nations, has been the victim.[5]

THE RISE OF PARTY POLITICS

"Our wigged and literate Founding Fathers were not immune to vulgar politics."
–*Christopher Hitchens,* Thomas Jefferson: Author of America

Students learn that the War of 1812 was caused by the British blockade of American ships and forced impressment of American sailors. But these were only the public excuses for war — under the slogan, "Free Trade and Sailors' Rights" — even though American privateers made millions from the war, and America welcomed British navy deserters.

British bullying was just a minor annoyance compared to other reasons behind the conflict: land hunger, a lust for political power by their supporters, the fear on the part of Jefferson and Madison that their republic was in danger of breaking up, and their slavish addiction to the French connection

Madison would later claim war as a political tool to protect the repub-lic from being torn in two by pro-British Federalists. Yet the Federalists were already on the decline, mainly due to a population shift to the south and west. In the two decades after 1795, they engaged in an increasingly bitter struggle with the pro-French Republicans, and they were losing.

The old original Federalists — John Adams, Alexander Hamilton, and John Jay — had sponsored the new federal constitution of 1787. Even James Madison, lead author of the Constitution and Bill of Rights, started out as a Federalist. But he and Thomas Jefferson broke away over Treasury Secretary Hamilton's national debt plan, which they naively thought was incompatible with their republican ideals.

They called themselves the Democratic-Republican Party and took the side of farmers and landowners against what they saw as Hamilton's big city scheming. They could not appreciate how he converted the crushing debt from the Revolutionary War into a national asset, one that created a whole new era of prosperity through lower tariffs and $65 million in new capital. But they petulantly offered to back Hamilton if the capital was moved south from Philadelphia to the Potomac, closer to their Virginia power base.

The 1791 French Revolution further hardened the split between these two factions. The northern Federalist states, which traded actively with Canada, Nova Scotia, and Britain, generally took the British side against France. Jefferson's Republicans wanted to keep alive the old romantic alliance with France, at the expense of good relations with Britain.

The Haitian Revolution, which started in August of 1791, also shattered American political unity. By November, 100,000 slaves had killed 4,000 whites and burned hundreds of sugar and coffee plantations. The revolution terrified American slave owners, including Jefferson, and quickly became a test of the ideology of the French Revolution that he so ardently supported.

As stories of growing atrocities in Paris reached the U.S. from France, Jefferson and his pamphleteers dismissed them publicly as British propaganda. When he heard privately that some of his Paris allies had been beheaded, he shrugged, arguing that such sacrifices were a small price to pay for the liberty he believed would follow the excesses of the Revolution.

> The liberty of the whole earth was depending on the issue of the contest, and was ever such a prize won with so little innocent blood? My own affections have been deeply wounded by some of the martyrs to this cause, but rather than it should have failed, I would have seen half the world desolated. Were there but an Adam and an Eve left in every country, and left free, it would be better than as it now is.[6]

The party split finally hardened as a result of the Jay Treaty of 1794, backed by George Washington and Alexander Hamilton. The British finally agreed to withdraw from pre-Revolutionary forts they had failed to give up in the Northwest Territory west of Pennsylvania and north of the Ohio River after the Treaty of Paris. The two sides agreed to arbitrate disputes over loyalist losses, wartime debts, and the boundary — one of the first times in history arbitration was used to maintain the peace.

The treaty went into effect on February 29, 1796, and was set to expire after ten years. It was an honest attempt to patch over some issues with the British and helped the U.S. economy boom, but the Jeffersonians hotly disputed it clause by clause. They claimed that closer ties with Britain would undercut republican ideals, promote aristocracy, and lead America back into the British Empire.

For Thomas Jefferson himself, it also meant that he might very well find himself in court over his debts — in a clause that must have deeply alarmed him, the treaty provided for compensation to British creditors from American debtors, many of whom were his fellow Virginians.

JEFFERSON AS VICE PRESIDENT

The United States presidential election of 1796 saw the pro-French and anti-decentralization Republicans under Jefferson and Aaron Burr fight bitterly against incumbent Vice President John Adams and Charles Pinckney's pro-British and pro-centralization Federalists.

It was the first contested American presidential election and the last one in which a president and vice president were elected from opposing tickets There were no "running mates." Although Adams won the presidency, Jefferson received more electoral votes than Pinckney and was elected vice president, according to the prevailing rules of electoral balloting.

After the election, Jefferson continued portraying the Jay Treaty as a betrayal of the old alliance forged in the Revolutionary War. The French republicans even started an undeclared "quasi war" against John Adams's government from 1798 to 1801, seizing over $20 million in goods from U.S. merchant ships.

Perhaps what enraged Thomas Jefferson most was that the treaty was so successful. The peace was a boon to manufacturing and boosted U.S. exports from $33 million in 1794 to $94 million in 1801.

THE REVOLUTION OF 1800

As the eighteenth century drew to a close, two momentous events happened in France and the United States, the coming to power of two quite different revolutionaries: Napoleon Bonaparte and Thomas Jefferson.

On November 9, 1799, Bonaparte mounted a coup in France with the support of the Marquis de Talleyrand and paid for by an army contractor named Collot, who advanced two million francs to the cause. Unopposed by a nation weary of chaos, Napoleon declared the French Revolution dead and installed himself as First Consul, thereafter governing as a dictator, and then, in 1804, Emperor.

Across the Atlantic, Thomas Jefferson also engineered a coup that he himself would call the Revolution of 1800, because it appeared to usher in so many radical changes.

Jefferson's rise to the presidency was perhaps inevitable. His supporters were more numerous, and better organized. They came more and more from the younger, dynamic western states and territories, overwhelming the New Englanders. In the state of New York, perhaps key to his success, there was also an active movement to the frontier and Great Lakes. The alliance between these two groups would control U.S. politics for a generation.

The Federalists could only hold on to New England, and John Adams was defeated. But the choice of president was deadlocked into 1801, until Alexander Hamilton himself recommended to the Federalists that they support Jefferson over the scheming Aaron Burr, because it was better to back a man who had principles, wrong though they might be, than a man who had none.

Benefitting from a public split between John Adams and Alexander Hamilton, and tied with Aaron Burr, Jefferson was elected president by a single vote in the House.

On March 4, 1801, Thomas Jefferson strolled the short distance from his residence, Conrad and McCunn's boarding house, to his presidential inauguration at the Capitol building, because he felt people would think taking a carriage was too aristocratic. It was symbolic of a new way of thinking in Washington.

Jefferson's election gave the anti-Federalist Republicans their first taste of real power.

As the United States entered the nineteenth century, Jefferson's country had a population of not much more than six million people. But settlements were thin and scattered, with only six people per square mile compared to seventy people today. Only 7 percent lived in towns of more than 2,500 people.

There were no large cities like London or Paris. A few big port towns had emerged to handle imports and exports, mainly to Britain and the West Indies.

In 1800 the largest were Philadelphia with 80,000 inhabitants, New York with 60,000 people, and Baltimore and Boston with about 25,000 people each.

Interests were local above all and there wasn't much national economic activity between cities. But all that was about to change as the centre of the American economy began to shift westward toward the Mississippi. And suddenly, in 1803, courtesy of Napoleon Bonaparte, America had an Empire, with Jefferson's purchase of Louisiana.

THE LOUISIANA PURCHASE

RELATIONS WITH SPAIN

> "This accession of territory affirms forever the power of the United States, and I have given England a maritime rival who sooner or later will humble her pride."
>
> *—Napoleon Bonaparte*

Once they had settled lands across the Appalachians, the Americans began to rely heavily on the Mississippi River and the port of New Orleans.

Pinckney's 1795 Treaty with Spain gave U.S. merchants "right of deposit" in New Orleans, meaning they could use the port to store goods for export. The treaty also recognized American rights to navigate the river, which was vital to the booming trade of their western territories. But Spanish power in the region was starting to collapse anyway, as Americans continued to pour into the Mississippi Valley.

In 1798, the Spanish revoked this treaty, but it was restored by Napoleon, who had captured Spain, and secretly returned the territory to French control in 1801. That year Jefferson sent Robert Livingston to Paris with instructions to purchase New Orleans for $10 million. Behind the scenes, gunpowder manufacturer Pierre du Pont de Nemours engaged in some back-channel diplomacy with Napoleon and came up with the idea of the much larger Louisiana Purchase. It worked. The cash-strapped Corsican agreed to offer all of Louisiana instead of just New Orleans, at the bargain price of $15 million.

On May 2, 1803, Livingston signed the Louisiana Purchase Treaty, acquiring the vast territory for 60 million francs ($11,250,000) plus cancellation of debts worth 18 million francs ($3,750,000), for a total sum of 15 million dollars ($225 million in 2012 dollars). The land totalled 828,800 square miles (2,147,000 km^2), and it more than doubled the size of the United States. At mere pennies an acre, it was the biggest real estate deal in history.

Back in Washington, both Federalists and Jeffersonians fretted about whether the Louisiana Purchase was unconstitutional, but land hunger trumped political philosophy. Suddenly the Americans had the beginnings of an empire, and Jefferson immediately sent Meriwether Lewis and William Clark up the Missouri River to explore the real estate and to find a route to the Pacific. That autumn he was reelected President.[7] To justify the Louisiana Purchase, Jefferson even drafted a constitutional amendment authorizing Congress to exchange lands in the West for eastern lands occupied by Indians, as long as they pledged allegiance to the United States. It was never ratified, but future practice ensured that troublesome Native Americans east of the Mississippi would have to be resettled west of the river.

Napoleon used a good chunk of the Louisiana money to put in place a new army, known as the Armée de l'Angleterre (Army of England), at camps at Boulogne, Bruges, and Montreuil. At his command, 200,000 French soldiers were to cross the English Channel on a fleet of barges and capture the Crown of Great Britain.

The British were furious over what they saw was an American subsidy to Bonaparte and immediately declared the War of the Third Coalition against France. With Admiral Nelson's crushing victory at Trafalgar in 1805, they won complete control of the seas, and with their thousand-ship navy held it for the next decade.

Some Britons still feared Napoleon might make an attempt to capture Quebec with the help of the Americans, but without sea power, with the victory of the slaves in Haiti, and the loss of an entire army to yellow fever, Boney's dreams of an American Empire were dead, along with the invasion of England. So he crowned himself Emperor of France, and fattened by 15 million American dollars, turned his energies to conquering the rest of Europe.

As for Thomas Jefferson, the rise of Napoleon of course offended his republican ideals. The old Roman Republic collapsed with the arrival of Augustus Caesar. And now the First French Republic was being led a strong, ambitious general. Could the same fate befall America?

On the other hand, Jefferson could work with the man. But he didn't want Napoleon to capture Canada; he wanted to do it himself.

Napoleon's Reverses

Napoleon had originally set his sights on commandeering Britain's colonial possessions, especially India, but a British fleet under Horatio Nelson booted him out of Egypt after the Battle of the Nile.

More naval defeats followed, at Toulon and Copenhagen, and on October 21, 1805, the Royal Navy again dashed Bonaparte's dreams at Trafalgar, winning complete mastery of the seas. The British soon blockaded France and seized over 1,000 U.S. merchant ships.

British attitudes enraged Jefferson and his followers, who protested that these actions were illegal under international law. But Britain was fighting a total war and shrugged off American protests. The British simply wanted no whining, no ingratitude, and no nonsense from their former colonies as they threw everything into the fight against Napoleon.

John Adams was dismayed by Jefferson's attitudes as president, which he felt would lead to disaster and war: "I shudder at the calamities, which I fear his conduct is preparing for his Country: from a mean thirst of popularity, an inordinate ambition, and a want of sincerity."[8]

Free Trade and Sailors Rights

> "Great empires are not maintained by timidity."
>
> —*Tacitus*

The United States was just twenty years old when Royal Navy captains began to stop and search U.S. merchant ships, looking for any British deserters who could be "pressed into service" (made to serve on ships of war).

It was important for the Jeffersonians to seize upon impressment as an easily understandable excuse for moving toward a war with Great Britain.

For all the fuss raised about impressment, it was not an issue important enough to go to war over. And the Americans were incapable of doing anything about it anyway. The Royal Navy refused to give up the practice because of desertions, and never would. It would leave their 1,000 warships hopelessly undermanned.

Jefferson's reasons were purely political. Pressing sailors was an easily understood issue in southern ports like Baltimore, where the slogan "Free

Jeffersonian propaganda.

Trade and Sailors' Rights" became a popular rallying cry. And it handily covered up all the real reasons for war, the first of which was land hunger on the northern and western frontiers. The alliance of the Virginians with states like New York and Kentucky was the key to his party's political power.

In fact, the British only claimed the right to impress from merchant vessels on the high seas, and then only British citizens. Very few naturalized Americans were taken. But here was the problem: only about 30 percent of the 70,000 sailors in the American merchant navy were British. And of these only 1,500 went through the bother of getting American citizenship and carrying naturalization papers. Many were indeed deserters who had happily escaped the brutal life of an ordinary seaman on a Royal Navy frigate, and without papers, they were fair game. In peacetime they would have been hanged, but the British captains simply whipped them back to work.

An estimated 7,000 American-born sailors were impressed between 1803 and 1812, because they were not carrying any papers at all.

A Prelude to War

When the time came to renew or renegotiate the Jay Treaty, with the Monroe-Pinkney Treaty, signed on December 31, 1806, Jefferson refused to send it to the Senate because he said it didn't deal firmly with America's neutral rights. It did not include any guarantees against impressment, although the British offered informal assurances.

On June 22, the British escalated the impressment debate and called Jefferson's bluff, with a simple act of war against a nation they considered to be allied with France.

When the British warship *Leopard* stopped the American ship *Chesapeake* off the Virginia coast looking for deserters, the *Chesapeake*'s captain refused to allow the British to board and search for deserters. The *Leopard* then fired on the *Chesapeake*, killing three American seamen and wounding eighteen others. British Marines then boarded the American ship and removed four alleged deserters.

Jefferson called an emergency cabinet meeting on June 25, and a week later closed American ports to all British ships except those with emergencies or on diplomatic missions. Meanwhile, state governors were ordered to call up troops for the federal army.

Jefferson then pushed through his own ill-considered Embargo Act, which passed the Senate on December 18. It was the moral equivalent of war.

The act closed all American ports to foreign ships, allowing only coastal trade. Of course, true to form, his act's purpose was to benefit the French by punishing the British. All it did was hurt his own country.[9]

The embargo drew a shrewd rebuke from Treasury Secretary Gallatin, who suggested that:

> As to the hope that it may ... induce England to treat us better,
> I think is entirely groundless ... government prohibitions do

always more mischief than had been calculated; and it is not without much hesitation that a statesman should hazard to regulate the concerns of individuals as if he could do it better than themselves.

But a cranky Jefferson was not to be turned aside from his idealistic goals. In 1808, he pushed through further measures to tighten the Embargo Act and prohibit exports by land. But fierce opposition to the Embargo Act was growing, and not just among New England merchants. Jefferson shrugged off the protests, and on April 19 went even further, and declaring the Lake Champlain region to be in a state of insurrection because of smuggling to Canada in violation of his Embargo Act.

This time Jefferson went too far, with his actions actually threatening the union itself. Jefferson's ill-thought-out embargo was ruining trade — in fifteen months, exports fell from $108 million to just $22 million. Ships rotted at the wharves, while smugglers got rich. Thirty thousand sailors were out of work. Frustrated Federalists were threatening to dissolve the union and talking seriously about creating a new federation in New England, and perhaps joining Canada. But Jefferson was irrepressible. On November 8, in his last lame-duck message to Congress, he spun his own version of events, saying that his Embargo Act had led to the "beneficial expansion of manufacturing." It had not, and Jefferson had never toadied to manufacturers before, regarding them as corrupt and tied to the British.

In the elections of December 7, Secretary of State James Madison was elected as Jefferson's successor.

The following March 1, in his last act as president, Jefferson signed the Non-Intercourse Act, which effectively repealed the Embargo Act of 1807 but kept restrictions on trade with Great Britain.

Thomas Jefferson then left Washington and returned to his home in Virginia, never to return to public life. Endlessly frustrated by his failure to put his pet theories into practice, the sixty-five-year-old founding father professed to be relieved: "Never did a prisoner, released from his chains, feel such relief as I shall on shaking off the shackles of power."[10]

Now he had his own domestic problems to face. Even after burning through a $25,000 annual salary for two terms, Jefferson left office with $10,000 in additional debt, and his finances would worsen during his retirement at Monticello.[11]

MADISON TAKES COMMAND

O N MARCH 3, JAMES MADISON WAS INAUGURATED PRESIDENT AND carried on his friend's legacy as if nothing had happened.

A modest mini-me to Jefferson's bulkier heft, James Madison was less of a philosopher and a far better politician, organizer, and manager, with a splendid wife who know how to work a room and charm frosty foreign envoys. In fact, Dolley Madison had previously served as Jefferson's White House hostess.

Madison faced a brash new Congress, led by Henry Clay's War Hawks, a group of westerners determined to put Jefferson's visions of conquest into action: to drive the British, Indians, and Spanish out of the new American Empire.

For all the spin about free trade and sailors' rights, the real reason America was preparing to go to war was timing, and the very special relationship the Jeffersonians had with Napoleon Bonaparte.

In December 1811, in the Elysée palace in Paris, Napoleon welcomed President Madison's new U.S. envoy, the ardent pamphleteer and poet Joel Barlow. Barlow and his wife were old and dear friends of both Jefferson and the Madisons.

In a private meeting, the Emperor confided in Barlow his plan to invade Russia. While he himself would subdue the Czar, the Americans, he suggested, should take advantage of the situation to make war against the British in North America and finally capture Quebec.

With a huge army tied up by Wellington in Spain, Napoleon urgently needed the Americans to open up a second front, and he clearly offered them another sweetener: Spanish Florida. Just three months later, on March 13, 1812, backed by President Madison, U.S. General George Mathews led a small flotilla of U.S. Navy gunboats with seventy-nine Georgian filibusters calling themselves "the Patriots of East Florida" across the St. Mary's River, where he read a manifesto establishing the American "Territory of East Florida."

Some lame opposition was mounted by local Seminoles and African Americans who sided with the Spanish, but at that moment the crown of Spain happened to be the property of Napoleon's brother Joseph, who was temporarily ruling the country as José I.[12]

BONAPARTE'S HEMP PROBLEM

It is fruitful to look at the main reasons why Napoleon invaded Russia, and, by no coincidence at all, why the Jeffersonians declared war on Great Britain at exactly the same time.

The War of 1812 was a war of trade as much as one of conquest. After its victory at Trafalgar, the Royal Navy started tightening the noose around France's neck, putting in place a stifling blockade of Europe and leaving Napoleon with very few maritime options.

But Bonaparte still controlled the continent, and he knew that Britain's Admiralty had an Achilles Heel: the Royal Navy ran on two major goods, timber from Quebec and Russian hemp. From hemp fibre, the navy got sails and ropes and oakum, which was tarred and hammered into the planking to provide a watertight seal. From Canadian timber the naval yards fashioned ships with tall, straight spruce masts and spars, and hard, durable oaken hulls. Not for nothing did the British tars sing their rollicking sea shanty that began, "Hearts of oak are our ships, jolly tars are our men, we always are ready, ready, aye ready."

But Britain's wooden warships had a short life span. Salt rot wore away at sails and rigging. Hempen sails and ropes only lasted two years at best before they started to tear and had to be completely replaced. Hulls lasted ten years at best.

Britain's bustling naval trade was seen first-hand by Isaac Brock at Quebec and U.S. diplomat John Quincy Adams at the major Russian port of Kronstadt. They marvelled at the harbours and quaysides, packed with hundreds of freighters and clipper ships loading rough-cut logs and bales of hemp fibre to feed the demands of the Royal Navy.

By 1806, Britain was buying 90 percent or more of its marine hemp from Russia. The 1,000 ships of the Royal Navy ran on Russian hemp, as each British ship replaced fifty tons of hemp a year, for sails, rope, rigging, and nets. France had its own hemp supply, but the British were almost completely dependent on Russian hemp. Russia was the low-cost producer because of its cheap serf labour.

Napoleon knew this perfectly well, and after defeating the Russian and Austrian armies at Austerlitz, he was determined to bring Britain's navy to heel. In 1807, he forced Czar Alexander of Russia to sign the Treaty of Tilset, promising to cut off all Russian trade with Britain. Bonaparte's intention was simple: to starve the Royal Navy of cordage and canvas. He reckoned quite rightly that inside of three years, he could bring Britain to its knees.

But the treaty with the Czar was a farce and the lucrative Russian hemp trade continued as before, with hundreds of ship captains easily dodging Napoleon's paper blockades and dictates. Irony of ironies, most of these vessels were from New England, enlisted in the crusade against Napoleon.

The Royal Navy had captured hundreds of Yankee clippers on the high seas and impounded their cargoes. The Admiralty quickly offered the captains a deal they could not refuse. They could either forfeit their ships and cargoes, or they could in effect take a double profit. They could trade their rum, sugar, spices, cotton, coffee, and tobacco to the Russians at Kronstadt, but on one condition only: they would have to return to an English port with naval supplies, and especially hemp fibre.

To sweeten the deal, the British paid the Yankees in gold, half in advance, and the balance when the hemp was delivered to the Royal Navy.

Alarmed by stories of American ships working against France, James Madison sent John Quincy Adams to St. Petersburg to investigate the problem. In 1809, Adams reported back to his chief that there were as many as 600 clipper ships in Kronstadt harbour, flying the American flag, loading hemp for the British and American markets.

The continuing Russian hemp trade made Napoleon apoplectic, and in 1810, he settled on a final solution to his problem. He would personally invade Russia, topple the Czar and stop the follow of hemp to Britain, while his Jeffersonian allies would invade Canada, capture Quebec, and stop the Royal Navy's prime source of timber.

The bomb was timed to blow up in June of 1812.

Slapping the Spaniel's Nose

> "The Declaration of Independence I always considered as a
> Theatrical Show. Jefferson ran away with all the stage effect of
> that; i.e. all the Glory of it."
>   –*John Adams, to Benjamin Rush, June 21, 1811*

John Adams always considered Thomas Jefferson something of a drama queen, indulging his desire for romantic conflict and personal glory at the expense of the nation. Now James Madison was following in the master's footsteps.

If they had been more mild-mannered and patient, the Jeffersonians and War Hawks would surely conclude that it was cheaper to pay the price of losing a few sailors than spending a fortune trying to beat British regular troops on the frontier.

Or if they had been more like John Jacob Astor, who happily traded with his Montreal partners during the war, they would have rubbed their hands and said, "The war in Europe is a cost of doing business; let's see if we can make a decent dollar out of it."

Or if America had been less of an adolescent nation, with a burning need to get into the ring with an old battle-hardened pugilist — Britain — they would have shrugged and toughed it out.

But Britain was otherwise distracted, in a life-and-death struggle with Bonaparte, who had massed armies ready to invade England, fed and armed with the $15 million that Jefferson and Madison paid to Bonaparte for the purchase of Louisiana. Now the Americans were threatening war. Most British saw this as just another event in a ten-year history of pure treachery, another back-stabbing American assault on the Mother Country in her hour of greatest need, when she was struggling to free the world from a monstrous despot.

The British were in no mood to humour a gang of Virginia squires infected with pious political ideals and a love of all things French. Admiral Cockburn thought the American president should be treated like a naughty spaniel. "If he misbehaves, slap him on the nose."

Indeed, the Americans were exactly like a wild dog that nips at the hind leg of the wildebeest while he is struggling with the lion. They were practical men who did not want to let a crisis to go to waste. They needed to get some value out of the European war while the lion was otherwise distracted, tightening its teeth on the windpipe of the wildebeest. That is pretty much why they declared war.

The Cries of the War Hawks

"We hear from the halls of Congress the cry 'On to Canada!' It is the fur dealer and the land speculator who want war, but it is we of New England who will pay the price.... The War Hawks of Tennessee and Kentucky are safe. I doubt if the English navy can reach them."

—Nicolas Smyth, letter opposing war

As the nineteenth century began, philosophers from Hegel to Schopenhauer to Nietzsche were infected by Napoleonic ideals, as monarchies fell like bowling pins across the landscape of Europe.[13]

Everywhere, politicians wanted to speed up the course of history through seeding conflict. Thomas Jefferson, philosopher king, was also aroused by his old romantic notion of smashing statues. Now in his declining years at Monticello, surrounded by his children and slaves, a safe distance from the hurly-burly of Congress, his pen still dripped with a lust for blood and change.

A new generation of politicians in the U.S. Congress was also affected by the rumblings of war in Europe. The so-called War Hawks grew up immersed in the glory of their fathers' revolutionary exploits. Now they wanted a national dustup to forge their own legends.

Conflict provided these men a chance to prove themselves, get rid of the Indians, and make themselves and their friends filthy rich selling land along the frontier running from Louisiana to Quebec. All their supporters, the young lawyers and newspapermen and state militia captains, likewise yearned for armed adventure and booty.

Led by John C. Calhoun of South Carolina, Felix Grundy of Tennessee, Henry Clay of Kentucky, and Peter B. Porter of New York, the War Hawks knew they had to convince their fellow citizens to fight for the honour of the United States, insulted long enough by the arrogant British.

In 1811, Grundy told the House that "This war, if carried on successfully, will have its advantages. We shall drive the British from our continent. They will no longer have an opportunity of intriguing with our Indian neighbors.... Her means of annoying us will be diminished."

House Speaker Henry Clay of Kentucky had another, more practical reason for going to war: profit. Born in Virginia, he moved to Lexington in 1797, where he became a well-known trial lawyer and husband to Lucretia Hart, the daughter of a rich slave owner and hemp manufacturer. Soon after his marriage, Clay began to promote the cause of Kentucky's hemp farmers, and as the war began, got the tariff on imported hemp doubled to forty dollars per ton.

Another committed War Hawk who stood to benefit handsomely from the war was Congressman Peter B. Porter, chair of the House Foreign Relations Committee. As quartermaster general of the New York state militia, his family shipping and forwarding company, Porter, Barton Company, were major road builders, land dealers, and suppliers to the U.S. Army.

THE VIEW FROM CANADA

"The expulsion was so thorough that the next generation of Americans, with few former loyalists as reminders, almost forgot the civil aspects of the war and came to think of it as a war solely against England. The loyalists disappeared from American history."
–*Carl Van Doren,* Secret History of the American Revolution

JUST AS THE AMERICAN REVOLUTION FORGED THE UNITED STATES, IT ALSO created A new pair of provinces called Upper and Lower Canada north of the border, populated by French Canadians and British Loyalists. It also set in motion the energy of a new North American people, with their own ideals of destiny and their own western vision.

By 1812, some in Britain were arguing for peaceful overtures toward America. But with the 1812 American declaration of war, most British grew even more resentful of the American Republicans. They saw Madison's war as a barefaced attempt to help out Bonaparte by forcing them to maintain a strong regular force in Canada. And they had few illusions about Madison's economic reasons for declaring war. It was a land grab, pure and simple, and the biggest part of the booty was British North America.

The British lion's response was to growl at the little spaniel, whack him on the nose, and deny him Canada.

Jefferson and Madison were fully aware that the British did not want to lose Canada. Canada had deep sea ports like Halifax and reliable timber supplies to feed the Royal Navy's insatiable desire for oak planks and spruce masts. The Canadians could export wheat to feed hungry Britons during bad harvest years. And they had a vibrant metropolis in Montreal, gateway to a continent rich in furs. Captains James Cook and George Vancouver had already scouted out deep-water ports for British ships in the Pacific, and Britain meant to hold on to this vast continental empire, controlled for the moment by the Hudson's Bay Company and the North West Company of Montreal.

Jefferson and Madison also knew perfectly well that if they tied up regiments of redcoats in British North America, they were giving Napoleon real concrete aid in his military campaigns in Europe, including his plan to invade Russia.

Britain had absolutely no fear of conflict with the United States, but the prospect of war terrified many of the native Loyalist families who had fled to Canada during the American Revolution. Many of these "Tories" had been mistreated, robbed, tarred and feathered, and lost homes and businesses to the "Patriots." Now they feared, with some cause, that new American invaders would compound their suffering.

Most Canadian settlers were attached to the British connection, especially with high prices for wheat, but there was also a growing north–south trade between the Canadas and New England. Many so-called "late Loyalist" Americans immigrated to Canada after 1790 in search of good land and commercial opportunity. One of them, Philemon Wright from Massachusetts, founded the Ottawa Valley timber trade. These American immigrants soon became loyal to the local authority and often served in their local militia. They wanted no quarrel with the republic to the south.

Even during the war the people of northern New York and Maine continued to trade with the British. The Vermonters were known for supplying most of the cattle consumed by the British army. They even sold them masts and spars used for British warships on the Richelieu River and Lake Champlain.

The French Canadians likewise wanted to be left alone and unmolested by the United States. They had already helped the British beat back American invaders in 1776 and were prepared to do so again. The British in general respected French rights, and when a martinet governor, James Craig, menaced their language and their rights of assembly, they protested, and he was recalled and replaced by a more sympathetic viceroy.

Some French Canadians had flirted with Napoleon, but as war approached, their loyalty was no longer suspect. Quebec militia captains enrolled 1,200 militiamen in Lower Canada to meet the growing American threat.

In Indian Territory

One of the great assets of the Canadian loyalists was their attachment to the Indian nations of the Northwest. This worried many Americans. On April 20, 1812, Thomas Jefferson wrote to John Adams about Tecumseh's brother Ten-squat-a-way, or The Prophet:

> The Wabash prophet is a very different character, more rogue than fool, if to be a rogue is not the greatest of all follies. He arose to notice while I was in the administration, and became, of course, a proper subject of inquiry for me. The inquiry was made with diligence. His declared object was the reformation of his red brethren, and their return to their pristine manner of living. He pretended to be in constant communication with the Great Spirit; that he was instructed by him to make known to the Indians that they were created by him distinct from the whites, of different natures, for different purposes, and placed under different circumstances, adapted to their nature and destinies; that they must return from all the ways of the whites to the habits and opinions of their forefathers; they must not eat the flesh of hogs, of bullocks, of sheep, &c. the deer and buffalo having been created for their food; they must not make bread of wheat, but of Indian corn; they must not wear linen nor woollen, but dress like their fathers in the skins and furs of animals; they must not drink ardent spirits: and I do not remember whether he extended his inhibitions to the gun and gunpowder, in favor of the bow and arrow. I concluded from all this that he was a visionary, enveloped in the clouds of their antiquities, and vainly endeavoring to lead back his brethren to the fancied beatitudes of their golden age. I thought there was little danger of his making many prose-lytes from the habits and comforts they had learned from the whites, to the hardships and privations of savagism, and no great harm if he did. We let him go on, therefore, unmolested. But his followers increased till the English thought him worth corruption, and found him corruptible.

One of the main grievances listed against George III in the Declaration of Independence was this: "He has excited domestic insurrections amongst us, and has endeavored to bring on the inhabitants of our frontiers, the merciless Indian savages, whose known rule of warfare, is undistinguished destruction of all ages, sexes and conditions."

In fact, most Native American tribes were untouched by the American Revolution. They were not parties to the treaty of peace, and chiefs like Little Turtle and Blue Jacket refused to recognize U.S. title to the area northwest of the Ohio River.

Under the Peace of Paris, the British agreed to give up their Great Lakes forts, such as Detroit, but they simply built new ones across the new frontier and kept supplying their old Indian customers with kettles and axes and guns in exchange for valuable furs. Some British traders, who intermarried with Native families, actively promoted the creation of their own neutral Indian territory.

Farther south, and west of the Alleghenies, lived five major Native American tribes which were gradually adopting European farming practices, domestic tools, and European clothing. They preferred more and more to raise livestock instead of hunting, and to buy clothes at a store instead of sewing deerskin. They came to adopt the cash system and supplied traders with millions of deerskins and beaver pelts that were made into shoes and hats or exported to Europe. And many of them intermarried with whites and free blacks.

One young Shawnee man named Tecumseh fell in love with a white girl. She taught him how to read and write and give him a rudimentary education in the classics. But when he asked if she would marry him, she turned him down.

At about this time, Tecumseh's brother, a man debauched by alcohol, one day had a revelation that the red man should turn away from the white man's ways and go back to

Tecumseh Wearing a Treaty Medal.[14]

his roots. He convinced his brother, still smarting from being rejected by a white girl, of his new vision. Tecumseh soon became a strong orator for the cause of Indian unity. By the 1800s, dressed in beautiful buckskin, he went from tribe to tribe promoting the vision of his brother, now called the Prophet. They gathered their followers in the Indian northwest at a village they called Tippecanoe.

Moral: To rally your tribes, speak with conviction and vision.

Dealing with the Indians

The United States was only an infant nation when it began to stretch its ambitions, rattle the bars of its crib, and set off to conquer a continent.

President Thomas Jefferson and his old friend James Madison were driven by a continental vision, and now they owned land stretching all the way up to the territory of the Hudson's Bay Company in present-day Canada.

Jefferson and Madison were not naive about the fact that Tecumseh and The Prophet also wanted their own territory in the northwest. They feared that he might ally with the British and prevent the Americans from claiming what they paid for, and was now legally their property.

A huge stretch of territory was at stake, running from Michigan through Illinois and Wisconsin and west.

Harrison at Tippecanoe.

First the French and then the British had tried to prevent land-hungry American settlers from moving west and clearing homesteads. Now was the time to civilize this land and make it American. They knew blood would have to be shed to make their title clear.

Western politicians soon found an excuse for war when some British muskets were found in several Indian villages, leading to the charge that the British were arming the Indians. Of course the British had always armed the Indians, in exchange for furs.

In 1811, enough outrage had been generated for Madison to order General William Henry Harrison to deal with the threat from Tecumseh. While Tecumseh was away visiting the Creek Indians in the south, Harrison slaughtered the natives of Tippecanoe, killing Tecumseh's brother and father.

Tecumseh himself survived, and a year later, James Madison declared war on Great Britain.

JOHN JACOB ASTOR

February 15, 1812, New York City. John Jacob Astor, the richest man in America, sat in his counting office on Albany Street, watching the changing political winds.

It was clear now that Madison and the War Hawks were intent on going to war, and nothing could stop the momentum. Astor understood the president perfectly. It was all about protecting his republic against British sympathizers. Little Jimmy (some called him the "Pygmy President") was a hardliner compared to Jefferson, but cut from the same Virginia cotton.

Astor was preparing his chessboard carefully, dividing his operations into three in order to maximize his profits from the war and survive intact. The American Fur Company was his U.S. base, the Pacific Fur Company would handle his west coast, and growing China operations and the South West Company would be his working partnership with the North West Company of Montreal.

The Norwesters were a many-headed monster, a shifting partnership of clanny Scots, and he often had to resort to the time-honoured practice of dividing to conquer.

Madison and the War Hawks were doing a good job drumming up the populace about the continuing British presence in the old North West. Astor considered the area west of the Great Lakes his natural territory, and he planned to put in place his own trading monopoly, while still dealing profitably with the Norwesters as they withdrew. They still had the cheapest and best supply routes via the St. Lawrence, and he needed their cooperation.

Born in Waldorf, Germany, the third son of a butcher, Astor arrived in Baltimore at age twenty, determined to make his fortune. Moving to New York City, he toiled as a bakery assistant and a peddler, and in 1787, with his wife's $300 dowry as capital, he entered the fur trade. By the 1790s, he was a major player and had enough capital to buy a licence to trade in any port monopolized by the East India Company. This meant China, the greatest market for furs in the world. He and a partner quickly pulled together a load of furs and shipped them to Canton. Astor's share of the profit was $50,000, much of which he invested in Manhattan farmland.

Astor was a sophisticated strategist who knew how to influence politicians in the United States, in Canada, and in England. He was the major beneficiary of Jay's Treaty, which got the British army out of U.S. territory and banned Canada-based traders from dealing south of the international boundary. This directly impacted his major rival, Montreal's North West Company, heirs to the old French fur trade. It also was good news for the Hudson's Bay Company, which controlled the northern trade and was itself locked in bitter combat with the Norwesters.

Astor was able to lever the Norwesters into a deal where his company could import trade goods from Montreal up the St. Lawrence in summer, and when the river was frozen they could export furs from Montreal to New York, where Astor shipped them to Europe. It was the best deal the Norwesters could get.

By 1800, Astor was thought to possess a quarter of a million dollars in capital — multiply that by at least 100 to get his worth in today's money. But he was not satisfied. He did not wholly trust the Norwesters, nor they him. He wanted a real monopoly of furs inside American territory. He still faced competition from pesky free traders like Robert Dickson of the Michilimackinac Company, who was exporting through Montreal furs that should be rightfully be Astor's. He wanted this bleeding to stop.

Astor strongly supported the Louisiana Purchase, as well as the Lewis and Clark Expedition to Oregon. Astor's great dream was to establish a single entrepot at the mouth of the mighty Columbia River, to serve as an outlet for entire American West and a gateway to China. In the spring of 1811, his ship *Tonquin* beat Montreal's Norwesters to the site and erected a post at the site of present-day Astoria, Oregon. From there he planned to build a small fleet of ships to transport his furs directly to Canton, and to get into the East India opium trade.

Astor's commercial plans neatly dovetailed with the nation-building vision of Thomas Jefferson and James Madison. Both Astor and the two presidents wanted to expand the boundaries of the United States beyond the Mississippi to the Pacific coast.

Jefferson's Embargo Act in 1807 disrupted Astor's import/export business and may have been an attempt to bring him to heel. To mollify Astor, Jefferson backed his creation of the American Fur Company on April 6, 1808. Astor also financed an overland expedition to Astoria in 1810–12, which discovered South Pass, later used by hundreds of thousands of settlers to pass through the Rocky Mountains.

Jefferson also assured Astor on April 13, 1806, that "You may be assured that in order to get the whole of this business passed into the hands of our own citizens & to oust foreign traders who so much abuse their privilege by endeavoring to excite the Indians to war on us, every reasonable patronage & facility in the power of the Executive will be afforded."

Astor was also an enthusiastic supporter of Madison's declaration of war, as the best way to kill off threats to his monopoly. He couldn't destroy the Norwesters, because they dealt in superior north country furs and had a shorter water route to the Great Lakes, out of North America to Europe. But one solution Astor imagined was for the United States to invade Canada, capture Montreal, and take over the entire Great Lakes Fur trade. And why not?

Six months earlier, on December 17, 1811, Astor passed detailed intelligence through his friend Albert Gallatin, Madison's treasury secretary, of British troop deployment in Upper and Lower Canada.

ASTOR AND THE NORWESTERS

For the time being, Astor had to maintain friendly relations with the Norwesters in order to beat up his rivals in St. Louis, Missouri. He knew a way to get leverage over the Norwesters at the bargaining table while still creating a climate where at least both sides could get some benefit, most of all himself.

After Jefferson and Madison enacted the 1803 Louisiana Purchase, the Montreal companies that continued their lucrative Indian trade in the Upper Mississippi region faced increasing interference. Washington formally banned British trade west of the Mississippi. The Americans placed duties on British goods entering the U.S., appointed Indian Agents, and built government trading posts (or factories) at key locations including Chicago and Mackinac.

In late 1807, Jefferson's embargo on the import and export of foreign goods forced the Norwesters to buy out their Mackinac partners and move their fortified trading post from Mackinac Island to St. Joseph's Island, forty miles north into British waters.

The Norwesters lobbied hard in Washington, and in 1810, Astor got them to enter a partial merger called the South-West Company, letting the Montrealers supply part of his U.S. business. When Madison ordered the embargo lifted, the Norwesters hoped the agreement could neutralize future sanctions, but they found they could never escape Astor's squeeze. The man was a human boa constrictor. Madison again slapped an embargo on British goods in 1811, and declared war in 1812.

On July 15, 1811, Norwester David Thompson reached the mouth of the Columbia River and the Pacific Ocean; he called it Cape Disappointment, because he realized it was in territory already occupied by John Jacob Astor's American Fur Company. What he didn't know was that on June 15, Astor's ship *Tonquin* had been attacked by local Nootka, who killed the sailors and burned the ship at anchor. This tragedy marked the end of the New York fur trader's hopes for northwest coast trade to China.

Two years later, on October 16, 1813, while war was raging in the east, Astor and his Pacific Fur Company partners came to an agreement with the Norwesters to protect their property from the Royal Navy. They quietly transferred ownership of their Fort Astoria fur depot to the North West Company. A month later, on November 12, Norwester John McTavish took possession of Astoria for the North West Company.

On November 30, when Royal Navy Captain William Black arrived off the mouth of the Columbia in his 26-gun sloop *Raccoon* to officially take possession of Fort Astoria for Britain, he found it was already in British hands. He renamed the new North West Company's Fort Astoria Fort George.

As a postscript, Astor was a major beneficiary of the Treaty of Ghent, negotiated by his old friend Albert Gallatin. The treaty restored borders and properties to prewar conditions, and of course Astor got back Fort Astoria, and eventually the Americans got Oregon.

Astor's Friends in Washington

> "Merchants have no country. The mere spot they stand on does not constitute so strong an attachment as that from which they draw their gains."
> —*Thomas Jefferson to Horatio G. Spafford (March 17, 1814)*

Knowing how to turn the levers of power, Astor easily secured concessions allowing him, in effect, to continue the fur trade in Canada throughout the war. He was able to buy up Norwester furs at a better price and less risk than London merchants by declaring they were U.S. property, owned in the northwest at the time of the outbreak of war.

In 1813, Astor had enough capital to help out his friend Treasury Secretary Albert Gallatin bail out a government on the brink of bankruptcy. In 1813, with a consortium of Philadelphia associates, he acquired high-interest bonds with debased currency, 85 cents to the dollar, emerging from the war in far better shape than Madison's government.

During the war, he also kept friendly relations with President Madison's wife Dolley, on one occasion sympathizing with her husband's illness and sending her a Chinese hat. (Astor also held a mortgage on Dolley Madison's Washington house.)

Jefferson and Madison never full trusted Astor's motives, especially if they related to the British in Canada or to his demands for government help in protecting his private property or his schemes to open trade with China. But most of Madison's colleagues, and many congressmen, including chief War Hawk Henry Clay, were indebted to Astor's cash in one way or another.

Moral: Even in wartime, you can still manage trading with the enemy, and keep everybody happy.

ISAAC BROCK

> "There is only one favorable moment in war; talent consists in knowing how to seize it."
>
> *–Napoleon*

In 1802, a young British officer named Isaac Brock was posted to Quebec to take charge as brigadier of the 49th Regiment. Born on the Channel Island of Guernsey, he was a veteran of several campaigns against the French, including with Nelson at the Battle of Copenhagen, and advanced rapidly in the service. He was a handsome, charismatic man, six foot three and a champion athlete, and was known for his ability to recruit.

Brock soon grew bored at Québec and yearned for glory in Spain and Portugal. He wrote often to his brothers, one of whom was a London banker. Like most of his fellow soldiers, he held strong feelings of animosity toward the Americans. In a letter of July 20, 1808, he told them it was clear they were edging toward war:

> We have completely outwitted Jefferson in all his schemes to provoke us to war. He had no other view in using his restrictive proclamation; but failing in that, he tried what the embargo would produce, and there he has been foiled again. It is certainly the most ridiculous measure imaginable, and was evidently adopted with the view of pleasing France; but no half measure can satisfy Napoleon.[15]

The following year Brock got a report that Americans along the border were starting to provoke the British:

> A few weeks since, the [U.S.] garrison of Niagara fired upon
> seven merchant boats passing the fort, and actually captured
> them. Considering the circumstances attending this hostile
> act, it is but too evident it was intended to provoke retalia-
> tion: these boats fired upon and taken within musket shot of
> our own fort [Fort George]; their balls falling on our shore,
> was expected to have raised the indignation of the most
> phlegmatic; fortunately, the commandant was not in the way,
> as otherwise it is difficult to say what would have happened.

Brock knew that for the time being it was wise to remain cautious, but prepared, because of the strategic importance of Canada to the British. He wrote
his brothers that

> the American government is determined to involve the two
> countries in a war; they have already given us legitimate cause,
> but, if wise, we will studiously avoid doing that for which they
> shew so great an anxiety.
>
> Their finances, you will perceive, are very low, and they
> dare not propose direct taxes. They must have recourse to
> loans at a time when they have only six frigates in commis-
> sion, and about five thousand men embodied. To what a
> state of poverty and wretchedness would the accumulated
> expenses of war reduce them!
>
> But they look to the success of their privateers for a sup-
> ply, and contemplate the sweeping away of all foreign debts as
> the means of reducing the calls upon their treasury. Whatever
> steps England may adopt, I think she cannot in prudence,
> avoid sending a strong military force to these provinces, as
> they are now become of infinite importance to her.[16]

Like most around him, Brock made the error of believing that Canada
was in more danger from Napoleon than from the Jeffersonians: "Bonaparte,
it is known, has expressed a strong desire to be in possession of the colonies
formerly belonging to France, and now that they are become so valuable to
England, his anxiety to wrest them from us will naturally increase. A small

French force, 4 or 5,000 men with plenty of muskets, would most assuredly conquer this province."

In July of 1810, Brock's attitudes changed after Governor Craig posted him to Upper Canada as military governor. Craig knew the current lieutenant governor, Francis Gore, had no experience raising and training militia troops. Brock had good experience recruiting, and he was just the man for the job.

SETTING THE TONE

Isaac Brock knew he was in the line of fire and that he faced huge challenges pulling together a credible defence of Upper Canada. The Assembly was apathetic and not inclined to cooperate. The population was scattered and unreliable. Brock reckoned that there were 80,000 men, women, and children in Upper Canada. More than half were families of American farmers, "late loyalists," who came north to homestead in the last twenty years. Only 13,000 were original Loyalists, and another 14,000 were British. Added to the 300,000 in Lower Canada, mainly French, there were another 80,000 British North Americans in Nova Scotia, New Brunswick, Prince Edward Island, and Newfoundland. The thriving states south of the border now had almost eight million citizens.

Any sane, unimaginative person would have given up Upper Canada for lost, but not a strategist like Isaac Brock, infected with the fighting spirit.

He knew he had the advantage if he moved quickly. Informers returning from the U.S. reported a lack of preparation for war. The Americans had not yet built good roads to Lake Ontario and Lake Erie, and Brock still controlled the lakes with armed ships of the Provincial Marine based at Kingston.

Detachments of Brock's old regiment, the 49th, were based in three places: at York, where Brock made his headquarters; at Kingston near the head of Lake Ontario (under Lieutenant-Colonel John Vincent); and at Niagara (under Roger Sheaffe, a hard-nosed officer who kept discipline by handing out hundreds of lashes for minor infractions).

That autumn Brock started pulling together and drilling a militia of about eight battalions — 4,000 men that he knew could be trusted. He also began work on a blockhouse at Point Henry to guard Kingston, and beefed up the stockades at Fort York as well as the forts built on British territory after the American

Revolution: Forts George, Chippawa, and Erie opposite Niagara, Fort Malden opposite Detroit, and Fort St. Joseph near American Fort Mackinac.

In the summer of 1811, Brock and Sheaffe were both promoted major generals, and Craig was posted back to England due to ill health. He was replaced that October by Sir George Prevost, a Swiss Protestant born in New York, who spoke flawless French and whose first job was to repair relations with the French Canadians, damaged by Craig's mistrust of their support for Napoleon.

Isaac Brock.

Lieutenant Governor Francis Gore also left Upper Canada on leave, and Brock became the civil governor as well. At this point he learned that the French blockades had ruined his family's business in Guernsey, close to the Brittany coast. To pay the debt incurred in buying his commission, Brock signed over his entire pay of £1,000 as administrator of Upper Canada to his youngest brother and lived frugally enough on his colonel's wage of 22 shillings and 6 pence per day.

Late that year, Brock's regiment was posted back to Montreal, while he was forced to stay at York, left for the time being with his militia, some of the 10th Royal Veterans, a few Royal Artillerymen, and the Royal Newfoundland Regiment of Fencibles. He wrote Governor Prevost that he was not very confident about the militia and found the people pessimistic. "Most of the people have lost all confidence. I however speak loud and look big."

Brock nevertheless had a plan, one based on speed, deception, and stagecraft.

DECLARATION

PRETEXTS FOR WAR

> "Many nations have gone to war in pure gayety of heart, but perhaps the United States were the first to force themselves into a war they dreaded, in the hope that the war itself might create the spirit they lacked."
>
> –*Henry Adams*

Countries declare war after they fail to solve real problems. Apart from lingering commercial problems cause by a decade of Jeffersonomics, Madison's major challenge was national unity, and yet political partisanship was more important than unity. War was pretty much a cheap patent medicine to purge the republic of un-republican ideals. Yet the Jeffersonians held a majority and controlled the levers of power, and were in a good position to pour this nostrum down the nation's throat.

Jefferson and Madison had tried to persuade France and Britain to treat them honourably. Instead of picking one side, say Britain, with its command of the seas after Trafalgar, they tried to deal with both and completely lost credibility. By 1812, neither France nor Britain trusted or respected the American government and treated Madison somewhat like harassed parents humouring a child having a tantrum.

Still, the War Hawks and land dealers grew more and more worried about whether Madison had the guts to risk national unity and go through with the war.

Calhoun wrote a friend that "our President tho' a man of amiable manners and great talents, has not I fear those commanding talents, which are necessary to control those about him. He permits division in his cabinet. He reluctantly gives up the system of peace." The South Carolinian also astutely observed that the coming conflict was "the first war that the country has ever been engaged in; there is a great want of military knowledge; and the whole of our system has to be commenced and organized." Eight months later, after disasters caused by "errors and mismanagement … of most incompetent men," Calhoun noted that the difficulties "lie deep; and are coeval with the existence of Mr. Jefferson's administration."[17]

Henry Clay was likewise nervous about the government's ability to wage war. In fact, with the war approaching, Madison had only about 130 employees in total, and his War Department had the Secretary and only seven clerks. Clay urged Madison not to reply on the old fogeys in the War Department. "The militia of Kentucky alone are able to place Montreal and Upper Canada at your feet."

Clay need not have worried about a declaration of war. In the years leading up to 1812, James Madison had actively ignored what could have kept the peace and became more and more the creature of the War Hawks. But he still owed favours to his old fogeys. And to Napoleon Bonaparte.

As for the British, they saw little chance of avoiding conflict with the Americans. British Ambassador Augustus Foster had several meetings with Madison and Secretary of State James Monroe in 1811 and 1812, trying to gauge how serious the Americans were about declaring war. He came away with the strong feeling that the Cabinet's mind was already made up, and that they were actively seeking pretexts for war.

Foster also had the distinct impression that nothing the British could do or say would make the slightest bit of difference. The persistence of Henry Clay and the War Hawks was too strong.

The Americans were now pretty much committed. With Napoleon preparing to invade Russia, now was the time to light the bonfire of conflict, and to expand the American frontier south, west, and north.

But first, a sense of outrage had to be generated to get popular support for the war and to promote national unity.

A DECLARATION OF SORTS

The year 1812 was a presidential election year. On May 18, Madison got the endorsement of his party in caucus. Still, about one third of Republican lawmakers boycotted the vote, vowing not to join in re-nominating the president. It was a brutal referendum on his leadership, and a clear message from the War Hawks to get cracking on the war.

For Madison, the time was not yet ripe, but almost. A month later, he started the wheels turning, with a special message to Congress listing American complaints against Britain. It was not a declaration of war. Such a declaration by a president would not be proper under Madison's strict interpretation of a constitution that he had a big hand in writing.

In his message he laid out his reasoning and asked Congress to decide the proper course of action.

During the war debate, Virginia Federalist Daniel Sheffey painted for the House a vivid picture of the horrors they faced, the loss of treasure and blood, and the dangers to civil society. He considered the war a naive, self-indulgent fantasy: "We have considered ourselves of too much importance in the scale of nations," he told his fellows. "It has led us into great errors. Instead of yielding to circumstances, which human power cannot control, we have imagined that our own destiny, and that of other nations, was in our hands, to be regulated as we thought proper."

When the votes were called, Congress split pretty much along party lines. The House quickly agreed to war by a vote of seventy-nine to forty-nine. The Senate took weeks to decide, but finally voted nineteen to thirteen in favour of the following motion:

> Be it enacted by the Senate and House of Representatives of the United States of America in Congress assembled, That war be and is hereby declared to exist between the United Kingdom of Great Britain and Ireland and the dependencies thereof, and the United States of America and their territories; and that the President of the United States is hereby authorized to use the whole land and naval force of the United States to carry the same into effect, and to issue to private armed vessels of the United States commissions or letters of marque and general reprisal, in such form as he shall think proper, and under the seal of the United States, against the vessels, goods, and effects of the government of the said United Kingdom of Great Britain and Ireland, and the subjects thereof.

APPROVED, June 18, 1812

PRELUDE TO WAR

> "The annexation of Canada this year as far as the neighbor-
> hood of Quebec, will be a mere matter of marching, and will
> give us experience for the attack of Halifax the next, and the
> final expulsion of England from the American continent."
> —*Thomas Jefferson to Duane, August 4, 1812*

Jefferson's bravado was shared by most of his countrymen, but War Hawks like Calhoun knew it was not justified.

By June 1812, the United States had a total population of about 7.7 million people, but the nation was not at all ready for war against well-trained British regulars, their Native allies, and the Royal Navy. Their military were more of a police force, and since most of the Revolutionary War leaders had retired, the regulars had seen little if any combat. Most state militias were the playgrounds of Sunday soldiers.

The War Department in Washington consisted of Secretary Eustis and eight clerks. He and Dearborn were old warhorses in their sixties. Most of the regular army and militia commanders were city politicians and country lawyers. With a few exceptions (Kentucky riflemen and Boston and Baltimore sailors) they were no match for battle-hardened redcoats.

But Madison and the War Hawks felt that the two sides were pretty evenly matched, since the British had been tied up in Spain and Portugal fighting Bonaparte for a full eight years.

The U.S. Regular Army totalled less than 12,000 officers and men, including 5,000 recruits, far less than the authorized strength of 35,600. They manned a very thin chain of four border stations along the Canadian boundary: Fort Mackinac, on the straits between Lake Michigan and Lake Huron; Fort Dearborn, on the site of what is now Chicago; Fort Detroit; and Fort Niagara, where the Niagara River meets Lake Ontario.

Britain had a navy of 1,000 ships and 140,000 sailors patrolling the globe and controlling the seas around Napoleonic Europe. The minuscule U.S. Navy consisted of only twenty vessels: three large forty-four-gun super-frigates, three smaller frigates of the Constellation class rated at thirty-eight guns, and fourteen others. But the crews were well trained, and a match for any British frigate one on one. Many of the captains had seen action against France during the "Quasi War" and against the pirates of Tripoli. The real naval war was waged by America's flotilla of privateers, who planned to level the playing field and get rich by doing severe damage to British merchant shipping.

THE NEWS REACHES CANADA

On June 24, 1812, a courier from New York reached Montreal bearing the dreaded news: the United States had declared war on Great Britain seven days earlier.

A total of 7,000 British and Canadian regulars in Upper and Lower Canada and the Maritimes began their preparations for war. The regiments on North American duty were the following:

- 375 officers and men of the Royal Regiment of Artillery;
- the 31st Royal Artillery Drivers;
- 3 Royal Engineers;
- the 10th Royal Veteran Battalion;
- the 8th (1st Battalion);
- the 49th, 100th, 103rd, and 104th Regiments of Foot;

and four Canadian regiments:

- the Royal Newfoundland Regiment;
- the Canadian Fencibles;
- the Glengarry Light Infantry;
- the Canadian Voltigeurs.

In Upper Canada, which was to bear the brunt of the fighting, Major General Isaac Brock, the civil governor and military commander, had only 800 militiamen to back up his 1,600 regulars.

The two Canadian provinces would eventually put a total of about 10,000 militiamen in the field, while the U.S. sent at least twenty times that number of state militia to the frontier of war. Many however, stood on their constitutional right not to fight outside their own state border.

Britain could spare little else for the defense of Canada, with its population of only 500,000. It might have to be a holding action, with potential fallbacks toward the fortress of Quebec, until Napoleon was finally brought to heel.

Mister Madison Goes to War

> "The sword once drawn, full justice must be done. 'Indemnification for the past and security for the future,' should be painted on our banners."
> —*Thomas Jefferson to Robert Wright, 1812*

The United States was not so united in 1812, and not all citizens were ready to close ranks behind the war effort. Not everyone was as hot for war as Jefferson and Madison and the War Hawks.

Congress was split along party lines: every northern Federalist cast a "nay" vote, but the Jeffersonians and War Hawks still got their most ardent wish. At a celebratory Fourth of July dinner in the White House, Madison and his cabinet rose for a toast: "To an infant Hercules destined by the presage of early prowess to extirpate the British race of pirates and free-booters."

Down in the street, violent riots broke out when war was declared. In Baltimore, mobs burned property and killed dozens of Federalists. In New England people greeted the news with boos and sneeringly called it "Mr. Madison's War." They lowered their flags to half-mast and draped their windows in black. In Plymouth, Massachusetts, the townspeople jeered at the news and kicked their congressman through the streets of the town because he had voted for war.

TWO

1812

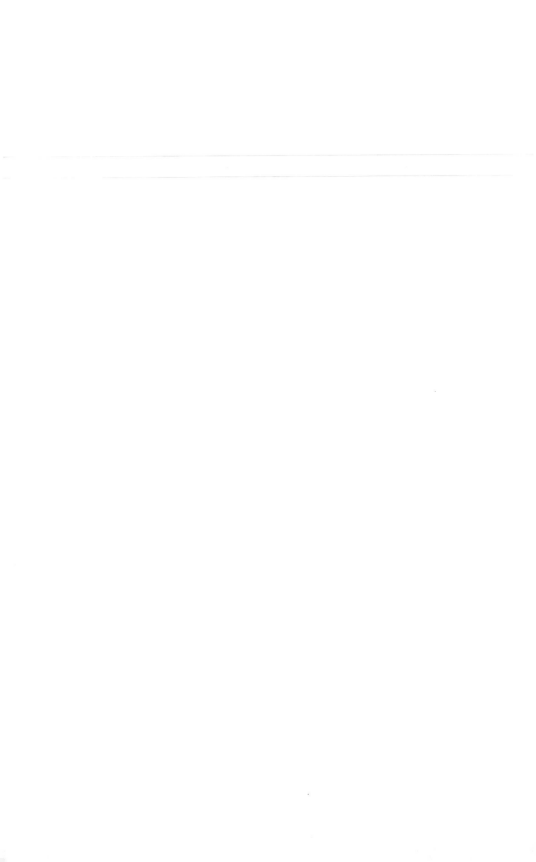

WAR PLANS

"An army which cannot be reinforced is already defeated."
–Napoleon Bonaparte

DEARBORN'S WAR PLAN

As the war began, James Madison had only about 130 employees in total, and his War Department had the Secretary, William Eustis, and a small office of clerks.

Madison and Eustis appointed seven old generals to lead the United States Army. All veterans of the American Revolution, way past their prime, some were overly fond of their whiskey, others grossly overweight. "Granny" Dearborn, as the troops called him, could no longer mount a horse and had to lead his troops from the back of a buckboard.

Dearborn, a northerner, had been Jefferson's Secretary of War, and had the cushy job of Customs Collector of the Port of Boston when Eustis tapped him to draw up a master plan for the invasion of Canada. The general saw in his mind's eye four powerful invasion forces crossing the thousand-mile frontier at about the same time — from Fort Detroit, Fort Niagara, Sackets Harbor, and Lake Champlain — who would then join up and capture Montreal, Canada's chief city. Dearborn had a problem. There were few roads, and whoever controlled the St. Lawrence River and Great Lakes would win the war.

RANKING THE ARMIES: THE AMERICANS

Henry Dearborn called for 50,000 volunteers to add to his 7,000 regulars in the invasion of Canada. Only 5,000 signed up. So much for "a mere matter of marching." The state militia was little better. There were over 100,000 men who had taken compulsory military training, but they could only be a called up by the state's governor, and then only in emergencies. And they could not be forced to serve outside their home states.

The British had their own problems and could only spare at the most 7,000 regulars from the campaign against Napoleon, out of a total of 300,000 men. But they were tough and disciplined and seasoned, unlike Madison's army, whose experience was limited to fighting the Prophet's deluded followers.

As it prepared to go to war, the U.S. Army's worst problem was not with its regulars, but at the top, with its command. There were virtually no professionals to choose from. Madison and Dearborn simply chose them all on the basis of friendship, their Republican Party loyalty, their planter heritage, their Revolutionary War experience and/or their ability to maintain the Virginia/New York nexus, which was the heart of the president's political success.

ISAAC CHAUNCEY

One of the brightest lights in the American side was Isaac Chauncey. Born in Black Rock, Connecticut, Chauncey was appointed a lieutenant in the Navy in 1793, fought in the West Indies and Mediterranean, and commanded two warships before being chosen to lead the naval forces on the Great Lakes. He also served twice as commandant of the New York Naval Shipyard.

By 1813, Sackets Harbor had become the U.S. Naval Headquarters on the lakes. Working at the Navy Point shipyard were 300 shipwrights and carpenters brought from New York City by Chauncey and shipbuilder Henry Eckford. Over the course of the war, they built eleven finely crafted warships.

Chauncey also mentored two young officers, Oliver Hazard Perry and James Macdonough, who were only in their twenties when they singlehandedly thrashed British fleets on Lake Erie and Lake Champlain.

On Lake Ontario, Chauncey had a harder time of it, especially after the British sent Sir James Yeo and 450 sailors and shipbuilders to Kingston in 1813. The two commanders operated under orders not to engage in any battle they might risk losing. Their war became a series of yacht races, interspersed by sharp episodes of extreme violence. At the end, it was nothing more than an arms race, with each bigger ship temporarily upsetting the balance of power. By the end of the war, Yeo had launched the biggest warship the British had ever built, bigger even than Nelson's Victory.

Ranking the Armies: The British

The British were outnumbered as the war began. But their senior officers outweighed this deficit with their skills, experience, training, and youth, plus the fact that very few were political appointees. They had either bought or earned their commissions. Those who had done both, like Isaac Brock, fought not just for pride and glory, but for a share of the prize money as well. Brock certainly was aware of the promise of booty in battle, to pay back the loan for his commission.

By contrast, the American commanders were by and large, rich, slave-owning planters, or had generous pensions or positions courtesy of the Republican Party of Jefferson and Madison.

In addition, many of the troops fighting for the Crown were pure mercenaries, Germans, Italians, Hungarians, Poles, and Russians in the Swiss Regiments that fought in Canada in 1812. One of first Royal Newfoundlanders killed in the war was a Dane. One 1812 British officer had to have his orders translated to German and French so the Swiss officers would understand. These mercenaries were pure professionals and very meticulous in their business, which was war.

Brock and his fellow British-born officers were all very competent in the field, except perhaps their commander. Dearborn's British counterpart was a mild-mannered, cautious, and as we shall see double-dealing staff officer named Sir George Prevost. He was the grandson of Augustine Prevost, a French-speaking Swiss mercenary, and a lieutenant-colonel in the British Army who had been wounded near Quebec in 1758. In 1765 Augustine Prevost, married Ann Grand, daughter of a wealthy moneylender whose brother was Benjamin Franklin's banker and chief financier of the American revolutionaries.

In the later 1760s, Augustine moved to New Jersey to speculate in land with his brother James. He and his wife Theodosia owned a large estate at Paramus, New Jersey, called the Hermitage. To protect the property during the American Revolution while her husband was fighting for the British, Theodosia offered George Washington the use of the Hermitage as his headquarters when he was driven out of New York in 1778. Two young officers, James Monroe and Aaron Burr, developed a friendship with Theodosia; when her husband James died in Jamaica in 1781, she mourned for a year then married Burr on July 6, 1782.

Brother Augustine Prevost had three sons: Augustine, William, and George. Augustine Junior joined his father's regiment, the 60th Foot (Royal

American Regiment), and became a land speculator with his father-in-law George Croghan, associate of Sir William Johnson. Croghan's other daughter married none other than Mohawk leader Joseph Brant.[1]

George was the youngest of the three brothers. At age eleven, he was commissioned in the family regiment, the 60th Foot (Royal American Regiment). He became a major at age twenty-three, and rose rapidly in the service, his commissions purchased for him by his rich grandfather. In 1805, he was created a baronet, and in 1808, Prevost was appointed lieutenant governor of Nova Scotia and tasked with improving the military defences of the Atlantic colonies. Responding to Jefferson's embargo, he set up "free ports" in Nova Scotia and New Brunswick, where American goods could be landed duty-free. While there, he mounted an expedition to Martinique, quarrelled with the Assembly, and slapped a tax on distilled liquors to pay for the militia.

Prevost spoke fluent French, and in 1811 the War Office ordered him to move to Lower Canada and replace Governor Craig as commander-in-chief of British forces in North America. One of his main duties was to conciliate French-Canadian political leaders, angered by the partisan alliance between Craig and the British oligarchy. Prevost charmed Bishop Plessis, exploited a split in the radical Canadian party, and bought off their leader Pierre Bédard with a judgeship. Working closely with his successor Louis-Joseph Papineau, he named five French speakers to the Legislative Council and pretty much brought the French Canadians onside.

Prevost was by nature a desk officer and was possessed of a shallow intellect. He initially did a decent job following orders from Lord Bathurst, far away in London, to fight a defensive war and not rile the Americans just yet, nor give them any excuse for invading the Canadas. Isaac Brock was to shatter these delusions.

The knock against Prevost is that he kept far too many troops downstream at Quebec, when it was at very little risk of invasion by sea. He starved the frontier of troops and supplies, resented the successes of his junior commanders, kept intelligence out of the hands of his generals, and actively tried to hog all the glory for himself and his place-serving friends.

Prevost seemed to revel in sitting in his office in Montreal, preventing his young Turks from ruining everything. And yet he nearly ruined everything himself. His hatred and jealousy of Voltigeur leader Charles-Michel de Salaberry nearly drove the young man out of the army. In his dispatches to London, Prevost actually claimed the victory at Chateauguay for himself.

Every army has its Prevost, a plodding and bloodless functionary, rusty in the field. Thinking himself more capable of glory than the next man, he couldn't resist putting himself in direct command at Sackets Harbor and Lake Champlain, where his rash actions and pig-headedness lost both battles for the British.

Sir George Prevost.

ISAAC BROCK TAKES CHARGE

I N SHARP CONTRAST TO SOUR-VISAGED SIR GEORGE PREVOST, ISAAC BROCK was a genial general, blue-eyed, six-foot-three, and still muscular at age forty-three. As a young man he could wrestle, box, and swim like a champion. When he was a young officer, he chased away a regimental bully who challenged him to a duel by accepting on the condition that they fight toe-to-toe with pistols. The bully was drummed out of the regiment.

Brock was also highly intelligent and knew how to manage civilians, and how to recruit militia, which was one of the main reasons he was sent to Upper Canada. He was also a natural-born master of psychological warfare. But was also desperately lonely living on the frontier and yearned to fight beside Wellington in Portugal and Spain. His passion was reading the classics and the lives of great men.

Brock lost his life gallantly in the first year of the war, after his amazing success at Detroit. And while his successors didn't have the same brilliance of command, leaders like Drummond and de Salaberry and Yeo were inspired by his example. Brock set the tone of the war on the British side. It was only a pity that Sir George Prevost smothered the spirit of Isaac Brock and led the British to two costly defeats.

MICHILIMACKINAC

On June 18, 1812, American President James Madison signed a congressional declaration of war against Britain.[2]

Brigadier-General Isaac Brock heard the news while he and his officers were hosting a dinner at Fort George for their American counterparts from across the river. They finished the splendid meal around a table covered with linen and candles glowing from the regimental silver, toasted each other with clinking wine glasses, then the Americans withdrew to their boats and were rowed back to Fort Niagara, so they could plan how best to kill each other.

Brock immediately went into action, ordering fast horses and runners to relay the news via York, then up Yonge Street to Georgian Bay, and then by fast canoe to Fort St. Joseph, at the head of Lake Huron, attention Captain Charles Roberts of the 10th Royal Veterans, commanding.

Isaac Brock had come to understand that gaining the friendship and trust of the western tribes was a key to his success in the forthcoming conflict.

Brock had met a Scottish trader in the U.S. northwest, supplied from Montreal, by the name of Robert Dickson, known as "Red Head" for his flaming red hair and beard. Dickson's brother Thomas had been one of Brock's militia officers in Niagara. In 1806, Dickson joined the Montreal-based Michilimackinac Company, whose silent partner was John Jacob Astor of the American Fur Company. Dickson had a Sioux wife, daughter of a powerful Dakota chief, who lived near the British fort on St. Joseph's Island, commanded by Captain Charles Roberts with forty-five soldiers of the 10th Royal Veterans Battalion.

Brock had already written to Dickson on February 27, 1812, asking if he and his friends could cooperate with the British in the likely event of war. Dickson immediately grasped what Brock needed — the capture of the American Fort Mackinac, formerly known by the British as Michilimackinac — the Gibraltar of the Great Lakes. He soon was leading a force of 150 Sioux, Ojibwa, Ottawa, Menominee, and Winnebago warriors, and about 180 Canadian voyageurs toward Fort St. Joseph. John Astin, Jr., the storekeeper for the Indian Department, also gathered a force of men, and by July 15 they reached Captain Charles Roberts at St. Joseph's Island, who told them that war had been declared less than a month earlier.

Roberts had earlier received conflicting orders from General Prevost at Quebec, who urged him not to go further, "if there is still a chance of peace." But now Brock's note told him that war was declared, and he had to "adopt the most prudent measures either of offense or defense which the circumstances might point out." This meant an attack the American fort while he still had the advantage of surprise. Fort Michilimackinac, sited on a secure promontory, was protected by a single nine-pounder gun and had a garrison of sixty-one U.S. regulars of the 1st American Artillery Regiment, commanded by Lieutenant Porter Hanks. In any equal battle, the British would lose.

The following day Roberts' force scrambled off in canoes, boats, and the North West Company schooner, *Caledonia*, bound for Mackinac Island, fifty miles away. They left only a caretaker garrison of six soldiers behind. That after-noon they came upon a Michigan militia officer, Michael Dousman, sent to spy on their activities, both for the Americans and for John Jacob Astor. Dickson knew Dousman well from his days at the Fort. Dousman told them nobody knew that war was declared. Nervously eyeing the Native warriors, he told Dickson he was concerned about his family and the safety of the people living in the small village below the fort. Seeing they were a serious threat to take the fort, he agreed to tell them the weaknesses of the American camp and not alert the garrison while he moved the villagers out of harm's way.

At three o'clock on the morning of July 17, Dickson and Roberts quietly landed their forces on the northwest side of the island, out of sight of the fort. Using Dousman's oxen, they hauled a six-pounder gun to the top of the hill overlooking the fort and prepared to do battle if necessary.

At ten o'clock, Roberts sent a message calling on Porter Hanks to surrender. The American commander, fearful of a massacre by the Dickson's warriors, agreed without too much urging, if Roberts permitted the regulars to leave for Detroit "on parole." This meant they pledged never to take up arms against Britain again.

Fort Mackinac.

Roberts then searched the fort and ordered a portion of the food and trade goods — valued at £10,000 — divided up among his soldiers and volunteers, with him taking the lion's share.

The result of this action? From that point on, British prestige rose in the eyes of the Amerindians, who had been indecisive up to that time. Without firing a single shot, the British had captured an essential strategic point that let them control the fur route to the upper lakes. At the same time they forced the Americans to abandon Fort Dearborn on the site of present-day Chicago.

Moral: There is nothing more important in war and business than dispatch.

DETROIT

"All warfare is based on deception. Therefore, when capable of attacking, feign incapacity; when active in moving troops, feign inactivity. When near the enemy, make it seem that you are far away; when far away, make it seem that you are near."

—Sun Tzu

RIGHT FROM THE START, THE U.S. TRIED TO CAPTURE THE WESTERN frontier of Ontario rather than the St. Lawrence Valley between Montreal and Lake Ontario. While some have argued the approach was a strategic mistake, the War Hawks were far more interested in driving the Indians west and capturing the rich lands of the Ontario peninsula between Lakes Erie and Huron. And Prevost had concentrated his regular troops at Montreal and Quebec.

HULL MAKES THE FIRST MOVE

On March 22, 1805, Thomas Jefferson appointed William Hull governor of the new Michigan Territory. Hull began to purchase Indian land for American settlers and negotiated the Treaty of Detroit with the Ottawa, Chippewa, Wyandot, and Potawatomi nations, who ceded their title to a large area around Fort Detroit.

When James Madison asked Hull to take command of the Detroit campaign, the silver-haired sixty-year old-declined. He told the president it was a job for younger men. But Madison insisted. Hull reluctantly agreed to serve, even though he had been arguing with Dearborn that America needed to build a naval fleet on Lake Erie to properly defend Detroit, but nothing had been done.

A few weeks before war was declared, Hull started gathering a 2,000-man army, with 400 regulars and the rest untrained Ohio volunteers. He also ordered a unit of several hundred foresters to move north and cut a 200-mile rough road from Ohio to Detroit, with bridges so the main force could move its cannon and wagons.

The army set off in mid-June into a green hell. Clad in long blue coats, their heads capped with round leather shakos, the soldiers trudged north like pack horses, pestered by clouds of blackflies and mosquitoes, each carrying a fifty-pound pack and a ten-pound muzzle-loading musket. They slept on the ground, woke to the sound of the bugle an hour before dawn, and immediately went into battle formation to prevent surprise attacks.

THE FIRST AMERICAN INVASION

Meanwhile, a courier from New York reached Montreal on June 24, bearing the news that the United States had declared war on Great Britain seven days earlier. Military governor Sir George Prevost immediately sent out fast canoes with dispatches, and on June 28, got word to the commandant of Fort Malden, Lieutenant-Colonel Thomas Bligh St. George, that the war was finally under way.

Fort Malden was an old firetrap with a stockade wall of pointed logs and a wood-shingled barracks. St. George had only a few hundred regulars and militia-men, and he was not confident of success. He sent a detachment of regulars and militia north to Sandwich, opposite the American Fort Detroit, and waited for the enemy to make its move.

Hull's soldiers got to Fort Detroit early in July, and after a few days' rest, the Americans start bombarding Sandwich. On July 12, they crossed the Detroit River with 2,500 regulars and militia. Hull commandeered the stone house of fur trader François Baby as his HQ. The next day he issued a proclamation that he had come with an army of friends, as a liberator:

"You will be emancipated from tyranny and oppression and restored to the dignified station as freemen ... If, contrary to the expectation of my country, you should take part in the approaching contest, you will be considered and treated as enemies, and the horrors and calamities of war will stalk before you."[3]

The local farmers soon found out what he meant: a company of fifty soldiers roaming the countryside, foraging for food, and liberating any supplies and stores they could find.

Hull soon sent scouts south along the road between Sandwich and Fort Malden. When they were stopped by a patrol of the 41st Regiment guarding the River Canard bridge, the two sides started skirmishing. On July 16, a British soldier named James Hancock was killed — the first person to die in the War of 1812 — and another soldier, John Dean, was wounded and captured.

HULL LOSES IT

It was in Sandwich that William Hull first started losing his nerve. He was beginning to feel more and more stranded, in a foreign country, with no way out. His 200-mile supply line was too long for comfort, and part of it skirted the shore of Lake Erie. He knew the British had complete control of the waterway, with six small gunboats. What he didn't know was that, on July 2, British Lieutenant Frederic Rolette of the Provincial Marine captured Hull's supply schooner *Cuyahoga*, the crew of which had not heard that war was declared. Rolette's crew found a trunk on board belonging to Hull. It contained letters to and from the Secretary of War in Washington, and Hull's complete battle plans. Rolette immediately sent the papers off by fast express canoe to General Brock at York.

When Hull's supply ship did not show up at Detroit, he feared the worst. Then on July 28, he was jolted by the arrival of some traders from the north who told him a British–Indian raiding party had taken Fort Mackinac.

Hull's mind soon filled with nightmarish visions of hordes of Indians cutting his supply line and massacring local settlers. To ease these worries, he ordered his dismayed young officers to pack up the army and cross back to the safety of Fort Detroit. He then sent a message ordering the garrison at Fort Dearborn, on the site of the future city of Chicago, to retreat to the larger Fort Wayne, which was safer from Indian attack.

The Indians were indeed busy. Just south west of Detroit, Shawnee chief Tecumseh had persuaded the Wyandot (Huron) people to switch their allegiance to the British. On August 4, a Captain Brush, escorting a supply column bringing cattle and other goods to Detroit, wrote Hull from River Raison that Tecumseh and some of his warriors were nearing the village of Brownstown. Brush asked for troops, and on August 4, Hull sent 200 Ohio militia south under the command of Major Thomas Van Horne.

On August 5, Van Horne's men were just fording Brownstown Creek when Tecumseh, Chickamauga war chief Daimee, Wyandot chief Roundhead, and twenty young warriors caught them in an ambush. Van Horne ordered a retreat, but his untrained militia scattered in a panic. Van Horne lost eighteen men killed and twelve wounded. Seventy other men simply disappeared.

Back in Detroit by August 8, Hull's jitters about the alliance between the British and the Indians increased daily.

The Wellington of Indians

The good news of the fall of Michilimackinac reached General Isaac Brock, wartime governor of Upper Canada, at York on July 29. He was at the time juggling his regimental staff to shore up the Niagara frontier, which he thought was the most vulnerable to attack. He asked Major General Roger Sheaffe of the 49th to take command at Fort George, and ordered the 41st Regiment at Kingston, under Lieutenant-Colonel John Vincent, to send six of his ten companies west to York and Niagara.

Now, armed with William Hull's battle plans, and with the knowledge that Tecumseh was nearing Detroit, Brock began to feel that he might have an even chance to gain the victory. He had already rushed Lieutenant-Colonel Henry Procter and most of the 41st Regiment ahead to Fort Maiden to relieve elderly Lieutenant-Colonel St. George, who had only 471 militia left to protect Amherstburg. Knowing Hull's fears, he also wrote a false letter, intending it to be captured, suggesting that he had 5,000 Indian warriors converging on Detroit and didn't need reinforcements from Mackinac.

In early August, Brock took 300 militia men from York and Niagara, raced southwest to Port Dover on Lake Erie, and then embarked on boats west to Amherstburg, arriving at Fort Malden on August 13. That night, a colonel brought Tecumseh and a group of warriors to the Fort. "This, sir," he said to Brock, "is Tecumseh, who desires to meet you." Brock saw a proud, solidly built man in buckskin jacket and leggings, with a single eagle feather in his black hair, and three silver coins dangling from his nose.

They liked each other immediately. Tecumseh turned to his aides and said, "This is a man!" The braves nodded in agreement, muttering "Ho! Ho!"

Without wasting a second, Tecumseh unrolled a sheet of birch bark and scratched a map of the area around Fort Detroit, with pathways for quick movement and ravines for cover.

Brock too was mightily impressed with Tecumseh, telling Prevost that he was "the Wellington of Indians ... a more sagacious or more gallant warrior does not exist."

Just two days later they moved against William Hull.

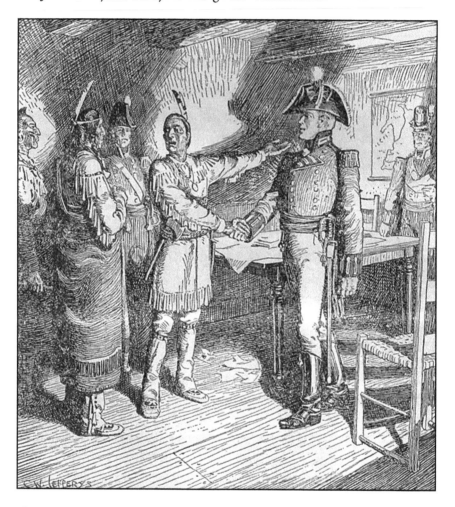

The meeting of Brock and Tecumseh.

The Capture of Detroit

That night, Tecumseh slipped back across the river south of Detroit to join his 600 warriors, who had quietly encircled the fort, cutting it off from the outside world. They then started their campaign of fear against the night watch on the stockades, howling like coyotes and signalling to each other with wild turkey calls.

Brock and Procter spent a day pulling together an attack force of 300 regulars and 400 Canadian militiamen. Most of the militia they dressed in old red uniforms from the fort to make Hull think they were regulars. They started crossing the river on August 15 and joined up with Tecumseh's braves. The warriors were all dressed for battle in moccasins and loincloths, their bodies painted in a kind of magical camouflage of garish black, white, and red designs meant to protect them in the forest. They were waving their muskets, tomahawks, scalping knives, and stone-headed war clubs, ready for a bloody battle. The whole band had been marching repeatedly in single file around a long loop, showing themselves briefly in a clearing, to convince the American sentinels that their numbers were far larger.

But Brock had no intention of exposing his men to the fearsome eight- and twelve-pounder guns of Fort Detroit, loaded like giant shotguns with canister shot that delivered hundreds of musket balls at a time. The Americans were well protected. From inside the stockade, soldiers could shoot their muskets through scores of loopholes without exposing themselves to return fire.

Brock marched his redcoats up the road toward the guns of Fort Detroit, and then ordered them suddenly to wheel left into a protective ravine discovered by Tecumseh's scouts.

He then sent Hull a letter warning that, unless the fort surrendered inside three hours, he might not be able to prevent an Indian massacre if it had to be taken by force.

While Hull pondered his message, Brock's gunners opened up with their artillery to soften up the fort. They did little damage until a ball bounded into the middle of a group of officers, cutting in half Lieutenant Porter Hanks, former commandant of Fort Mackinac, and horribly mutilating two others, their blood and body parts splattering the wall of the barracks.

Seeing this, Hull became paralyzed with fear. His young officers waited for the order to return fire. Nothing. Hull sat in his office stuffing his cheeks with his favourite chewing tobacco. His officers found him with a glazed look on his face, yellow-brown saliva dribbling down his shirt.

Suddenly he made his decision, and Detroit's defenders watched in amazement and horror as they witnessed their flag flutter down the flagpole and their fort surrendered without a shot. Many of Hull's officers openly wept or broke their swords in anger for being so dishonoured.

When Brock led his officers into Fort Detroit, some knelt and kissed the cannon captured from their countrymen long ago. Brock's first deed was to personally release soldier John Dean, who was wounded and captured at the River Canard bridge, and congratulate him in front of the troops.

Brock treated the American prisoners well, releasing the militiamen on parole, while Hull and his regulars were sent to prison camp in Quebec. For his part, Tecumseh kept his bargain and made sure that warriors who felt cheated out of a battle did not take their frustrations out on American civilians.

Hull was later sent home in exchange for British captives. He was tried at a court-martial presided over by General Henry Dearborn and sentenced to be shot for cowardice, although the court recommended mercy. President Madison agreed and pardoned him because of his services during the Revolution.

Moral: Make the best use of your lucky breaks, know what terrifies your enemy, and mount a classic bluff.

THE DEARBORN MASSACRE

Perhaps William Hull was the only sane man in Fort Detroit, for by surrendering peacefully to an army whose Indians were under the control of Tecumseh, he avoided a dreadful massacre of the civilians in the fort, including his own daughter and grandchildren.

The dangers of an Indian massacre were all too real on the American frontier.

At nine o'clock on the morning of August 15, the very day that Isaac Brock was crossing the Detroit River, Tecumseh's allies were committing a horrible massacre 500 miles to the west at Fort Dearborn, deep in Indian territory.

Chief Catfish, a friendly Potawatami, had warned Captain Nathan Heald that it would be suicidal to leave Fort Dearborn, but when he received General Hull's orders, he went against the pleas of his officers and men and ordered a retreat to Fort Wayne.

As Heald led a hundred soldiers and civilians from Fort Dearborn, the militia band struck up a funeral march. Near some sand dunes a mile along the shore of Lake Michigan, 500 Potawatamis suddenly streamed out of the woods in their war paint and opened fire on the wagons. The drivers whipped their horses to a grove of trees to make a last stand, where Heald was able to call a truce and negotiate a terrible deal: he and the unwounded survivors would become prisoners of war until the government paid for their release. The Potawatamis then went over the ground killing and scalping the fifty-four remaining wounded, including twelve children in a single wagon. They then burned Fort Dearborn to the ground.

After the Dearborn Massacre, a ragged madman named John Chapman — the famous Johnny Appleseed — went about the territory warning settlers if dangerous Indians were near, with this chant:

"I sow while others reap. Be sure my warning keep.

Indians will come by break of day. Indians hunting scalps, I say."

The Indians let Chapman come and go at will, believing he was possessed by the Great Spirit. His warnings were rarely wrong, and he saved many lives.

Moral: Sometimes Do or Die really does mean Die.

QUEENSTON HEIGHTS

"Courage cannot be counterfeited. It is the one virtue that escapes hypocrisy."

–Napoleon Bonaparte

Prevost's Armistice

Brock happily left Detroit and its immense quantity of booty behind and sailed back to Niagara and York. His share of the prize money would be generous, and he would send it on to his brother in London and the family in Guernsey, who were suffering from the blockade against Napoleon.[4] Following him were boatloads of guns and ammunition from Detroit, to arm his loyal Upper Canada militiamen.

On board the schooner *Chippawa* en route to Fort Erie, he discussed the upcoming campaign with the young militia officers. Brock told them, "If this war lasts, I am afraid I shall do some foolish thing, for I know myself, there is no want to courage in my nature — I hope I shall not get into a scrape."

Halfway back, he learned to his dismay that Sir George Prevost had arranged a truce with Granny Dearborn, before the news reached Montreal of his victory at Detroit. Prevost's ceasefire was a naive attempt to engage President Madison in peace talks, but it was partly to rein in Brock and prevent him from invading the United States. From Prevost's point of view, Brock's aggressive personality and tendency to stretch orders might derail delicate peace parleys, now that the British had backed off impressing U.S. sailors.

Brock thought it a foolish decision that would backfire. Madison and the War Hawks had far more on their minds than bullying on the high seas. Now the Americans would have time to reinforce their forts and supply their army at Niagara. A real danger was that Tecumseh and the western Indians would start to desert the British when they heard the news.

Indeed, when Brock's second-in-command General Roger Sheaffe relayed Prevost's ceasefire proposal at Niagara on August 16, the Americans were secretly delighted. Lieutenant-Colonel Solomon van Rensselaer of the New York Volunteers crossed to Fort George, and after a poker-faced standoff with Sheaffe, wrung a valuable concession from the British: free passage of the Great Lakes. This disastrous giveaway by Sheaffe let the Americans move a flotilla of nine trapped boats up the St. Lawrence to Sackets Harbor. They also ferried several batteries of heavy cannon, six regiments of regulars and five of militia, a battalion of riflemen, and what Brock called "a prodigious quality of Pork and Flower," from the port of Oswego at the eastern end of Lake Ontario, which had road connections to Albany.

A frustrated Brock reached Fort George on August 24 and immediately took charge. This so-far bloodless war made him yearn to cross the Niagara and thrash the Americans, but he threw himself into the work of building new fortifications and readying his soldiers for battle in spite of the ceasefire. On August 24, he paraded the regulars of Hull's army from Detroit along the river road from Fort Erie to Fort George, with men shuffling along and the wounded in open carts. Brigadier-General Peter B. Porter, a local congressman, War Hawk and quartermaster general of the New York state militia, wrote New York Governor Daniel D. Tompkins that the sight "made my heart sick within me, and the emotions it excited throughout the whole of our troops along the line are not to be described."

As expected, Madison nixed the truce on September 8, but the damage was done. Brock was now in a worse position because of the actions of Roger Sheaffe, following the orders of their timid commander downriver in Montreal. Now Sir George Prevost was speculating about abandoning Detroit — Brock warned him not to — it would be a grave mistake to alienate the Indians.

Brock was being hailed everywhere as the "saviour of Upper Canada," and perhaps some of the praise was going to his head. He wrote to his brother Savery, "if I should be beaten, the province is inevitably gone; and should I be victorious, I do not imagine the gentry from the other side will be anxious to return to the charge."

Perhaps Prevost knew better. Under orders from England, he vetoed any cross-border invasion plans. For the moment, the war would be strictly defensive. There would be no more Detroits for Isaac Brock.

POLITICS ON PARADE

By early October, the weather worsened, with raw winds and cold rain lashing up the Niagara gorge between Lewiston, New York, and Queenston, Upper Canada. U.S. Militia Major General Stephen van Rensselaer and his cousin Solomon had gathered 900 regulars and 2,600 militia for the invasion of Upper Canada. They believed they were facing the same number of British. In fact, Brock's force along the Niagara numbered only 400 regulars and 800 militia, most of them at home harvesting their crops. More regulars were on the way, as well as a mercenary force of 300 Iroquois from the Grand River, persuaded to join the fight by John Norton of the Indian Department.

Stephen van Rensselaer was the horse-faced forty-eight-year-old scion of a wealthy old New York Dutch family who owned a 1,200 square mile (3,072 km²) estate named Rensselaerswyck. A supporter of the Federalists, he had little military experience and was intending to run for the governorship of New York before the war began. But his younger cousin Solomon was an experienced militia officer and did the bulk of the real soldiering.

Urged on by Granny Dearborn, who told them "we must calculate on possessing Upper Canada before winter sets in," the van Rensselaers were ready to cross the river, but they had a serious problem of a political nature.

Up the river at Buffalo, Brigadier-General Alexander Smyth had arrived on the frontier at the head of 1,600 U.S. regulars. The brigadier was also inspector general of the Army, ordered north by his friend in Washington, Secretary of War William Eustis. Smyth was another intensely political Virginia Republican, and as such, would have nothing at all to do with the Federalist van Rensselaers. He wouldn't even answer van Rensselaer's letters and told everybody within earshot that Stephen van Rensselaer was a craven coward.

Smyth's real role for the time being was not to conquer Canada, but to see van Rensselaer disgraced, so that he was not a threat to the re-election of Republican stalwart Daniel D. Tompkins as governor of New York.[5]

So Smyth stayed put, refusing to march over muddy roads, knowing full well that the optimal place to land an army was above the Falls, while van Rensselaer's plan, approved by Granny Dearborn, was to cross at Queenston and Fort Niagara.

On October 8, van Rensselaer told Dearborn that "the blow must be struck soon, or all the toil and expense of the campaign will go for nothing, and worse than nothing, for the whole will be tinged with dishonor."

Van Rensselaer had to act quickly. His army was atrociously equipped, with up to half of the men sick from living in the open in the cold and wet weather. Three or four soldiers were dying each day from camp diseases, and there was a shortage of coffins. He couldn't pay his troops, desertion was rife, and he was low on ammunition, medical supplies, and food. All his militiamen wanted to do was go home to their families for the winter. But like Hull in Detroit, he was being pushed by his younger officers to fight.

Brock shook his head at the baffling intelligence coming across. Would this military melodrama give him an advantage? Brock kept his focus on fortifying the village of Queenston. He brought in two companies of the 49th Regiment, led by captains John Williams and James Dennis, backed by two trusted companies of green-jacketed Lincoln Militia. Up the steep southern slope, and out of sight of the Americans, his engineers quickly cleared a long field of fire and built a redan, or earthwork battery, with a hefty eighteen-pounder. On Vrooman's Point halfway to Fort George, they installed a massive twenty-four-pounder super mortar called a carronade, to shoot up the river. The British were ready to fight.

Bold Action at Black Rock

1812, October 10, 3:00 a.m.

Meanwhile, above the Falls, young U.S. Lieutenant Jesse Elliot was planning a bold move. Just before midnight on October 9, he stealthily launched two boatloads of American sailors from Black Rock and led them across the Niagara River to Fort Erie. They completely surprised the crews of the British brig *Detroit* and schooner *Caledonia* at anchor under the protection of the guns of the fort. They quickly freed forty American prisoners aboard the two ships and captured seventy British and Canadian sailors. In ten minutes they were away from the dock and heading across the Niagara River. *Caledonia* made it to the American naval base at Black Rock, but *Detroit* ran aground, and all that day, the angry guns of Fort Erie pounded the ship. That night Elliott took what stores he could off the ship and fired the rest.

In one audacious action, Elliott had sharply reduced the strength of the British squadron on Lake Erie and seized a fighting ship for an American squadron that had previously had none. The British would pay dearly for this negligence.

The Battle Begins

Lieutenant George Ridout of the 3rd York Militia had been on duty five nights straight, up on Queenston Heights, waiting for the attack. Suddenly the quiet was shattered by jets of flame and cannon fire from the two eighteen-pounders on the mountain across at Lewiston. The British replied with cannon and musket fire, and Ridout raced down to the redan, "from whence the view was truly tremendous, the darkness of the night, interrupted by the flash of the guns and small-arms."

Van Rensselaer finally decided to make his crossing without Smyth, who was refusing to commit on an attack on Fort George from Niagara. To van Rensselaer's dismay, he found they only had thirteen boats to ferry the troops. And for some reason, possibly sabotage, an experienced boatman named John Simms had disappeared with a boat containing all the oars from Barton, Porter & Co.'s dock at Lewiston. After a two-day scramble to make new oars, van Rensselaer ordered his army to move on the night of October 13. Since there weren't enough vessels to carry the whole army across, they had to shuttle back and forth in the darkness, carrying twenty-five men per boatload. Several boats overshot and were swept down the river.

The Americans cross the Niagara at Queenston.

By about 4:00 a.m., only half his army had landed on the beach. Suddenly a redcoat sentry saw them and sounded the alarm. Soon tongues of flame from British muskets flashed in the darkness, from Captain Dennis and his forty-six regulars, while Captain Williams' gunners opened fire with grapeshot on the American boats. The roar of artillery woke General Brock out of a light sleep at Fort George seven miles away. He immediately sprang into action — in battle conditions, you slept in your clothes. Brock ordered a general alert and told his second in command General Roger Sheaffe to start bombarding Fort Niagara in case the action at Queenston was a feint. He then mounted his grey horse Alfred and with his aides Major Glegg and Lieutenant-Colonel Macdonnell headed south toward Queenston.

Dawn was breaking as Brock arrived at the village and galloped up to the redan to survey the field. The morning was grey and a light drizzle was falling, but Brock could see this was not a feint, and that the main body of Americans were lined up at Lewiston waiting to cross. He immediately sent back an order to Sheaffe to follow at the double.

At that very moment, Captain John Wool of the 13th U.S. Infantry was feeling somewhat like Wolfe at Quebec in 1759. He had found a fisherman's path up the cliff behind Brock, and his sharpshooters were scrambling up the escarpment. Brock and his officers seem to have made a fatal mistake. Now the Americans were digging in on the high ground 300 feet above the town, checking their ammunition pouches, ready to repel the enemy.

Suddenly Brock heard Wool's troops cheering overhead. Horrified that he was being outflanked, he had to think quickly. He ordered the eighteen-pounder spiked with a ramrod and made a fast downhill retreat to the village.

Brock was in a slow panic. He did not have enough hard information on which to act. He had to visualize several scenarios, and then move very fast. Assuming that the Americans on the heights were an advance body, he needed to beat them before they were reinforced. So he took a calculated risk, believing he might be able to rely on his usual speed and boldness. And luck.

Quickly assembling a party of 200 regulars and militia behind a stone wall, he cried "Follow me, boys," and started back up the steep hill to dislodge the invaders. Wool's riflemen saw them coming up and started a murderous fire. One of them targeted Brock and hit him with a ball in the wrist. He hardly noticed. A few seconds later, he felt a sharp, hot burn in his heart as another American sniper found his mark. Isaac Brock slumped to the ground and quickly expired.

He had been lucky with Mackinac, lucky at Detroit, but here at Queenston Heights his luck ran out, and the glory he had always sought grasped him to her breast.

Under a withering assault, the rest of his volunteers crouched down out of sight of the Americans and waited for backup. Captains John Williams and James Dennis arrived to try another charge up the hill, but both were seriously wounded. Brock's aide Macdonnell arrived with two companies of York militia, but he too was shot and died the next day.

Up on the heights the Americans were suffering as well. Captain Wool had taken a British musket ball through the buttocks. He was happily relieved by militia Brigadier-General William Wadsworth and an aggressive young colonel from Smyth's army named Winfield Scott, who had raced downriver without permission to join the fight. Scott quickly took charge.

By noon, the Americans had the momentum, Queenston seemed lost, and the defenders were retreating. At this point, Major General Roger Sheaffe was halfway to Queenston with the main body of British regulars. He had wisely sent John Norton's Mohawks on ahead to reconnoitre. When scouts came back to report on the U.S. position, Sheaffe coolly commenced a long flanking action along a trail that climbed the escarpment to the west. Norton and eighteen-year-old Mohawk chief John Brant then led the Iroquois through the forest up to the American lines and started terrifying them with war whoops, stopping enemy scouts from tracking Sheaffe's army.

Then the tide changed. Across the river at Lewiston, van Rensselaer no longer had an army to command. The sight of the returning wounded, many badly mangled by ball and shot, now horrified his militia. They could hear war whoops from the heights across the river. They were now quite properly refusing to cross, claiming their right not to fight outside their home state.

At mid-afternoon, British regulars from Chippawa and Captain Runcey's platoon of black troops joined the main army, and they drew up west of the Americans in Elijah Phelps's harvested field. At Sheaffe's command, they started advancing with fixed bayonets toward the Americans, now thoroughly terrorized by the Iroquois. Hundreds were cowering in caves under the very edge of the escarpment, or sliding back down to the river, crazed with fear. Some lost their footing on the slippery shale and flew onto the rocks below.

Winfield Scott's troops were nearly out of ammunition, and they had failed to take the spike out of Brock's eighteen-pounder. After failing to rouse his men,

Scott knew the first real battle of the War of 1812 was lost. He commandeered a white shirt, waved it from his sword, and surrendered, just as a Mohawk was about to plant a tomahawk in his skull.

By sundown 250 of the Americans who had landed in Canada were dead or wounded; 100 of the wounded would die back in camp at Lewiston. Almost 1,000 were prisoners. Sheaffe sent the militia home under parole. The rest, including Wadsworth, Scott, and seventy-three other officers, were shipped to the prison camp at Quebec.

The British lost only fourteen killed, including their beloved commander Isaac Brock, who did his duty and did it well. On the day of his funeral and burial at Fort George, the guns at Fort Niagara boomed out a seventeen-gun salute for Isaac Brock. It was the American officers he had supped with barely three months ago, giving him a moving farewell to arms.[6]

Moral: Have the depth to carry on regardless, even when your charismatic commander gets himself killed.

AFTERWARD

Roger Sheaffe became commander-in-chief of British forces and administrator of Upper Canada on Brock's death. He served for less than a year before he was posted out of the province on June 19, 1813.

Brigadier-General Alexander Smyth, who had ruined van Rensselaer's invasion attempt and sabotaged his campaign for governor of New York, fared no better. In late November, after posturing for weeks, he bungled two attempts to invade Canada near Fort Erie. He then got into a furious argument over strategy with Brigadier-General Peter B. Porter, a lead War Hawk and local businessman whose family firm, the Porter, Barton Company, were major road builders, land dealers, and suppliers to the U.S. Army. When Porter called him a coward in public, Smyth challenged him to a duel. The two met on Grand Island. "Unfortunately," quipped one historian, "both missed." However with his political duties done, Smyth was able to slip away to his home in Virginia. His name was removed from the U.S. Army rolls, and by war's end he was back in the state legislature and the Congress.

As for Queenston, it was easily captured the following year by American troops on their way to take Fort George.

The Real Uncle Sam

One of the Porter family's favoured suppliers was Samuel Wilson, a prosperous old meat-packer from Troy, New York, who had a contract to supply salt beef and pork to the Army. Wilson's rations were supplied in government barrels branded with the initials "U.S." The teamsters and soldiers joked that the initials referred to "Uncle Sam," which was Wilson's nickname. Soon cynical locals started to refer to all U.S.-marked goods, from brass buttons to bullets, as belonging to Uncle Sam (the federal government).[7]

OLD IRONSIDES

John Adams's Pro-British Federalists built the first real American Navy during the mini war with France in the 1790s, and took action against the Barbary pirates. After Trafalgar in 1805, there was little pressing need to construct American ships of the line. They could only be used against Britain anyway, since the French threat was gone. The British would have interpreted any building program as a hostile act, tipping the scales in favour of Napoleon.

However, Americans could rejoice in a few brilliant individual maritime victories, which were heavily milked as morale boosters.

THE *CONSTITUTION* BATTLES THE *GUERRIERE*

On August 19, 1812, three days after William Hull turned into a nervous wreck and gave up Detroit, his favourite nephew and adopted son Isaac Hull was busy making a wreck of the British frigate HMS *Guerriere*.

Born in Derby, Connecticut, Isaac would join his mariner father, Joseph, as cabin boy on trips to the West Indies. When his father died of yellow fever, young Isaac was adopted by his famous uncle William, a hero of the Revolutionary War. During the mid-1790s, he captained several merchant vessels, losing some to French privateers. When the United States Navy was founded in March 1798, he served on board the super frigate *Constitution* in the Quasi-War with Revolutionary France, and went to the Mediterranean to fight the Barbary Pirates as First Lieutenant of the frigate *Adams*. Promoted to captain in 1806, he supervised the building of gunboats with Isaac Chauncey, of the Boston naval yard, and then realized his dream, in 1809 and 1810, with command of the frigates, *Chesapeake* and *President*.

At age thirty-three, he found himself posted as captain of the *Constitution*, one of the finest ships built in Boston. In August, 1812, Hull was out hunting for British prey when he came upon the impressment ship *Guerriere* 600 miles (1,000 km) east of Nova Scotia. The two ships manoeuvred all night and came to blows the following day.

British tars were virtual slaves, whereas Yankee sailors in the tiny American Navy were well treated, very well-trained, and itching for a fight. The navy's four super-frigates were thoroughbreds, made of the hardest oak available, their seven-inch planks carefully curved and reinforced to deflect cannon balls. Where the average British frigate had thirty-eight guns, *Constitution* had forty-two. In fact, Hull had crammed fifty-two cannons into the vessel.

It was really no contest, and when the two warships engaged in close and violent action, the *Guerriere* was de-masted and rendered a wreck in less than half an hour. When the *Constitution*'s boarding officer asked Captain Dacres if indeed he had struck *Guerriere*'s colours, the shattered commander replied, "Well I don't know; our mizzen mast is gone, our main mast is gone, and upon the whole, you may say that we have struck our flag."

Guerriere was too badly damaged to take in tow, so Hull ordered his sailors to take out the wounded and set her on fire before returning to Boston.[8]

USS Constitution *smashes HMS* Guerriere.

In a war where bad news was the norm, Hull's victory electrified the Americans and showed the world that the small U.S. Navy was a dangerous opponent for Britain's thousand-ship navy, in single vessel action at least. Witnesses later claimed that the British shot merely bounced off the *Constitution*'s sides, as if the ship were made of iron rather than wood. Soon nicknamed Old Ironsides, the *Constitution* defeated or captured seven more British ships during the war, and ran the British blockade of Boston twice.

The USS *Constitution* is the oldest commissioned ship afloat in the world and is still in service in the U.S. Navy.

Moral: Training and hearts of oak conquer all. Also, make sure you have more guns than they do.

At Sackets Harbor

On September 1, 1812, capable Boston navy yard director Isaac Chauncey was appointed a commodore in command of U.S. naval forces on Great Lakes, with his headquarters at Sackets Harbor, New York. He had already been involved in construction of the lake fleet, and his yard was completing the 243-ton brigantine *Oneida*, with sixteen long range twenty-four-pounders, and the *Julia*, a refitted schooner armed with one thirty-two-pounder gun and some swivels.

By early November, Chauncey had seven warships under his command, giving his fleet the ability to dominate Lake Ontario and bottle up the British fleet in Kingston Harbour.

The British Provincial Marine, under the command of Captain Hugh Earle, was also busy building a battle fleet, but was not as far advanced. Earle's fleet consisted of HMS *Royal George*, his flagship, a corvette with twenty-two twenty-four-pounder short range carronades; the brigantine *Earl of Moira*, with sixteen twenty-four-pounders; two large armed schooners, *The Prince Regent* and *The Duke of Gloucester*; and two small armed schooners, *The Simcoe* and *The Seneca*.

On November 9, to show who was boss, Chauncey waited with his fleet by the False Duck Islands, then chased the *Royal George* into the Bay of Quinte, The following morning, Earle escaped to Kingston in a light wind, followed closely by Chauncey's fleet. That afternoon at the Battle of Kingston Harbour,

Chauncey bombarded the town for a few hours, exchanged respectful gunfire with the five batteries of long-range shore cannon at Point Henry, and then, with a November gale coming up, steered back to Sackets at dusk.

It was the first and last time the Americans would dare the wrath of the gunners of Kingston.

GRANNY DEARBORN

As the 1812 campaigning wound down, the course of the war seemed all to the advantage of the British Army, with the glorious exception of Old Ironsides. It was no longer "a mere matter of marching," in the immortal words of Thomas Jefferson. On October 1, he wrote his friend Colonel William Duane, that he feared Hull's surrender was

> more than the mere loss of a year to us. Besides bringing on us the whole mass of savage nations, whom fear and not affection had kept in quiet, there is danger that in giving time to an enemy who can send reinforcements of regulars faster than we can raise them, they may strengthen Canada and Halifax beyond the assailment of our lax and divided powers. Perhaps, however, the patriotic efforts from Kentucky and Ohio, by recalling the British force to its upper posts, may yet give time to Dearborn to strike a blow below. Effectual possession of the river from Montreal to the Chaudiere, which is practicable, would give us the upper country at our leisure, and close for ever the scenes of the tomahawk and scalping-knife.

As for Granny Dearborn, he was well aware that the American public demanded action, especially after Hull's treason, especially during an election year — James Madison was re-elected that November.

With the agreement of Eustis and the president, Dearborn decided to take one more stab at glory and capture Montreal before winter. In early November he set off from Burlington, Vermont, with an army of 2,000, leaving behind a third of his troops, laid low with measles and flu, and 200 dead from typhus and pneumonia. On November 10, at Odelltown, Lower Canada, he was driven back sharply by Lieutenant-Colonel Charles de Salaberry, with his Canadian Voltigeurs, a regiment of the British Army raised for service in Canada. Other smaller raids followed, but the American militia refused to cross the border, and the regulars couldn't handle the Voltigeurs.

Charles de Salaberry recruiting.

By November 23, Dearborn was back in his cozy quarters at Albany, warming his toes before the fire. The only Americans left in Canada were prisoners of war.

Ten thousand miles away, outside Moscow, Napoleon's Grande Armée, once 690,000 strong and the largest army in European history, was beginning its bitter retreat. As many as 400,000 of his soldiers would die of cold, disease, and Russian cannon shot during the appalling campaign. Along with them was the great friend of Jefferson and Madison, U.S. Ambassador to France Joel Barlow, who froze to death in a Polish village.

Prince Regent William addressed Britain's Parliament on November 30. He regretted that efforts to restore peace between Great Britain and the United States had not been successful; that America had attempted, without success, to invade his Canadian provinces and "seduce the inhabitants of them from their allegiance." Until peace could be restored "without sacrificing the maritime rights of Great Britain," he would expect parliamentary support for "a vigorous prosecution of the war."

THREE

1813

"Poor little half-starved Upper Canada alone could carry on a war against the whole gang of cowardly, stupid Democrats to all eternity."

–Nathan Ford, Ogdensburg, NY, July 5, 1813

BATTLES IN THE WILDERNESS

A FTER THE DEBACLES OF MACKINAC, DETROIT, AND QUEENSTON, CYNICS in the north doubted the ability of Madison's old soldiers to mount any decent campaigns, but Granny Dearborn soldiered on. He had developed two major scenarios for the coming season — the recapture of Detroit and an attack on Upper Canada across Lake Ontario — and ran them by the secretary of war, William Eustis.

REMEMBER THE RAISIN

Eustis's choice to lead the Detroit Campaign was obvious: Brigadier-General William Henry Harrison, the hero of Tippecanoe. Harrison was in the mold of George Washington, another leader of Virginia planter stock who knew Latin and Greek and who tirelessly promoted western settlement. When Federalist John Adams wanted to appoint him governor of the Indiana Territory in 1801,

Harrison first checked with the Jeffersonians to see if they approved of him taking the job. They did.

At age thirty-nine, Harrison was an implacable and dedicated military man. He knew he was in for a brutal campaign, with Tecumseh's warriors still at Detroit. Without wasting a minute, or waiting for spring, he started north at the end of October 1812. He needed to build a fort closer to Lake Erie on the Maumee River as soon as possible, and then prepare for a spring campaign.

William Henry Harrison.

His army of 6,000 men advanced in three columns so enemy scouts would not know the extent of his total force. Nearing Lake Erie in a snowstorm in January 1813, he ordered Brigadier-General James Winchester to move ahead with an advance column of 800 Kentucky volunteers. When Winchester reached the frozen Maumee, he received a call for help from frightened settlers at Frenchtown, a village on the River Raisin twenty-six miles south of Detroit.[1] They were terrified about a small camp of British troops and Indians in the area.

In sub-zero temperatures, with the wind howling off the lake and the snow deepening, Winchester's men trudged north to the Raisin River as fast as they could. On January 18, the Kentuckians attacked the British camp and forced them to retreat, and then reached shelter in Frenchtown in an exhausted state. Never expecting a major attack in winter, and with help on the way from Harrison, Winchester neglected to send out patrols to watch for enemy movements.

Meanwhile, Major General Henry Procter, Brock's replacement on the Detroit frontier, had been tracking Harrison's progress. He quickly left Fort Malden leading a force of 600 regulars from the 41st Regiment of Foot and Royal Newfoundland Fencibles, with 800 warriors and six light three-pounder guns drawn on sledges. They swiftly crossed the frozen Detroit River and converged on River Raisin. At four o'clock in the morning of January 23, they reached Frenchtown and completely surprised the 800 Kentuckians. Said Canadian volunteer John Richardson: "Such was their security and negligence, our line was actually half formed within musket shot of their defenses before they were even aware of our presence." As the British cannons started spewing fire, the redcoats stormed into the village with fixed bayonets, while Native warriors attacked from behind with tomahawks and war clubs. Wyandot chief Roundhead quickly captured General Winchester, stripped off his uniform and delivered him to Procter in his nightshirt.

After a brutal three-hour encounter that saw more than 400 Americans killed, Winchester sent a message to his force to surrender, since Procter was suggesting they would all be killed by the warriors. As part of the surrender terms, Procter agreed that the most badly wounded Americans would be treated fairly as prisoners of war, and would receive food, shelter, medical attention, and protection from the Native warriors.

Unfortunately, Procter was no Isaac Brock, and his word lacked clout.

Unable to control his warriors (and with Tecumseh hundreds of miles away to the south) Procter shrugged as the Indians stripped the Americans of their warm winter clothing and made them pull the sledges back to Fort Malden. Most survived, but many fell by the wayside and froze to death in snowdrifts. The surviving 550 Americans, mostly from Kentucky, were sent to Quebec for fifteen months then freed in a prisoner exchange.

The seriously wounded, sixty-four officers and men, were left behind in the settlers' houses. Procter feared he had to get away quickly because Harrison's main force might be approaching, but he promised Winchester his men would return and get the wounded out the following day. Again, he spoke with a forked tongue. The remaining warriors, left to guard the wounded, soon smashed into the dwellings and torched them, murdered the Americans, and sent the scalps on to Fort Malden.

When Harrison heard the cruel news, he shut down operations for the winter. On February 1, on the south bank of the Maumee River at the present day site of Toledo, Ohio, his men began to build a huge protective stockade, Fort Meigs, named after his friend the governor of Ohio.

Up at Fort Malden, more horrors awaited the imprisoned Kentucky volunteers. One of them, A.G. Austen, wrote to his mother:

> Never, dear mother, if I should live a thousand years, can I forget the frightful sight of this morning, when handsomely painted Indians came into the fort, some of them carrying half a dozen scalps of my countrymen fastened upon sticks, and yet covered with blood, and were congratulated by Procter for their bravery. I heard a British officer tell another officer that Procter was a disgrace to the British army and a blot upon the British character.

This brutal massacre of wounded Kentuckians made "Remember the Raisin" a rallying cry for Harrison's army that season, and back in Kentucky, enlistments soared.

Massacre at Fort Meigs

The suffering of the Kentucky volunteers was not over yet.

By early spring, Harrison's men had nearly finished the fifteen-foot pickets around Fort Meigs. The eight-acre site was well situated, with deep ravines to the east and west and the river to the north. South of the fort, axe-men were clearing an open field of fire while the carpenters completed eight large blockhouses.

Up Lake Erie at Fort Malden, Major General Henry Procter had to make a choice. He could attack Presque Isle, today's Erie, Pennsylvania, where a road had been cut from Pittsburgh, and a young American naval officer named Oliver Hazard Perry had arrived on March 27 to start building a flotilla of ships to control Lake Erie. Or he could attack Harrison at Fort Meigs, disrupt his summer campaign, and capture some badly needed supplies. Procter, as turned out, made entirely the wrong decision and prepared to attack Harrison as soon as the bad weather ended.

Harrison soon got wind of Procter's plans and ordered another 300 troops down the Maumee to Fort Meigs, increasing his garrison to 1,100 men. Kentucky Governor Shelby also sent north a brigade of 1,200 militia under Brigadier-General Green Clay.

Procter started disembarking his army at the mouth of the Maumee on April 26. He brought thirty-one Royal Artillery, 500 regulars of the 41st Regiment of Foot and Newfoundland Regiment of Fencibles, 462 Canadian militiamen, and about 1,250 Native warriors led by Tecumseh himself. For artillery he landed two big twenty-four-pounder guns from Fort Detroit and nine lighter guns. He had also towed along two gunboats with nine-pounders to bombard Fort Meigs from the river.

By the end of April, the British batteries were set up on the north side of the river, while Tecumseh's warriors had silently scoped out the south shore around the fort. Inside, Harrison's troops threw up "traverses," twelve-foot-high embankments to catch the cannon balls and limit their damage.

Tecumseh then sent a letter into the fort, challenging the hero of Tippecanoe to come out and fight:

> I have with me eight hundred braves. You have an equal number in your hiding place. Come out with them and give me a battle. You talked like a brave man when we met at Vincennes (the capital of Indiana Territory), and I respected you, but now you hide behind logs and in the earth, like a groundhog. Give me your answer.

Harrison did not respond to Tecumseh's taunting, but he decided to act quickly before the British could start their bombardment. Most of General Clay's Kentuckians had arrived and they developed a plan. Clay's force would cross the river, spike the British guns on the north bank, and then withdraw into the fort, while Harrison's force attacked a single British battery on the south bank.

Before dawn on May 5, Colonel William Dudley led almost 900 Kentucky militia and regulars across in boats, and they completely surprised the British. But they were poorly trained and spiked the guns with musket ramrods instead of handspikes, which meant that the British could quickly unspike their cannons with drills. Then, instead of retreating quickly to the fort, some of Dudley's men started firing back at Tecumseh's snipers, who retreated and led them deeper into the woods into a bloody ambush. When Dudley followed to warn them of the danger, four British companies under Major Adam Muir counterattacked and forced the Kentuckians to surrender.

That day, only 150 of Dudley's 866 officers and men made it back to Fort Meigs. He left eighty dead on the field, and the rest were made prisoners and taken by British and Indians toward the ruined Fort Miami near the British camp. On the way to the fort, some of the Indians started to steal the prisoners' clothes and possessions, and they jabbed them with spears to make them move faster. Arriving at the fort, the Kentuckians found themselves having to run the gauntlet as the Indians hit them with war clubs and slashed them with scalping knives. Those who stumbled or fell unconscious were tomahawked and their bodies tossed into a ditch for scalping later. One British officer standing nearby joked with the Indians, "Oh, nichee wah!" ("Oh, brother, quit it!")

Just as some of the braves were threatening to turn the gauntlet into a massacre worse than the River Raisin, a furious Tecumseh galloped up with Lieutenant-Colonel Matthew Elliott and Captain Thomas McKee of the Indian Department.

A British colonel later recalled the scene: "His eyes shot fire. He was terrible." When he saw a warrior standing over a prisoner with an uplifted tomahawk, he rode straight at the brave and whacked him over the head, knocking him senseless. Then he leaped from his horse, grabbed another warrior by the throat, and threw him to the ground. He slapped another in the face and cried, "Are there no men here?" Finally the warriors snapped out of their bloodlust and hung their heads in shame.

When the bloodthirsty mob was gone, a look of sadness came over Tecumseh's face and he moaned, "My poor Indians! My poor Indians!"

When he had pulled himself together, he marched across the camp and confronted Procter, asking him in front of his officers why he had not protected the prisoners. When Procter replied, "Your Indians cannot be controlled; they cannot be commanded," Tecumseh, who had just proved the opposite, glared at the general and roared, "Begone! You are unfit to command. Go and put on petticoats." Proctor simply turned away while his officers stared down at their boots.

On May 7, Procter gave up the siege of Fort Meigs when eight militia captains from the Kent and Essex regiments told him they had to go home immediately to plant their crops or their families would face starvation. He would try again in July, but Harrison was dug in too well, and he was prepared to wait to wage war until the times were riper. Meanwhile, a hundred miles east, Commodore Perry was starting to launch his Lake Erie fleet.

The War of 1812 was now one year old, and James Madison had little to show for his war except an empty treasury. That state of affairs was about to change.

Moral: The laws of war mean nothing when you are travelling through wild country in winter."

THE TAKING OF YORK

As the 1813 campaign year began, Henry Dearborn had a new secretary of war to deal with. Somebody had to walk the plank after the previous year's military reversals, and it was his old friend William Eustis.

Madison originally offered the job to Major General Morgan Lewis, former New York governor and quartermaster general of the U.S. Army. But Lewis declined and suggested his brother-in-law Brigadier-General John Armstrong, Jr. The two men were old friends, both having been aides to General Horatio Gates at the Battle of Saratoga. Both their fathers were valued friends of George Washington, and both were leaders of the Society of the Cincinnati.[2]

Another Armstrong brother-in-law was prominent Republican and Founding Father Robert Livingstone. One of Armstrong's daughters married John Jacob Astor's son, William Backhouse.

Jefferson was impressed with Armstrong and had appointed him minister to France from 1804 to 1810. However, as Henry Adams wrote of the man, "Something in his character always created distrust. He had every advantage of education, social and political connection, ability and self-confidence; he was only fifty-four years old, which was also the age of Monroe; but he suffered from the reputation of indolence and intrigue."

Armstrong was appointed on January 13, 1813. He met Dearborn shortly afterward at Albany, went over Granny's plans, and quickly approved his scenarios. Dearborn's strategy was reasonably sound. A force of 7,000 regular soldiers would leave Sackets Harbor on April 1. With the help of Chauncey's squadron, they would reach Kingston over the ice before the Saint Lawrence River thawed, then destroy the Royal Navy dockyard and capture the fleet of the Provincial Marine. In one blow, this would starve the British posts west of Kingston of ammunition and war supplies. Next on

Granny's shopping list was capturing the Upper Canadian capital at York. Then they would join up with troops from Buffalo and take the British forts along the Niagara River.

Dearborn decided to lead the Lake Ontario campaign himself, even though he was not in the best of health. His first item of business was to order his northern army to move across country from Plattsburg to Sackets Harbor.

THE ATTACK ON YORK

> "We cannot doubt but that in all cases in which a British commander is constrained to act defensively, his policy will be that adopted by Sheaffe — to prefer the preservation of his troops to that of his post, and thus, carrying off the kernel leave us only the shell."
>
> –*John Armstrong, Jr., U.S. Secretary of War*

When the time came to execute his plan, Dearborn's caution overcame his ardor. When he heard news that the British force in Kingston had been reinforced, he grew timid and decided to bypass Plan A entirely. He would attack York instead. The capital of Upper Canada was an easy target, with very little military significance. Two British ships were based there, the *Prince Regent* and the *Duke of Gloucester*, and a powerful thirty-gun frigate, *Sir Isaac Brock*, was being built in the naval yard. These would be easy prey, and taking the ships would prevent Yeo from tipping the balance of naval superiority on the Lake against Chauncey. But the symbolism of capturing the provincial capital would surely be a boost to American morale.

Indeed, the British had been watching Dearborn's moves closely, and Kingston definitely needed reinforcing. Prevost ordered six companies of the 104th Regiment of Foot, plus 4th New Brunswick Regiment, to march overland from New Brunswick in the dead of winter and reinforce the garrison at Kingston. After a grueling fifty-two-day march overland up the Saint John River valley to the St. Lawrence, travelling on snowshoes, and pulling supplies on toboggans, they arrived at Quebec on March 15 and Kingston on April 12.

On March 19, an experienced and dynamic Royal Navy officer, Sir James Lucas Yeo, stepped into the breach as commander-in-chief of the Lake Squadrons.

On April 25, Chauncey's fleet left Sackets Harbor and ferried Dearborn's 1,700-man army in fifteen boats up along the north shore of Lake Ontario. The fleet arrived off Toronto Island on the afternoon of April 26. Feeling indisposed, Dearborn stayed on board the flagship USS *Madison* and turned over command to Brigadier-General Zebulon Pike, the explorer of the southwest whose name is commemorated in Pike's Peak.

General Roger Sheaffe, the hero of Queenston Heights, commanded the defence of York. He knew how badly the town was defended. It had a semicircular earthwork battery containing only two twelve-pounders, and another battery 600 yards further west that held two elderly eighteen-pounders off their mounts that were virtually useless. Inside Fort York, it had a "grand magazine" to store ammunition and 500 barrels of gunpowder. Sheaffe's 600-man garrison consisted of two companies from the 8th Regiment, a company of Royal Newfoundlanders, a company of the Glengarry Light Infantry Fencibles, as well as some men from 3rd York Militia Regiment, backed by 300 dockyard workers and less than 100 Mississauga and Chippewa warriors.

Sheaffe correctly assumed the Americans would land west of the town, by the old French fort. When a sentry on the Scarborough Bluffs sighted Chauncey's fleet, Sheaffe dispatched the Indians and a company of the Glengarrys to meet them. But on the morning of April 27, strong winds pushed the American boats past this area, and Pike's force had to land a mile further to the west. Pike brought ashore his regulars and militia as well as a company of blue- and grey-clad riflemen under Major Benjamin Forsyth. They were virtually unopposed except for some sniping by Indians in the woods. Sheaffe's regulars tried to slow them down, but Pike's large body of regulars and sharpshooters quickly overwhelmed the western battery, and then started to march toward Fort York.

Sheaffe had already lost sixty-two dead and ninety-four wounded in the battle, and the hardnosed general was not interested in wasting any more lives. And he had no intention of letting the Americans capture hundreds of barrels of British powder and large quantities of arms and ammunition. He ordered his men to detonate the grand magazine. They may or may not have timed it to explode just as the Americans were entering the fort. The stone building blew with a thunderclap that rattled windows as far away as Niagara and sent a mushroom cloud into the sky. The ammunition inside poured out a deadly hail of shot, and the blast sent huge chunks of masonry flying into the air, one of them landing on General Pike, crushing his back and chest.

Thirty-eight men were killed instantly and another 222 injured, including some local militia. Pike died within hours on board Chauncey's flagship, clutching the British standard.

By that point, Sheaffe and his regulars were already heading east toward Kingston, disbanding the militia and leaving them to fend for themselves. They torched the *Sir Isaac Brock*, a warehouse full of valuable naval stores for Lake Erie and fired the bridge over the Don River as they went. The *Prince Regent* had sailed away to Kingston several days before the attack, and the Americans were only able to capture the schooner *Duke of Gloucester*.

When the Battle of York ended on the afternoon of April 27, the Americans felt cheated by the quick redcoat retreat and angry at the booby-trapped magazine that killed their general.

Dearborn, resplendent in a uniform that "would not have shamed Napoleon," came ashore the following day to begin six hours of negotiation with the local militia and leaders of the town. Apparently enraged by the explosion, he vowed to "make the town smoke for it." The Reverend John Strachan calmed him down, promising that the explosion was an accident, citing the deaths of Canadian militiamen as proof.

Pike's death at York.

Dearborn agreed that the town would not be razed. The surrender document they signed guaranteed the safety of private property but said nothing about government property. As was standard practice, the captured York militiamen were released on parole. They could return to their homes by promising not to take any further part in the fighting, at least until they had been officially swapped for a similar number of parolled enemy militia.

Dearborn was feeling ill and went back to his ship, the corvette USS *Madison*. That night, a leaderless mob of soldiers and sailors roamed about York looking for revenge. They burned down the Assembly and snatched the parliamentary mace (President Franklin D. Roosevelt returned it in 1934 as a goodwill gesture), then torched the governor's residence and Court House, as expected. But then, joined by turncoat Canadians, some of them turned to stealing and pillaging private property. They looted St. James Church of many religious treasures, took books from the town library (later returned by order of General Dearborn), robbed several stores and all the empty homes, smashed the town's only printing press, and grabbed any livestock they could find to roast over their fires.

This went on for two days, until the Reverend John Strachan complained bitterly to Dearborn. On May 1, Granny ordered the soldiers to return to their ships.

The American fleet had to stay put until May 8, when the weather cleared. Isaac Chauncey then ferried Dearborn and his troops across the lake to attack Fort George. Dearborn delayed the attack for three weeks due to sickness in his ranks, and the need to organize old Fort Niagara as his HQ and to get enough food and medical supplies. He gave the honour of leading what would surely be the momentous capture of Fort George to his old friend, former New York governor and now Quartermaster General Morgan Lewis, while he would survey the action from the deck of the *Madison*.

Moral: Avoid pausing beside a live ammunition dump.

THE CAPTURE OF FORT GEORGE

Like Fort Malden on Lake Erie, Fort George on Lake Ontario was a dilapidated old firetrap, with barracks and palisades made of logs and shingles. The main powder magazine was not solid enough to withstand a direct hit. The fort had five guns inside: a twelve-pounder, two twenty-four-pounders, and two mortars. North of the fort, facing U.S. Fort Niagara, was a battery with six cannon and five mortars, and another small battery guarding the mouth of the Niagara River. The fort itself was not much of a prize. What Winfield Scott was after was the outflanking, capture, and complete surrender of Brigadier John Vincent and his regulars.

Vincent faced a totally unequal contest. Counting the naval guns on Chauncey's flotilla of seventeen warships, with the cannons and mortars of Fort Niagara, and the artillery on the heights at Lewiston, which could lob cannon balls directly into Fort George, over seventy heavy guns and mortars were aimed directly at his army. But Vincent and his staff were well-trained and resourceful, in the mould of Isaac Brock, and he meant to give the Americans a fight.

Vincent had a little over 1,000 regulars from the Glengarry Light Infantry, the 8th King's and 49th regiments of Foot and the Royal Newfoundland Fencibles, along with 500 militia, including Captain Runchey's Company of Coloured Men, a unit of escaped and freed slaves, as well as fifty tribal warriors. He positioned one-third of his force, led by Lieutenant-Colonel Myers, north of the fort along near Lake Ontario. Another third, under Lieutenant-Colonel Harvey, waited south of the fort beside the Niagara River. His own third were camped in reserve on the large plain west of Fort George.

The attack began on May 25 with a softening up by sixteen large caliber guns and mortars from Fort Niagara, which bombarded Fort George with fire shells — red-hot cannon balls heated in the ovens at Fort Niagara. By the following day, all the British guns were out of action, and most of the buildings in cinders.

Early on the foggy morning of May 27, Lieutenant Oliver Hazard Perry of the U.S. Navy, temporarily serving as one of Chauncey's senior officers, surveyed the landing sites at the mouth of the Niagara River, took bearings, and placed marker buoys. After a naval barrage took out the nearby British batteries, Colonel Winfield Scott and Benjamin Forsyth landed in heavy surf with 800 men and quickly secured the beach at about nine o'clock. Vincent immediately ordered Myers and Harvey to meet the Americans with a bayonet charge as they disembarked. But the redcoats were cut up by grapeshot from Chauncey's schooners, and quickly outnumbered, as wave after wave of 4,000 U.S. regulars poured ashore from more than 100 small transports. They drove the British troops back to a ravine held by the 8th Regiment. At noon, when the 49th Regiment and militia failed to halt further American advance, Vincent knew he was in grave danger of being outflanked and had to put his escape plan into action sooner than expected. The whole force had to retreat at double speed south down the road to Queenston, leaving behind many women and children of the 49th and other corps huddled in the stone casements of the fort.[3]

Colonel Winfield Scott was just forming up to pursue Vincent when he was approached by a messenger with a note from his CO, General Morgan Lewis, to return to Fort George. He read it quickly, hiding his disgust, knowing it let the British survive to fight another day.

When scouts told General Vincent the Americans were not pursuing, he moved more comfortably, turning southwest to Beaver Dams, near present-day Thorold, Ontario, where he called in the other British regulars from Fort Erie to boost his force. When the coast was clear, Vincent disbanded the local militia so they wouldn't be made prisoners of war. Then he cut north to Burlington Heights with 1,400 British and Canadian militia and their families.

It was a costly battle for the British. The Americans reported only 150 total casualties, compared to 358 for the British. The 8th (King's) Regiment lost 196 killed or wounded out of their total contingent of 310. The Glengarry Light Infantry lost seventy-eight out of 108, and the Royal Newfoundland suffered sixteen casualties out of forty men.

The Americans had failed in their intent to destroy Vincent's army, but the Niagara peninsula was for the time being under their control.

Moral: Use overwhelming force if you want to win.

PAYING FOR THE WAR

THE BUSINESS OF WAR

> "War is not so much a matter of weapons as of money."
>
> *– Thucydides*

One of the biggest battles of the War of 1812 was the fight to keep the United States Treasury afloat. As the year 1813 began, Madison was finding that waging war was far more expensive than he envisaged.

A new problem was Napoleon. In January, Madison wrote to Jefferson that "Bonaparte, according to his own shewing is in serious danger; and if half the official accounts of the Russians be true, his own escape is barely possible, and that of his army impossible. The effect of such a catastrophe on his compulsory allies may once more turn the tables quite round in the case between France & Engld."

The twin disasters of Napoleon in Russia and America's own troops in Canada finally woke the Americans from their torpor. If they wanted to win this war that they themselves had declared, they would no longer have Napoleon as a silent ally. They could no longer rely on the Emperor of France to keep the British busy as they went off to capture Canada.

To do a more credible job than a repeat of the disasters they inflicted on themselves in 1812, they needed money, more money.

Unfortunately, as Treasury Secretary Albert Gallatin told Congress in March, 1813, the United States had expenses of $39 million and revenues of only $15 million.

ALBERT GALLATIN TO THE RESCUE

Credit for sorting out the Republic's finances goes to Albert Gallatin, a true hero of the War of 1812 on the American side.

The U.S. was financially unprepared for war in 1812. The Republicans had piously allowed the First Bank of the United States to expire in 1811, over Gallatin's objections, claiming it was not authorized in the Constitution. He had to ship $7 million to Europe to pay off foreign lenders just when money was needed for war.

Now Gallatin was faced with crushing military expenditures, at the same time as the U.S. faced a steady decline in tariff revenue caused by Jefferson's and Madison's foolish embargoes and the British blockade.

The answer, as always, was a deft combination of debt and taxes.

The United States of America was founded on $75 million of Revolutionary War debt. Alexander Hamilton, the first United States Secretary of the Treasury, once famously said, "A national debt, *if it is not excessive*, will be to us a national blessing."

The war debt was paid off quickly and America enjoyed several years of budget surpluses, letting Jefferson abolish the Federalist system of internal taxation in 1802. To pay for Madison's War, Gallatin was forced to bring them back in. An angry Congress finally voted for a direct tax on houses, lands, and slaves, and apportioned the money to the states on the basis of the 1810 census. Congress also brought in duties on liquor, carriages, refined sugar, salt, whisky, and other luxuries.

Without a national bank, and with New England financiers refusing to loan money for the war effort, Gallatin had to innovate in order to go back into debt. But the amount was peanuts — less than $90 million.[4]

In March 1813, he brought in a public bidding system, which worked well. A financial syndicate led by John Jacob Astor, Girard, and friends finally took 57 percent of the $16,000,000 loan, and Gallatin handled the deficit of $69 million by bond issues.

Moral: You still can pay for a war even when your country is bust and your political colleagues don't have a clue about finance.

The Lucrative War of the Privateers

Thomas Jefferson generally turned up his nose at liberal enterprise, but in the case of privateering against the British, he was prepared to make an exception, writing to James Monroe,

Privateers will find their own men and money. Let nothing be spared to encourage them. They are the dagger which strikes at the heart of the enemy, their commerce. Frigates and seventy-fours are a sacrifice we must make, heavy as it is, to the prejudices of a part of our citizens. They have, indeed, rendered a great moral service, which has delighted me as much as anyone in the United States. But they have had no physical effect sensible to the enemy; and now, while we must fortify them in our harbors and keep armies to defend them, our privateers are bearding and blockading the enemy in their own sea-ports. Encourage them to burn all their prizes, and let the public pay for them. They will cheat us enormously. No matter; they will make the merchants of England feel, and squeal, and cry out for peace.

Indeed, I would argue, the potential spoils from privateering, not the losses from impressment, were the best revenge against the British, and a key reason why America declared war in 1812.

Before 1812, from 1803 on, both Britain and France seized nearly 1,500 American trading vessels bound for Europe. The Americans wanted to get in on the action. Indeed, a lust for booty trumped "Free Trade and Sailors' Rights!"

Privateering was big, big business for the United States during most of the war. American practitioners captured 1,300 merchant ships and military vessels worth almost $40 million, a truly colossal sum of money in those days. Not being bound by the rules of war, they were required to share a modest portion of the booty with Washington.

As Jefferson suggested to Monroe, the U.S. had almost no navy during the war — twenty-three ships at most, with 556 guns. But a rag-tag fleet of 517 privateers with almost 3,000 guns operated happily from U.S. shores, sailing as far as the English Channel and Irish Sea, and from the coast of Africa to Brazil and into the Pacific to take their prizes.

When the Royal Navy started blockading the U.S. seaboard from its bases at Halifax and Bermuda, speedy rake-masted Baltimore clippers, the greyhounds of the seas, easily evaded the lumbering frigates. Many of the sailors were free blacks, who participated equally when it came time to hand out the prize money.

The British, not to be outdone, encouraged their own fleet of Bermudian privateers, capturing 298 American and French merchant ships near the end of the war. And in Nova Scotia, three partners in Lunenburg purchased a privateer schooner and captured seven American vessels. The *Liverpool Packet* caught over fifty ships, and the prizes taken by one young privateer named Samuel Cunard gave him the capital to finance a future shipping empire.

Privateers had to be bold and daring in order to survive and reap the financial rewards for bringing prizes to port.

One ship, the *Paul Jones*, left New York in 1812 with 120 men but only three guns, and soon captured enough merchantmen with guns to easily fill her gun mounts.

Thomas Boyle of Baltimore, sailing a clipper named *Comet*, once captured a Portuguese warship big enough to carry on the *Comet* on her deck. His second ship, the *Chasseur*, known as the Pride of Baltimore, captured eighteen valuable British merchant ships, and many times outran British brigs sent to hunt him down.

Declaring a "blockade of the British Isles," Boyle did so much damage to British ship owners and insurance companies that many complained directly to Whitehall. His actions doubtless shortened the duration of the war.

The privateer *America* was such a threat to the British merchant marine that Her Majesty's government built a frigate, the *Dublin*, to chase *America* from the seas. *America* easily evaded the *Dublin* on several occasions.

Joshua Barney of Baltimore, a Revolutionary War hero, soon got into the privateering business, capturing over a million dollars in prizes on one trip. He and his fellows effectively ruined the British sugar trade in the West Indies. Another Baltimore privateer, to the supreme annoyance of the Duke of Wellington, captured one of his pay ships off the coast of Portugal. The loss slowed his progress against the French because he couldn't pay his bills to suppliers.

Privateering worked for a couple of glorious years, and big fortunes were made. But such bonanzas never last. In 1813, the Royal Navy beefed up its fleet and put in place an effective convoy system, protecting as many as 250 merchant ships in a single flotilla. The navy also built a few super-frigates and went after the largest American vessels. On June 1, 1813, off Boston, Captain Philip Broke of HMS *Shannon* captured the USS *Chesapeake* in only eleven minutes, and towed her to Halifax. In 1814, USS *Essex* and Stephen Decatur's USS *President* were both hunted down and beaten.

By the spring of 1814, lesser British frigates freed from the fight against Napoleon were effectively blockading the whole American seaboard, and driving most U.S. naval vessels and privateers off the high seas.

Moral: You too can make a fortune privately in wartime.

ATTACK ON SACKETS HARBOR

SIR JAMES YEO GOES TO WORK

Late in 1812, the Admiralty knew it had to beef up defences on Lake Ontario to counter American action at Sackets Harbor. Sir George Prevost was complaining about the problems he faced in maintaining such a long line of communications. He asked for supplies and men from the Royal Navy to turn what was essentially a transport service — the Provincial Marine of Upper Canada — into a freshwater navy. With Napoleon reeling from his disastrous foray into Russia, the Admiralty felt comfortable enough in sending one of its top young officers, a dynamic thirty-year-old captain, Sir James Lucas Yeo, who had served on board His Majesty's vessels since the age of eleven.

Yeo was used to unconventional sea warfare, so he was a good choice to replace Captain Earle in command on the Great Lakes. Yeo had captured privateers and pirate ships, stormed heavily fortified ports, and personally evacuated the Portuguese royal family to Brazil in the face of a French invasion of Portugal. In 1809, Yeo boldly captured Cayenne, French Guiana, expelling the last of Bonaparte's forces from South America, for which action he was knighted.

Yeo received his commission on March 19 as commander-in-chief of the Lake Squadrons. He arrived at Quebec on May 5 with a large party of 437 naval officers, sailors, and shipwrights. They proceeded up the St. Lawrence toward Kingston. Past Montreal, they joined Sir George Prevost, who was also making his way to Kingston, to deal with replacing General Sheaffe, who had outraged some of the citizens of York by his overly rapid departure a month earlier.

Prevost and Yeo arrived at Kingston on May 15, and Yeo got to work with commanders Robert Heriot Barclay, Robert Finnis, and Daniel Pring, from Admiral Warren's naval establishment at Halifax. The first order of business was to complete a new sloop of war, the twenty-three-gun *Wolfe* and refit the twenty-two-gun *Royal George*, the sixteen-gun *Prince Regent*, the fourteen-gun brig *Earl of Moira*, two eight-gun schooners, and a number of gunboats in an effort to match or surpass Isaac Chauncey's flotilla at Sackets.

Yeo's fleet was superior for the time being, but under-strength in men. His prime weapon was the thirty-two-pounder carronade, a marine mortar lethal in close combat but of limited range. Chauncey's twenty-four-gun *Madison*, sixteen-gun *Oneida*, and ten schooners were armed with long twenty-four-pounders, which gave them a big advantage at a distance. The Americans also had ample manpower, and were actively improving their wagon roads from the south to Lakes Erie and Ontario.

Sir James Lucas Yeo.

The Landing at Sackets Harbor

On May 25, only ten days after Yeo's arrival, Prevost got a dispatch from General Vincent at Fort George, informing him that Chauncey's fleet was offshore supporting a major attack by the U.S. Army. Prevost knew he had a golden chance to relieve Vincent at Niagara, take Sackets Harbor, and with one blow win naval supremacy on the lake. But he had to scramble before Chauncey's return.

Two days later, Yeo's instant squadron left Kingston carrying the grenadier company of the 100th Regiment, two companies of the 8th (The King's) Regiment of Foot, four companies of the 104th Regiment, one company of the Glengarry Light Infantry, two companies of the Canadian Voltigeurs and a detachment of Royal Artillery with two six-pounder guns. Since no general officer was available to command the troops, Prevost took the job, while delegating command ashore to his adjutant general, Colonel Edward Baynes, an officer with minimal battlefield experience. If Granny Dearborn could command an expedition, why not himself?

Yeo and Prevost arrived off Sackets Harbor early the next morning. The wind had died down, making it dangerous to steer too close to the shore. Since he had no charts or soundings, and little lake experience, Yeo was properly cautious.

Just as Prevost's force started rowing ashore before midday, some sails were sighted in the distance. Nervous that the sails belonged to Chauncey, Prevost called off the attack and ordered the troops to go back to their ships. It was a false alarm. The sails belonged to twelve bateaux carrying U.S. infantry from Oswego to Sackets Harbor. The British sent out three large canoes of Iroquois warriors and a gunboat with a detachment of Glengarrys to intercept them. The Americans quickly headed for shore and fled into the woods, pursued by the Iroquois, who killed thirty-five soldiers. Their senior officer rowed out to Yeo's fleet and surrendered his remaining force of 115 officers and men.

This episode gave the Americans plenty of advance warning. Under the command of Brigadier-General Jacob Brown of the New York state militia, with Lieutenant Woolcott Chauncey, younger brother of the commodore, their 400 regulars and 750 local militia worked feverishly to shore up their defences, which consisted of Fort Volunteer and Fort Tompkins, several strong blockhouses and a line of earthworks together. The hill to the fort also featured an abatis engineered from felled trees and branches by Alexander Macomb, one of the smartest generals in the U.S. Army, who was now in command of a unit at Fort George.[5]

Prevost resumed the attack the following morning May 29, landing his troops south of the town on Horse Island, under fire from two six-pounder field guns and a naval thirty-two-pounder firing at long range from Fort Tompkins. Once the landing force was assembled, the British charged across the flooded causeway linking the island to the shore, chasing the fleeing militia. They then swung left to take the town and dockyard from the landward side, but the American regulars with some field guns held fast, and fell back behind their blockhouses and earthworks.

It was "ticklish work," said Lieutenant John Le Couteur of the 104th Foot, who was armed only with an officer's sword.

> We had turned the battery, and got up to a stockade around the barracks. The Yankees were poking the muzzles of their guns, on each side of me while I made myself as flat as I could edgewise behind one of the posts of the stockade. It was really an uncomfortable position, there was neither glory nor pleasure in being riddled, or rather fringed with balls.

Out on the lake, none of Yeo's larger vessels could sail into attack range, until sailors carefully rowed the sixteen-gun *Beresford* close enough to bombard Fort Tompkins. One of the balls flew over the fort and landed in the naval yard. The sailors, thinking the fort had been taken, followed orders and set fire to the unfinished *General Pike*, now being built as Chauncey's flagship, as well as a huge quantity of naval stores. By this time, the Americans had repelled two attempts by Colonel Baynes to storm their lines, and without field guns Baynes was unable to breach the American defenses.

Prevost grew less and less confident that the British could win the day. When Brown's militia started attacking the British right flank and rear, their extremely risk-averse commander decided it was time to cut and run. He ordered his bugler to sound the retreat.

Major William Drummond, a brave Canadian who was worshipped by his men, was appalled at Prevost's call to withdraw. He pleaded with his commander, "Allow me a few minutes, Sir, and I will put you in possession of the place."

Prevost growled at Drummond, "Obey your orders and learn the first duty of a soldier."

Moral: "Know when it is better not to risk a fight, because if you fight, you might lose."

What Went Wrong

Back in his Montreal office, Prevost put a positive spin on the operation, reporting to Bathurst that the enemy had been beaten and that the retreat was carried out in perfect order.

He didn't supply his superior in London with the whole truth. When the bugle sounded, many soldiers misunderstood its meaning and responded with long cheers. Then, realizing that it meant retreat, they bitterly obeyed.

In fact, the retreat was not a pretty sight, as different British units had to jostle over who would re-embark first.

Did the British get away lightly? Prevost's gut instincts may have served them well: an entire U.S. infantry regiment was racing to Sackets and would arrive within hours. What was a rout could have turned into a bloodbath. But as Drummond argued, British valour might just as easily won the day.[6]

Prevost kept to his defensive playbook. He pointedly forbade Yeo from taking any further action against Sackets, arguing that if it failed it could leave Kingston fatally weakened; but Yeo was an experienced Royal Navy officer — from the other service — and clearly had more military savvy than Prevost. He respected his opponents, and it is not likely he would have jeopardized his ships unless he had the upper hand.

From then on, the naval arms race continued, but each side took extreme care to avoid battle under risky conditions. For much of the rest of the war, the battles on Lake Ontario resembled well-ordered regattas.

News of the British assault on Sackets did cause Chauncey to recall his entire squadron from Niagara, leaving the American victors at Fort George lacking in support and supplies. It would cost them dearly.

As for Sir James Yeo, he lost a battle on the *Wolfe* on September 28 against Chauncey's newly repaired flagship *General Pike*. In a yachting event that came to be known as the Burlington Races, the outgunned Yeo was able to escape into the safety of Burlington Bay, to fight another day. Shortly afterward he learned to his dismay that his squadron on Lake Erie, commanded by Robert Heriot Barclay, had been beaten by Oliver Hazard Perry at the Battle of Lake Erie.

For his services at Sackets Harbor, Jacob Brown was commissioned as a Brigadier-General in the United States Army. As for Sir James Yeo, if he was appalled by Sir George's Prevost's hasty actions at Sackets Harbor, he kept it to himself for the moment. As for Prevost, he escaped with his command intact for another year, yet with his prestige on the wane, until one final battle in 1814 buried his reputation for good.

STONEY CREEK AND BEAVER DAMS

THE BATTLE OF STONEY CREEK

On May 29, the very day Prevost and Yeo were mounting their attack on Sackets Harbor, Dearborn came ashore at Fort George to bathe in the glow of victory. Scott and his young generals wanted to go after the retreating British. They argued that a quick pursuit might seal the victory or even win the war, but many of the troops were sick, and the wounded had to be moved to the Fort Niagara hospital. Dearborn decided to stay put for several days, and the momentum went out of the campaign.

When the Americans found the British were along the lake at Burlington Heights, Dearborn agreed to send brigadiers William Winder and John Chandler with a depleted force of 1,350 men after the enemy. Winder was a Baltimore lawyer and Republican politician whose uncle was a close friend of Madison, Chandler was a blacksmith and Republican politician from Maine.

Winder and Chandler advanced to within ten miles of the British and camped for the night of June 5 at Stoney Creek. They were confident that victory was theirs the next day. Poorly trained in the arts of war, they had little regard for their men's security and little grasp of the kind of battleground audacity taught to British officers.

The British were well alerted by John Norton's Mohawks and by a local farmer, nineteen-year-old Billy Green.[7] Vincent and his adjutant, Lieutenant-Colonel John Harvey, quickly decided to make a surprise attack on the Americans. Harvey had already found out from Lieutenant James FitzGibbon of the 49th Regiment, who disguised himself as a farmer and went into the American camp selling butter, that "the enemy's guards were few and negligent; his line of encampment was long and broken; his artillery was feebly supported; several of his corps were placed too far to the rear to aid in repelling a blow which might be rapidly struck in front."

Harvey mustered 700 regulars from the 49th regiment, under Major Charles Plenderleath, some from the 8th Regiment, under Major James Ogilvie, and the Canadian Provincial Dragoons under William Hamilton Merritt. Leaving Burlington Heights at 11:30 p.m., they followed the Mohawks through the woods toward Stoney Creek, with a single field gun and the flints removed from their muskets to make sure that there were no accidental firings. It was a moonless night. The troops silently disarmed a sentry post and somehow got the password, "Wil-Hen-Har" (an abbreviation of Harrison's name), which let them approach more closely.

At 2:00 a.m., one of the American sentries cried out as he was being tomahawked, and some British began to give Indian war whoops to frighten the Americans. The British officers knew they had lost the element of surprise. They ordered their troops to fix flints to their muskets and move right to the attack. Seeing some fires in the distance, they charged with bayonets fixed into what they thought was the American camp, but found only a few cooks preparing the morning meal for the American troops. The U.S. 25th Regiment had moved to higher ground for the night, with orders to sleep on their arms. So Harvey and Fitzgibbon kept going straight up the road, Plenderleath cutting to the left and Ogilvie to the right.

The battle became chaotic, with the Americans trying to get into formation in the darkness as the British started firing. A fog of smoke from the black powder billowed around the camp. While the British paused to reload their muskets, many could not hear their officers' commands in the din. The Americans had time to recover their poise and mowed down many of Harvey's regulars with buckshot ammunition.

Momentum suddenly shifted to the British when General Winder ordered the U.S. 5th Infantry to protect the left flank, creating a gap in their line that left the artillery unsupported by infantry. Plenderleath was able to figure out their position when two field guns fired in quick succession. Gathering volunteers, they charged up Gage's Lane at a run, reached the four field pieces before they could fire, and overran the position.

Sergeant Alexander Fraser, age twenty-three, was the hero of the action, bayonetting seven enemy soldiers and their horses, all in a matter of minutes. Fraser's younger brother, Peter, killed four Americans in the assault.

Over on the right, Major Ogilvie and his men drove the American 5th Regiment back onto their cavalry, who charged into their own soldiers, killing many with bayonets.

In all this chaos, General Vincent, commanding the British artillery position, went missing. While Merritt's militia were searching for him, young Alexander Fraser and his fellows captured the two U.S. brigadiers, first Winder and then Chandler, who had been knocked unconscious when he fell off his horse.

The loss of their commanders decapitated the invasion force, and after forty-five minutes, the battle sounds eased off. Command of the U.S. troops fell to Colonel James Burn of the 2nd Light Dragoons. Lacking naval support from Chauncey, he was short of ammunition and backed away along the Niagara road toward Forty Mile Creek.

Harvey wisely decided to head back to Burlington Heights before dawn broke so that the enemy would not see how few soldiers had defeated them. The British carried with them two of the American guns and spiked the other two when they did not have the horses to pull them away.

The British suffered twenty-three killed and 136 wounded, as well as fifty-five missing, most of them captured. Plenderleath was one of the wounded, taking two musket balls in the thigh, which earned him the Order of the Bath. The Americans had seventeen killed, thirty-eight wounded and seven officers (two brigadier-generals, one major, three captains and one lieutenant) and ninety-three enlisted men missing and likewise captured.

The next morning, June 7, the British commander, General Vincent, was still missing and assumed taken, but later that day a scouting party found him wandering in a daze a few miles from Burlington Heights, hatless and dusty, convinced that the entire British force had been destroyed. He too had fallen off his horse and on his head, his mount had galloped away, and he had lost his sword.

A day later, Sir James Yeo arrived off Forty Mile Creek with his fleet from Kingston to help chase the Americans. He succeeded in getting close under the enemy's batteries, and "by a sharp and well-directed fire soon obliged him to make a precipitate retreat, leaving all his camp equipage, provisions, stoves, etc. behind, which fell into our hands. The Beresford also captured all his bateaux laden with stores, etc. Our troops immediately occupied the post."

Winder and Chandler's two brigades, minus their generals, were back at Fort George that evening, their tails between their legs.

Moral: "Respect the enemy you think you have defeated."

IROQUOIS VICTORY AT BEAVER DAMS

On June 21, to keep his soldiers in fighting trim, Fort George commander General John Parker Boyd, a former Dearborn aide, ordered Colonel Charles Boerstler to make a surprise attack on Lieutenant James Fitzgibbon's British supply depot at the village of Beaver Dams, fifteen kilometres to the west of Fort George near present-day Thorold.

Leading 570 regulars and militia, Boerstler halted at Queenston for the night. Three of his officers went to the house of wounded Loyalist James Secord and his wife Laura, demanding lodging and supper. As the night wore on, the soldiers became rowdy and talkative, and the Secords overheard the American plans. Since her husband was still recovering from wounds suffered during the Battle of Queenston Heights, Laura stole away at 4:00 a.m. the next morning to warn the British. She made her way west through swamps and woods, avoiding main roads for fear of American sentries, then climbed the heights at Twelve Mile Creek to St. David's. After passing three American sentries, late in the day on the 22nd, she was captured by some Iroquois scouts, who led her to Fitzgibbon's headquarters, where she passed on her message. After a thirty-kilometre trek, the heroine of Upper Canada collapsed from exhaustion.

Fitzgibbon had forty-six regulars of the 49th Regiment at his post, but his major weapon was a large body of 100 Mohawks from the Six Nations under Captain William Johnson Kerr and 300 Kahnawake Iroquois from Montreal, commanded by Captain Dominique Ducharme of the Indian Department, with Lieutenants Isaac LeClair and J.B. de Lorimier.

On June 24, before dawn, Colonel Boerstler made his move toward Beaver Dams, climbing up the hill toward St. David's and proceeding along the Mountain Road leading to the Beaver Dams settlement, while the Iroquois watched silently from the woods. As they approached Ten Mile Creek, they became aware of some of the warriors closing in on their flanks and rear. Boerstler then made a serious mistake and moved forward at the head of his troops, unwilling to change his plans. Suddenly shots rang out, and one of them hit Boerstler, who was placed in one of the wagons with a flesh wound. For the next three hours, trapped in a ravine in wooded country, the terrified Americans were being picked off one by one.

At this point, FitzGibbon intervened and approached Boerstler under a flag of truce. In language reminiscent of Brock at Detroit, he told the colonel that the Americans were outnumbered and surrounded, and that if they did not surrender he would be unable to restrain the natives from slaughtering the entire American force.

British Major de Haren of the 104th Regiment then arrived with his regulars from Twelve Mile Creek, took Boerstler's surrender, and marched the twenty-three officers and 489 enlisted men to Burlington Heights, where they were sent on to prison in Halifax.

While John Norton quipped that "The Caughnawaga got the victory, the Mohawks got the plunder and FitzGibbon got the credit," FitzGibbon reported to Captain Kerr:

> With respect to the affair with Captain [sic] Boerstler, not a shot was fired on our side by any but the Indians. They beat the American detachment into a state of terror, and the only share I claim is taking advantage of a favorable moment to offer them protection from the tomahawk and scalping knife. The Indian Department did the rest.

Having seen all his hopes dashed, Dearborn was again hit by illness and resigned his commission in early July. Indeed, both armies were hard hit by disease and welcomed the end of hostilities on the Niagara frontier. The American forces were soon ordered to move west to join Harrison, and east to Sackets Harbor and Plattsburgh, to participate in an attempt against Montreal. Fort George was left with a skeleton staff of New York Militia, demoralized by the loss of Boerstler, and terrified by Indians in the vicinity.

On December 10, U.S. Army Major George McClure was ordered to evacuate Fort George and cross to New York, leaving Upper Canada in the hands of an anti-British band of brigands calling themselves the Canadian Volunteers. They were led by a turncoat member of the provincial assembly, Joseph Willcocks.

Moral: Expect to be attacked when you least expect it.

FIRE ON LAKE ERIE

Oliver Perry Prepares for Battle

Pacing the floor of his HQ at Fort Meigs in June 1813, William Henry Harrison stopped and glared at the map before him. After the disaster of May 5, when he had lost 400 men, Tecumseh and Procter had tried to besiege him again, but left after ten fruitless days. He suspected that the tide of war was turning and that they might not be back. The attack on Niagara would disrupt the British supply line. But how much? Was Procter running low on food and ammunition?

To make any impact on the enemy and to retake Detroit, Harrison knew he HAD to have ships on Lake Erie to protect his own supplies, so he could starve and disarm Procter and the 10,000 Indian allies still around Detroit and Fort Malden.

Along the lake, a hundred miles east, Oliver Hazard Perry was still working to complete two brigs and four schooners on the beaches of Presque Isle, littered with coils of rope, barrels of tar and gunpowder, anchors, sails, shot, muskets, and cannons, all supplied up a rough new wagon road from Pittsburgh. Only a few months earlier, the tall, gawky young man had been in charge of in charge of eight gunboats stationed at Newport, Rhode Island, but he was itching for real action. His younger brother Matthew was already a lieutenant aboard the super-frigate *United States*.[8] And now, tapped to lead by Chauncey in February, and fully briefed by Harrison, Perry was already the man in charge of an operation that could change the course of the war.

The young commodore took advantage of his first lucky break on June 9, when General Vincent ordered the British to abandon Fort Erie after the American capture of Fort George. Perry moved quickly to free five armed schooners trapped up the river in Black Rock, then sailed them down to Presque Isle, cloaked by a thick fog.

Henry Procter tried to take Fort Meigs with still another siege at the end of July, but quit after less than a week, still unable to dislodge Harrison, and with his supplies running critically low. Procter now had to turn his energy to helping Commodore Robert Barclay of the Provincial Marine, who had arrived from Lake Ontario after a hard overland journey, keep control of Lake Erie.

Barclay, a one-armed veteran of Trafalgar, had served in the Royal Navy since the age of eleven. He was the second choice for the job, after Mulcaster refused to take it. He knew he had a nearly impossible job, with only the sixteen-gun ship *Queen Charlotte* and a small schooner squadron. He was short on trained seamen and had to make do without the naval stores destined for Malden that Sheaffe was forced to burn up at York. But he scrounged what he could, putting his shipwrights to work building a larger flagship he named *Detroit*, and fitting it with thirty-five long range guns from the ramparts of Fort Malden.

Barclay knew the key to victory was a land attack on Perry's shipyard, but Procter said he could not risk it. And after the British lost control of the Niagara Peninsula, Prevost had to focus entirely on Lake Ontario, and refused him any further help. He was on his own and increasingly resigned to his fate.

All Barclay could do was blockade Perry inside the sandbars of Presque Isle, which lay only six feet under the water. The two large brigs Perry was building drew nine feet of water, and he would have to drag them over the sandbars to get them out on the open lake.

By the end of July, Perry had his two twenty-gun brigs nearly ready for action. He named his flagship the *Lawrence*, after his heroic friend James Lawrence, captain of the *Chesapeake*, killed in action June 1 in a battle with HMS *Shannon* off Boston. Lawrence's last message to his crew was, "Don't give up the ship." His other brig he called *Niagara*.

At dawn on July 31, Perry's sentries peered out into the morning mist and found the lake empty; the British fleet had sailed away. Barclay later reported that had to go back to Malden to resupply. Another story said that he was bored with blockade duty and stopped on the way back from Malden to enjoy public dinner at Port Dover, where he responded to a toast saying, "I expect to find the Yankee brigs hard and fast on the bar at Erie when I return, in which predicament it will be but a small job to destroy them."

According to Amelia Ryerse's diary, the real story was this: "There was a pretty widow of an officer of some rank in Amherstburg, who was very anxious to go to Toronto. Captain Barclay offered her a passage in his ship and brought her to Ryerse and then escorted her to Dr. Rolph's, where he and some of his officers remained to dinner the following day."

So did Barclay's little love dalliance turn the tide of war? Indeed it did.

Perry's sailors jumped at the chance to get out onto the lake and worked feverishly to take off the heavy guns and drag and float the two brigs out over the sandbars, all the time carefully guarded by the smaller boats. That done, Perry sailed the flotilla west to Put-in-Bay in the Bass islands, very close to Harrison's supply line. The general wanted him to mount his own blockade of Barclay's squadron at Fort Malden. Spies reported that Procter and Barclay were running perilously low on ammunition and food. Their militia and Indian allies were deserting in droves.

The twenty-seven-year-old boy wonder knew he had pulled together a fleet superior to Barclay's in every respect except long-range guns. He was ready to fight, hopefully at close quarters. He also knew Barclay had no choice but to come out and engage. Once he got in close, he planned to devastate Barclay's ships with his twenty short range carronades, or "smashers."

Perry had brought up about a hundred sailors from his Newport gunboats and some veterans from Old Ironsides, as well as farmhands and free blacks, but he was still undermanned. For the next month he drilled his crews relentlessly to get them used to the brigs, and pressed his officers to grasp the fact that they had to engage with the enemy very quickly or be shot to pieces by the long-distance guns.

In mid-August, Harrison gave him a hundred "marines" — buckskin-clad Kentucky sharpshooters who had never been near a ship of war. Their job was to mow down Barclay's sailors from perches high in the riggings.

Moral: Avoid escorting pretty widows to Toronto when the fate of British North America hangs in the balance.

Barclay Versus Perry

For the next three weeks, Perry's fleet ranged the western part of Lake Erie, picking off British supply boats, daring Barclay to emerge. But British shipwrights were still putting finishing touches on Barclay's flagship *Detroit*, making do with old ropes and guns from the fort. In spite of Procter's unrelenting pressure, Barclay wasn't ready to emerge just yet from his lair at Malden.

Perry had a distinct advantage before the battle. An American spy at Fort Malden had learned Barclay's battle order, calling for each ship to fight an enemy vessel of its own class, one on one. Thus Perry's *Lawrence* would oppose Barclay's new *Detroit*; *Niagara* would take on the *Queen Charlotte*, and so on.

Finally, Procter could take no more and ordered Barclay to take the battle to the Americans. At 5:00 a.m. on September 10, a lookout on the *Lawrence* spied six ships on the horizon about ten miles away, the rising sun shimming off their red hulls. He woke Perry, who was sleeping in his uniform. He ran topside to see then calmly ordered the sails unfurled and the anchors raised. On this magical morning, they sailed slowly out of Put-in-Bay over the glassy surface of Lake Erie, inspired, legend says, by a lone bald eagle wheeling above the flagship.

With Barclay closing about six miles away, Perry divided his fleet in two, with the *Lawrence* and two gunboats attacking first, and then Lieutenant Jesse D. Elliott following in *Niagara* with the rest of the fleet as quickly as possible.

Perry then brought out his blue battle flag, which a shipwright's wife had sewn at Presque Isle. It said simply: DON'T GIVE UP THE SHIP. He then stood on a gun carriage and asked his men, "My brave lads, this flag bears the last words of Captain Lawrence. Shall I hoist it?"

"Aye, aye, sir!" came the reply, followed by three cheers.

The wind picked up only slightly, and at about 10:30 a.m. Perry ordered a meal of bread, beans, and hard cheese, washed down with a tot of whisky, to dull the fear.

Suddenly they heard a bugle sound from Barclay's, followed by cheers, and then some choruses of "Rule Britannia, Britannia Rules the Waves."

Barclay held his fire, and when *Lawrence* came closer, Barclay ordered a test shot, which flew short. Closer now, *Detroit*'s second shot slammed into the *Lawrence*, and then Barclay's ship started pounding Perry's with broadside after broadside from his long range guns, trying to finish off the *Lawrence* before Elliot could come up on the *Niagara*.

Perry's smashers were still falling short as Barclay's *Detroit* smartly held back out of range and for two hours pounded the *Lawrence* to pieces with her long guns. Perry grew worried, because Elliott on the *Niagara* was deliberately avoiding battle, whether through fear or stupidity, Perry didn't know. By the time the *Detroit* came within carronade range, all of the guns on *Lawrence* were wrecked, and her sails and rigging were in shreds. Most of his 100 crew members were dead or badly wounded, and only seventeen men were still fit for duty.

U.S. Commodore Perry rowed from the crippled Lawrence *to the seaworthy* Niagara.

Yet Perry remained cool, seemingly untouchable, protected by some invisible angel. When he looked over his shoulder and saw Lieutenant Elliot coming closer, he shouted, "I'll fetch them up!" He had four sailors lower the gig, a tiny rowboat, onto the lake's surface. As he stepped aboard, a sailor named Hosea Sargent tossed him the DON'T GIVE UP THE SHIP banner.

He was partly hidden by clouds of gun smoke, and the British didn't see him give up his ship just yet. "Pull!" he ordered the oarsmen.

When Barclay spied the gig and realized what Perry had in mind, he trained every gun on the *Detroit* at Perry's little boat. One piece of grapeshot found its mark, but Perry plugged the hole with his coat. Fifteen minutes later they came alongside Niagara. Perry was miraculously unhurt.

"How goes the day?" stuttered Lieutenant. Elliot.

"Badly enough!" snapped the commodore, who immediately hoisted his battle flag to signal that he was back in the action.

The wind had freshened, and in a sudden gust *Niagara* leaped forward to the centre of the British line, her smashers loaded with two balls apiece, raking the ships on either side as she came through, driving toward *Detroit*.

One fusillade caused the *Queen Charlotte* to lose a topsail and then swerve into Barclay's flagship, locking the two vessels together. Perry passed at right angles, his smashers delivering fiery hailstorms of shot across both ships. With a deafening crack, *Detroit*'s mast came down, and in short order, Barclay, badly wounded in his thigh and his remaining arm, struck his colours, knowing further fighting would be futile.[9]

In fifteen minutes it was over. Perry had engaged and defeated Barclay's British fleet and gained control of Lake Erie. Perry's casualties were twenty-seven killed and ninety-six wounded, most on the *Lawrence*. Barclay's casualties were forty-one fatalities and ninety-four wounded.

Taking a pencil and a scrap of paper, Perry scrawled a message to General William Henry Harrison:

> Gen'l. We have met the enemy and they are ours -
> two ships, two brigs, one schooner and one sloop. Yours
> with the greatest esteem and respect,
> O. H. Perry.

He later dutifully reported to the Naval Department in Washington that his squadron had won "a signal victory ... after a sharp conflict."[10]

Moral: There are times when you MUST give up the ship, especially if yours is sinking and there is a better one nearby.

BATTLE AT THE THAMES

HARRISON MAKES HIS MOVE

It was obvious now to Henry Procter that he had precious little time to move. He wrote Prevost that he would have to "retire on the Thames without delay." He had no doubt Harrison would take Detroit by land from the south and west, and probably mount a naval assault on Fort Malden. Prevost had penny-pinched his operations all that year. His supply lines were in tatters, Erie was an enemy lake, thousands of Indians were begging the fort for food and ammunition, and his only escape was up the Thames River toward Burlington Heights. Angered at the high command in Montreal and exhausted by the struggle, "*Sauve qui peut,*" was now his working motto.

On September 18, as predicted, Kentucky Colonel Richard M. Johnson galloped around the lakeshore with almost a thousand cavalry and forced the British to evacuate Fort Detroit.

Across the river at Fort Malden, Tecumseh was furious on learning of the planned retreat. He feared that his dream of an Indian nation would be forever lost. He would rather die fighting than bring such a tragedy on his people. Calling together a pow-wow on the Fort Maiden parade ground, he jumped up on the "standing stone," a large boulder where announcements were made, and began to make a fiery speech.

> I speak in the names of the Indian chiefs and warriors to General Procter as the representative of the great father, the King. You have arms and ammunition which our great father sent for his red children. If you have an idea of going away, give them to us, and you may go and welcome. Our lives are in the hands of the Great Spirit. He gave to our ancestors the lands which we possess. We are determined to defend them, and if it be His will, our bones will whiten on them, but we will never give them up.

He turned to Procter, and reminded him of the British promise.

> But now we see you are pulling back. We are sorry to see that
> you are getting ready to flee before you ever caught sight of
> the enemy. We must compare your conduct to a fat animal
> that carries its tail on its back, but, when frightened, drops it
> between its legs and runs.

Procter's face went pale then bright red as he realized Tecumseh was calling him a coward in front of his own officers.

"Listen, father!" cried Tecumseh. "The Americans have not yet defeated us by land. We therefore wish to remain here and fight the enemy if they make an appearance. If they defeat us, we will retreat with you."

By this time, Tecumseh's braves were ready to massacre Procter and his officers. The British general calmly promised to pull back only as far as Moraviantown, near an Indian mission on the Thames River, where the Americans could be ambushed. Procter evacuated the fort the following day at dawn, ordering a rearguard to set fire to the navy buildings and storehouses.

THE BATTLE OF MORAVIANTOWN

Two days later, on September 26, Perry's squadron ferried William Henry Harrison's 4,500 troops across Lake Erie. They landed on a pebbly beach south of Fort Malden, found it deserted and half burned, and in short order started to move up the Thames River road after Henry Procter, leaving behind a detachment to garrison the fort.

It was beautiful Indian summer weather, with the leaves all scarlet and gold. Harrison took with him a force of about 3,500 men, including his Kentucky cavalry regiments, five brigades of Kentucky volunteers, and a part of the 27th Infantry. Facing him, Procter had about 2,900 men, of whom about 900 were British regulars and the remainder Indians loyal to Tecumseh.

After a short skirmish with some of Tecumseh's warriors on October 4 at McGregor's Creek, the site of present day Chatham, Ontario, the Americans caught up with Procter and Tecumseh at Moraviantown the next day. Procter set up two columns facing west along the road, while

Tecumseh's followers waited in the swamp and bush to the north ready to close the ambush.

Tecumseh was now resigned to his fate, telling his closest warriors, "We are about to enter an engagement from which I shall not return." Then he went to see Procter. "Father," he said, "have a big heart. Tell your young men to be firm and all will be well." Then he went to shake the hands of the officers, smiling at each and saying: "Be brave! Stand firm! Shoot straight!"

Perhaps he saw Procter was now clearly focusing on flight and using all available wagons to send his papers and personal effects on to Burlington Heights. His soldiers were not impressed and grumbled among themselves.

Harrison ordered a surprise cavalry assault by the Kentuckians, and not the expected infantry action. "Charge them, my brave Kentuckians," he cried as a bugle sounded the attack. The cavalrymen, carrying long rifles instead of swords, spurred their horses into action, shouting "Remember the Raisin!"

Johnson's charge succeeded brilliantly, and 600 British barely gave them a fight, dropping their muskets and throwing up their hands in something close to disgust.

Another bugle sounded, and the cavalrymen dismounted to meet the Indians advancing from the north, engaging them in a desperate hand-to-hand struggle. Colonel Johnson fell unconscious after shooting a brave who struck him with a tomahawk. Tecumseh was in the thick of the battle, shouting to his followers, "Be brave! Be brave!" His friend Nawkaw, fighting beside him, saw a red stain on his buckskin shirt and saw that blood was trickling from his mouth. Suddenly there was no sound from Tecumseh, and a hush fell over the battlefield. His followers, knowing their chief was dead, stopped their struggle and slipped back into the woods, leaving the bodies of thirty-three warriors behind on the ground.

The Americans and British had few casualties, numbering in the twenties. Only a small remnant of the British force — less than 250 soldiers and a few Indians — escaped capture at the Thames and followed their fleeing general overland to the head of Lake Ontario. Harrison did not follow, content to pack up the weapons, field pieces, ammunition, personal baggage, and other booty left behind by Procter.

At midnight that night, the cavalrymen were wakened by a panicked cry: "Indians! O Lord! O Lord! Indians!" The whole camp sprang to arms, ready to fight off an ambush. But it was only a young Kentucky private who was having a nightmare.

Next morning, news of the Shawnee chief's death spread quickly, and with U.S. control of the western frontier, Indian resistance south of the lakes began to wither away. On October 17, Harrison felt confident enough to issue a proclamation letting civil servants in the Western District of Upper Canada remain in office if they took an oath of allegiance to the United States. There were, surprisingly, few takers.

Back at Fort Malden, a Kentucky volunteer named Isaac Shelby took from his tunic an American eagle banner, the battle flag of his state, ordered by the Kentucky legislature to commemorate those fellows killed fighting the British and Indians, and pinned it to the barracks wall. He remembered a year before, after Hull's disgrace, hearing Andrew Jackson's advice: "Kentuckians should plant the standard which bears your country's eagle on the walls of Malden."

Harrison soon discharged his Kentuckians and sent the militia home. Then he got on board Perry's flagship *Niagara*, and they sailed east, ready to join a two-pronged drive on Montreal.

As for Henry Procter, he was tried by court martial a year later for his conduct during the retreat. He was found guilty of "deficiency in energy and judgement" and suspended for six months without pay. The Prince Regent insisted the findings and sentence be read to every regiment in the British Army. Procter's sentence was later reduced to a reprimand, but his military career was effectively over.

An Indian Post Mortem

Andrew J. Blackbird, or Mack-e-te-be-nessy, son of the Ottawa Chief, Mack a-de-pe-nessy, in his history of the Ottawa and Chippewa, related that

> in the history of the United States, there are some mistakes concerning the accounts of the Indians, particularly the accounts of our brave Tecumseh, as it is claimed that he was killed by a soldier named Johnson, upon whom they conferred the honor of having disposed of the dreaded Tecumseh. Even pictured out as being coming up with his tomahawk to strike a man who was on horseback, but being instantly shot dead with the pistol.

Now I have repeatedly heard our oldest Indians, both male and female, who were present at the defeat of the British and Indians, all tell a unanimous story, saying that they came to a clearing or opening spot, and it was there where Tecumseh ordered his warriors to rally and fight the Americans once more and in this very spot one of the American musket balls took effect in Tecumseh's leg so as to break the bone of his leg, that he could not stand up. He was sitting on the ground when he told his warriors to flee as well as they could, and furthermore said, "One of my leg is shot off! But leave me one or two guns loaded; I am going to have a last shot. Be quick and go!"

That was the last word spoken by Tecumseh. As they look back, they saw the soldiers thick as swarm of bees around where Tecumseh was sitting on the ground with his broken leg, and so they did not see him anymore; and, therefore, we always believe that the Indians or Americans know not who made the fatal shot on Tecumseh's leg, or what the soldiers did with him when they came up to him as he was sitting on the ground.

Moral: When you are losing everything, know at least that your soul is in the hands of the Great Spirit.

CHATEAUGUAY AND CRYSLER'S FARM

> "The thirst of military glory will ever be the vice of exalted characters."
>
> —*Edward Gibbon*

While Barclay was being thrashed by Perry on Lake Erie and Procter chased up the Thames by Harrison, the Emperor Bonaparte was having some heavy weather of his own. The Duke of Wellington's storming of San Sebastien on August 13 marked the end of the Peninsular War and the flight of Napoleon's army back to France. On October 19 he was soundly beaten at the Battle of the Nations, and a month later he was fleeing to Paris, where, declining an offer to sail to the United States, he would be captured the following March, 1814.

The news from Europe gave James Madison and his Secretary of War John Armstrong Jr. a sense of impending doom. Clearly the British would soon start shipping whole regiments of battle-hardened regulars to Canada. Surely it was time for one big thrust against the Canadian metropolis of Montreal before winter set in.

And yet the Americans in the field felt pretty damned good about themselves after taking back Niagara, Detroit, and the Michigan Territory. They had stopped Sir George Prevost in his tracks, preventing him from taking Sackets Harbor. Best of all, a new cohort of scrappy younger leaders like Jacob Brown, Winfield Scott, and even boy commodore Oliver Perry were proving they could win big battles. And they were succeeding even in spite of doddering old lawyers and Republican congressmen who fussed and fretted and got in the way of their glory.

As autumn fell over Lake Ontario and the Valley, Armstrong moved up to Sackets Harbor and started planning his St. Lawrence campaign. It was simple and credible: two forces from the west and south of Montreal would unite in a pincer movement and then capture the city.

The southern lever of the pincer was an army of about 4,200 men assembling at Plattsburg on Lake Champlain under the command of sixty-one-year-old Brigadier-General Wade Hampton, another wealthy planter and Republican politician from South Carolina. Hampton was not a typical southern squire. He grew up on a farm and saw his parents and most of his kin killed in a Cherokee raid. During and after service in the Revolutionary War and in Congress, he had amassed a fortune speculating in land and owned hundreds of slaves. In fact, he had brought some of them along on the campaign to be his personal servants.[11]

The western lever was a force of about 7,000 men under the command of Granny Dearborn's replacement, Major General James Wilkinson, another privately tutored Maryland planter and land developer who had served with Benedict Arnold in the 1776 attack on Quebec. Wilkinson actually had some decent military experience, but he was a thoroughly untrustworthy character. After the Revolution he had moved to Kentucky and started dealing secretly with the Spaniards to get trading concessions at New Orleans. At that time he became a paid agent of the Spanish Crown, getting a pension of four thousand dollars a year. In 1793–94 he apparently betrayed his country, informing the Spaniards of plans for General George Rogers Clark to attack New Orleans. Wilkinson was doubtless a double dealer. After the Louisiana Purchase, Jefferson appointed him first governor of the Louisiana Territory. Even then, he lured Aaron Burr into a plot to set up an independent nation in the west, then betrayed Burr to Jefferson.

Armstrong gave Wilkinson two options: either attack Kingston first, or move directly down the St. Lawrence River to join up with Wade Hampton at the mouth of the Chateauguay River, and together they would take Montreal.

The problem was in the execution of Armstrong's grand plan. It was another poor recipe for success, because the two main ingredients didn't mix well at all.

A few years earlier, President Madison had replaced Wilkinson with Hampton as governor of New Orleans, and Wilkinson couldn't stand his rival. For his part, Hampton was appalled by the choice of Wilkinson and suspected the War Department of setting him up for a fall. He came close to resigning when he found out that Armstrong might give Wilkinson overall command, and only accepted if Armstrong stayed in charge.

In addition, both old generals were overly fond of the bottle. However, in those days, when whiskey was used as mouthwash, the love of alcohol was not grounds for dismissal from military service.

Moral: Old politicians make lousy generals.

Hampton Makes His Move

When Major General Wade Hampton took command of the Americans around Lake Champlain that July, he found thousands of badly trained troops, led by officers with no battle experience. The British had taken control of the lake and were raiding the towns for food supplies. U.S. Navy commander Lieutenant Thomas MacDonough had failed to get his flotilla of gunboats built until late August.

Charles-Michel de Salaberry.

On September 19, Hampton was able to move by water from Burlington to Plattsburgh, escorted by MacDonough's gunboats, and he made a half-hearted feint north from Lake Champlain down the Richelieu River, but had to turn back not just because of British strength, which was considerable, but because it was unseasonably hot, and his troops failed bring enough drinking water for themselves and the horses. His council of officers agreed to take the longer but safer route, along the Chateauguay River southwest of Montreal, where there would be a good supply of drinking water. The American force doubled back to Lake Champlain, and then marched forty miles west to reach Four Corners, on the Chateauguay River just south of the border, to wait for news from Armstrong.

Facing Hampton was Lieutenant-Colonel Charles-Michel de Salaberry, a scrappy thirty-five-year-old French Canadian aristocrat from an old military family. His father was a personal friend of the Duke of Kent, father of Queen Victoria, who was appointed military commander-in-chief in North America in 1799. Salaberry *père* was famous for standing up to Governor James Craig, who wanted to take away the rights of the French in Lower Canada. Craig was soon replaced by Sir George Prevost, a French speaker who soon mollified the feelings of the Canadiens.

Young de Salaberry was commissioned in the British army in 1794 and served in the Napoleonic Wars. In 1810 he returned to Lower Canada and two years later raised a regiment of French Canadian Voltigeurs, or light infantry. He was a tough and demanding but fair-minded leader, and a perfect foe. He had lost three brothers in combat, had been scarred for life in a sword duel, and was now eagerly awaiting another chance to drive back the Americans. He had already sent Granny Dearborn and 2,000 troops packing in November 1812 at Odelltown, but when Prevost made no mention of his leadership in dispatches, he seriously considered leaving the army. Then he got the order to proceed to Chateauguay with his troops.[12]

Mohawk scouts sent by Salaberry watched Hampton's progress carefully. Once de Salaberry knew the route they would take he moved his force up the Chateauguay to prepare defensive positions, build a rough fort and create a whole jungle of obstacles to slow the Americans. He had with him 1,630 Voltigeur regulars, about a hundred Mohawk warriors, and two groups of militia: the Sedentary Militia from nearby Beauharnois, and two companies of the 5th Battalion of Select Embodied Militia (the Devil's Own), recruited from the slums of Montreal.

When Armstrong reported that Wilkinson's expedition was still not ready, Hampton fumed at Four Corners for the next three weeks. The delay was depleting his supplies. Clearly the British knew exactly where he was and were preparing a nasty reception.

Hampton was seriously thinking of resigning when Armstrong wrote him that Wilkinson's force was "almost" ready to set out. He took that as an order and on October 18 began advancing along the south east bank of the Chateauguay River. At the Canadian frontier, his 1,400 New York militia stood on their constitutional rights and refused to fight outside their home state.

Hampton wasn't surprised. It was not a promising beginning, and it could get worse. But he was still left with two brigades of regulars, about 2,600 in all, plus 200 mounted troops and ten field guns. Was that enough? He doubted it.

Crossing the border, his force advanced slowly along a road that was not much more than a dirt track along the river. The Voltigeurs and militia had destroyed all the bridges, and the American engineers had to rebuild them before the ammunition and supply wagons could cross. Trees had been felled across the trail, and these had to be laboriously chopped and dragged out of the way with horses.

On October 25, his scouts came upon what they reported was the British front line. They told him it was not a large body, but they had sensed Indians to their left, and retreated, failing to discover de Salaberry's main contingent of 1,300 Voltigeurs, waiting downstream.

De Salaberry had hidden most of his men on the northwest bank of the Chateauguay River, defending the road past the ford in several protected fall-back positions in the ravines. On the front line that Hampton's scouts saw were fifty Canadian Fencibles, 150 Voltigeurs, and 100 sedentary militia, behind a line of breastworks and protected by Mohawks lurking in the woods. Another force of 160 militiamen waited on the opposite bank of the river, where they built a barricade (*abatis*) of fallen trees to protect the ford where they expected Hampton to cross. Finally, de Salaberry kept 1,130 men behind his own front line and out of sight.

An Extraordinary Affair at Chateauguay

Hampton decided to attack in two prongs in order to outflank the British position. Colonel Robert Purdy was to take 1,500 of the best light infantry across a ford to the southeast bank, then advance fifteen miles through the woods at night beyond the apparent British front lines, and take them from the rear. Once he heard firing, Brigadier-General George Izard would then attack the British front line directly with 1,000 troops, while Hampton would hold back with the rest of the force and guard the wagons and artillery.

A few hours after Purdy's brigade had left camp and crossed the river, a messenger rode up to Hampton with a short letter from Secretary Armstrong, dated 16 October, informing him that Armstrong was giving overall command of the combined American forces to Wilkinson. He also ordered Hampton to construct winter quarters for 10,000 men at Four Corners.

Not Montreal? Hampton took the secretary's vague missive to mean that there would be no attack on Montreal that year. So the whole campaign was pointless. But he could not retreat, because Colonel Purdy was already committed and would probably get to the ford the next morning. He had to make a move to protect the troops already under way.

Today's Chateauguay River is a popular place for canoeists and kayakers who adore its meandering waterway. The surrounding countryside is flat, with corn and soybean fields as far as the eye can see. But in 1813, the territory was thinly settled, and much of the woodland was swampy and cut by ravines. Purdy's men found the going so rough that they could only move six miles

The Battle of Chateauguay by Henri Julien.

through the tangled jungle by the time dawn broke. Poorly guided, and with cold rain pouring down, they lost their way and never got close to outflanking the British. At mid-morning, they stumbled out of the bush at a point on the river bank opposite de Salaberry's forward defences and immediately came under fire from militia on the far bank, who were spacing themselves out and blowing hunting horns to make the Americans think they were facing a larger force. Purdy's force was still able to proceed toward the ford, but soon was hotly attacked by a light company of the 3rd Select Embodied Militia under Captain Daly, who drove the Americans back upriver.

On the northwest bank, General Izard had been waiting for some good news from Purdy, but when there was none he marched his troops into the ravine facing de Salaberry's defences and deployed them into line. At that point, a story goes, he sent one of his French-speaking officers ahead on a horse to demand de Salaberry's surrender, with these words, "Brave Canadiens, surrender yourselves; we wish you no harm!" But because the man had forgotten to carry a flag of truce, he was shot dead, apparently by de Salaberry himself.

At that point the two sides started what could almost be described as play fighting. Izard's troops lined up, firing by platoons, as if they were on a parade ground. They started a steady, rolling volley into the trees and breastworks and abatis. The Canadians ducked, and with each lull in the firing, got off a few of their own shots, rarely hitting any of the Americans.

One of Izard's companies tried to outflank a light company of the Fencibles, but the reserves and Mohawks advanced with bugle calls, cheers, and war cries to rescue their companions. It was beginning to look like a scene from an Italian opera as De Salaberry sent his buglers into the woods to sound the "Advance." This completely unnerved Izard and his officers, who though they were facing 5,000 men.[13] They began to fall back along the road to their camp, where they found their commander Hampton in a daze, sitting beside the unused field guns, a whisky flask in his hand,

As for Purdy, he fell back to a position opposite where he though Izard would be, so he could ferry over his wounded. But finding nobody there, and under fire again, he retreated back through the swampy woods to camp, arriving as night fell. Hampton's army was already withdrawing in good order, seemingly glad to be rid of the place. De Salaberry did not bother to pursue the tired and dispirited Americans.

Chateauguay was a strange battle, with very little fighting. De Salaberry lost a mere two dead, with sixteen wounded, including militia captains Daly and Brugiere. Hampton suffered only fifty-six casualties, twenty-three killed, thirty-three wounded, and twenty-nine missing, including sixteen who were taken prisoner by de Salaberry.

Back in New York State, Hampton held a council of war with his officers and decided to enter winter quarters in Plattsburgh to await further instructions from the Department of War in Washington. He had already submitted his resignation to Armstrong the day before the battle, and would never again serve in the field.

De Salaberry held his position for a few more days until he was sure the Americans were truly on the way home. At this point he wrote to his wife that he thought they had "saved Montreal for another season." To his father, he modestly noted, "Without arrogating to myself too much credit, I am proud to think that this defence, on our part, has at least prevented the American army from penetrating to La Prairie. We are here situated about thirty-five miles from Montreal. This is certainly a most extraordinary affair."[14]

It would get even more extraordinary for the leader of the Voltigeurs. Just as he was about to retire his army downriver to Montreal, who should arrive in camp but Major General de Watteville and Sir George Prevost, who quickly surveyed the ground, forbade him to follow the Americans, and then just as rapidly returned to HQ in the city, submitting their own dispatches to Lord Bathurst. Prevost said that he himself had been present at the battle. He gave de Watteville credit for the strategy employed, saying that de Salaberry had been negligent. They two claimed the victory entirely for themselves, marvelling that due to their exertions, a mere 300 Canadians had put 7,500 Americans to flight.[15]

Prevost had done this to de Salaberry before. On November 27, 1812, the Voltigeurs Canadiens had fought back an attempted invasion near Lacolle. De Salaberry later learned that Prevost had sent the British government a weasely dispatch on the events, claiming he was at the battle, making no mention of de Salaberry's name and congratulating the adjutant general, Edward Baynes, and Major-General Rottenburg, who had taken no part in the action.

At first furious at his superiors, de Salaberry was mollified by an official expression of gratitude signed by the Quebec Assembly, and the ribbon of a Knight Commander of the Bath, doubtless arranged by his old friend the Duke of Kent.

Moral: If you don't have enough good data, don't attack.

BATTLE AT CRYSLER'S FARM

At the American naval base of Sackets Harbor on Lake Ontario, Isaac Chauncey's men were building Wilkinson a large flotilla of twelve gunboats and 300 transports to attack Montreal down the St. Lawrence. All was ready by October 4, but bad weather and illness in the ranks delayed their departure.

Almost a thousand men were sick with dysentery and typhus in the camp hospital. Camp surgeon William Ross blamed bad food, which he said "had destroyed more soldiers than have fallen by the sword of the enemy." The meat supplied from Albany was bad and the men's flour was so rotten "it would kill the best horse in Sackets Harbor." The sanitation was appalling, and the bread was baked with water taken from the lake near some latrines.

Wilkinson was plagued by more than bad digestion. He claimed to be ill from an ague he had caught in New Orleans, but in actual fact he was a hopeless drunk and probably addicted to the opium he relied on to relieve his stomach problems. Perhaps this clouded his judgment. His men were cold and hungry and ill-prepared for battle, but on October 16 he gave Major General Morgan Lewis, Armstrong's brother in law and Quartermaster General of the U.S. Army, the order to launch the flotilla against Montreal.

The troops embarked on a dark night just as a storm was brewing over the lake. As Lossing relates,

> They were packed in scows, bateaux, Durham boats, and common lake sailboats, with ordnance, ammunition, hospital stores, baggage, camp equipage, and two months' provisions. The voyage was among islands and past numerous points of land where soundings and currents were known to few. There was a scarcity of pilots, and the whole flotilla seemed to have been sent out with very little of man's wisdom to direct it. The wind was favorable at the beginning, but toward midnight, as the clouds thickened and the darkness deepened,

it freshened, and before morning became a gale, with rain and sleet. The flotilla was scattered in every direction, and the gloomy dawn [October 17, 1813.] revealed a sad spectacle. The shores of the islands and the main were strewn with wrecks of vessels and property. Fifteen large boats were totally lost, and many more too seriously damaged to be safe. For thirty-six hours the wind blew fiercely, but on the 20th, there having been a comparative calm for more than a day, a large proportion of the troops, with the sound boats, arrived at Grenadier Island. These were chiefly the brigades of Generals Boyd, Brown, Covington, Swartwout, and Porter (the three former had encamped at Henderson Harbor), which had arrived.

On the 24th, Wilkinson wrote Secretary Armstrong:

The extent of the injury to our craft, clothing, arms, and provisions greatly exceed our apprehensions, and has subjected us to the necessity of furnishing clothing, and of making repairs and equipments to the flotilla generally. In fact, all our hopes have been nearly blasted; but, thanks to the same Providence that placed us in jeopardy, we are surmounting our difficulties, and, God willing, I shall pass Prescott on the night of the 1st or 2d proximo.

On October 29, General Jacob Brown's brigade, with some light troops and heavy artillery, managed to start the American advance down the St. Lawrence from Grenadier Island.

American flotilla on the St. Lawrence.

THE BRITISH CANADIAN RESPONSE

When news of the American movement reached Kingston, Sir George Prevost ordered Lieutenant-Colonel Joseph Morrison of the 89th Regiment to take up the pursuit and harass Wilkinson's army.

A thoroughly professional soldier, Morrison was born in New York in 1783 during the British occupation, the son of a senior Commissariat officer. He joined the British Army at age ten as an ensign and was wounded in the Anglo-Russian Invasion of Holland in 1799. After service in Ireland, the West Indies, and Gibraltar, he was posted to Canada in 1812.

Morrison had 630 well-trained rank-and-file regulars. His own nine companies of the 89th totalled about 450 men, plus about 160 men from Brock's old regiment, the 49th Foot, sadly reduced by casualties. He had less than twenty artillerymen with two six-pounder field guns, but they would have to do. On November 6 this "corps of observation" left Kingston on two of Yeo's armed schooners, the *Lord Beresford* and the *Sir Sydney Smith*, escorting seven gunboats and a number of bateaux under the command of Royal Navy Captain William Mulcaster. Mulcaster's job was to bother the American rear.

General Wilkinson finally ordered his main force of 6,000 to proceed downriver on November 5, following Jacob Brown. On a glorious Indian summer day, the huge American flotilla of 350 bateaux and gunboats majestically made its way down the St. Lawrence in a five-mile-long procession, with flags flying and the bands playing "Yankee Doodle." When they reached Prescott, they had to evade the guns of Fort Wellington by landing above Ogdensburg, portaging the supplies in wagons, and floating strings of empty boats past in the dark.

The next day, Hampton's adjutant Colonel William King arrived with news of the debacle at Chateauguay. "Damn such an army," Wilkinson exploded. "A man might as well be in hell as command it." Wilkinson was getting more and more nervous about prospects, and wild stories were coming in about British gunboats ready to attack him from the rear, Iroquois war parties ready for action downstream, and a huge army of 5,000 British regulars and 20,000 militia waiting outside Montreal.

As the Americans swept downriver through Loyalist country, local militia continually sniped at them from the far shore. Their fire forced an angry Wilkinson to split his army, and he sent Jacob Brown and Forsyth with an elite force of 1,200 riflemen to land on the Canadian side at Iroquois and drive off the Canadian settlers.

Wilkinson paused at the Long Sault Rapids on November 8. He ordered Winfield Scott (who had ridden all the way from Niagara to enjoy the fight) to cross to the Canadian shore and fight off any attempt to interfere with the movement of the bateaux through the rapids. Two days later, Scott began to march downriver toward Cornwall with Jacob Brown's brigade, leaving John Boyd's brigade of 4,000 men to deal with Morrison's smaller force.

Boyd was universally despised by his other generals. A onetime soldier of fortune, he had spent twenty years in India fighting for the Nizam of Hyderabad and the Peshwa of Poona before signing up as a brigadier-general in 1812. Scott thought he was an imbecile, and Lewis "a combination of ignorance, vanity, and petulance." At least he had field experience.

Morrison Gets into Position

Meanwhile, Morrison's pursuing force had landed at Prescott on the morning of November 9. His "corps of observation" was boosted by men from Fort Wellington and a detachment of 240 troops from Montreal commanded by Lieutenant-Colonel Pearson. These consisted of two flank companies of the 49th Foot, a detachment of Canadian Fencibles, three companies of Canadian Voltigeurs, a handful of militia artillerymen with a six-pounder gun, and a half dozen Provincial Dragoons to serve a couriers. Captain Morrison now had about 900 officers and men.

Captain Mulcaster had to leave his armed schooners at Fort Wellington, but his smaller gunboats kept following the American bateaux, peppering them with fire as they began to move toward the rapids.

The next day, November 10, Morrison set up headquarters in a farmhouse belonging to militiaman Captain John Crysler at the head of the Long Sault Rapids, thirty kilometres west of Cornwall. From his window, Morrison and his staff ran their practiced eyes over the terrain and smiled with satisfaction. The farm had a dirt road that ran at a right angle to the river up to an impassable black ash swamp one kilometre inland. There were big cedar fences and gullies to protect exposed soldiers, and in front of them was a long muddy field of winter wheat cut by small ravines — a fine field of fire against the

Americans, who would have to land at the foot of the farm to portage around the dangerous Long Sault rapids that roared down to Cornwall.

John Crysler's farm was one of the few battle sites in the war that was fought in textbook field conditions, where British regulars knew best to operate.

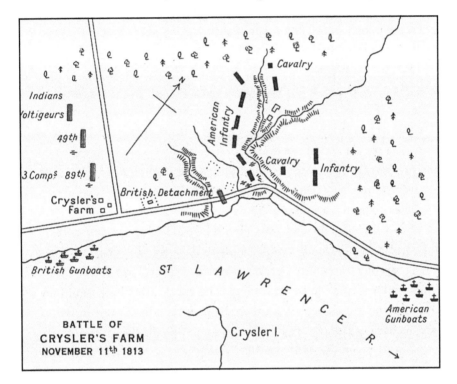

Battle map of Crysler's Farm.

THE BATTLE BEGINS

That night, both Generals Wilkinson and Lewis were knocked out by sickness, in no condition to lead any battle.

At 8:00 a.m. on the chill morning of November 11, an American scouting party exchanged shots with some of the Tyendinaga Mohawks. Convinced that the British were attacking, General Wilkinson roused himself and ordered his rear guard — 1,800 Americans of the 25th Infantry Regiment — to clear away the British troops before moving down the rapids.

At the same time, Mulcaster's gunboats kept firing shrapnel and grape-shot at John Boyd's waiting flotilla of 4,000 Americans. Boyd was getting conflicting orders from Wilkinson about whether to proceed. When a report reached Wilkinson about the presence of British redcoats on Crysler's field, he finally ordered Boyd to land, outflank the British, and capture their field guns. Boyd then landed 2,000 troops with artillery at the foot of the farm and started advancing on the British in three columns.

Waiting for him was Morrison, now with 800 British regulars of the 49th and 89th Regiments, with three guns and crews of the Royal Artillery, the Canadian Fencibles,[16] Voltigeurs Canadiens, and 30 Mohawk warriors from Tyendinaga, as well as the Dundas County Militia, totalling 1,200 men. The Canadian militia and Mohawk warriors guarded the woods on either side of the field, while the Voltigeurs, almost invisible in their homespun grey, got ready for skirmishing behind rocks and fences. The British regulars drew up in two lines up from the river to await the American assault.

Boyd first sent Lieutenant-Colonel Elzear Ripley's regiment to probe the skirmishers on the British left near the swamp. They were surprised by the Voltigeurs, who suddenly rose up and fired two volleys in their direction. They panicked and hid behind stumps and rocks, firing back until they ran out of ammunition. Ripley got them back in order and they finally started driving back the Voltigeurs, threatening to turn the British left flank.

At this point, the 49th and 89th, facing east, were swung around ninety degrees to the north, and ripped into the Americans with volley after volley, sending them into retreat. John Crysler's children, hiding in the cellar, could even tell the British guns from the American ones. The U.S. troops fired individually, their guns making a pop-pop sound. When the British opened fire, at intervals, it was like "a tremendous roll of thunder."

Boyd then tried advancing his three main brigades against the British right directly across the open wheat fields, but they were stopped by six-pounders and rolling volleys from the 49th, disguised in grey coats, who killed Brigadier Covington and several other American officers.

Morrison then ordered Stoney Creek veteran Charles Plenderleath to move the 49th against the U.S. guns before they could attack his troops with grapeshot. A troop of American Dragoons suddenly galloped toward their position to get behind them, but Captain Ellis performed another British drill book manoeuvre, left-wheeling his company backward to face the U.S. cavalry.

By holding his fire to the last moment to maximize the effect, he shattered the American charge. His company then wheeled back to the advance and took the American guns before they could go into action.

In the end, the American officers proved no match for the battle-hardened British regulars, backed by the deadly shrapnel of the artillery and withering fire of the Canadian skirmishers. It was over in less than three hours. Despite the Americans' overwhelming numerical superiority, General Boyd withdrew from the field leaving 400 casualties — 102 killed, 237 wounded, and more than 100 missing — and crossed to the U.S. side.

Morrison reported his own casualties for the Battle of Crysler's Farm as being twenty-two killed, 148 wounded, and nine missing, or about one-sixth of his total force. The greatest losses were suffered by the Canadian Fencibles, a Quebec regiment whose ranks were about 50 percent francophone. They suffered a casualty rate of nearly 33 percent. Two thirds of the 270 Canadian regulars under Morrison's command that day were French-speaking soldiers from Quebec.[17]

Lieutenant-Colonel Morrison's troops had beaten back the Americans against overwhelming odds, but one American unit caught his eye: the U.S. 25th infantry. He was so impressed by their steadiness in battle that he sent a note to their commander, Colonel Edmund Gaines, hoping that they might meet after the war as friends.

The battle over, Wilkinson scribbled a note back to Armstrong that "although the imperious obligations of duty did not allow me sufficient time to rout the enemy, they were beaten." He roused himself from his sickbed, and then pushed down the St. Lawrence with the remnant of his demoralized army to join Hampton's army beyond the Long Sault for the push to Montreal. But he soon got word that Hampton was refusing to meet him below the rapids at St. Regis, as planned, and was already on his way to Plattsburgh.

When this news reached Wilkinson, it was a golden excuse to abort his own attack as well. Ill and discouraged after the mauling at Crysler's Farm, out of supplies, and with the roads almost impassable, he led his army into winter quarters at French Mills (present-day Fort Covington), ending the threat to Canada that year.

There his men passed a miserable winter on hard rations. Some crossed the river and raided Loyalist farms, stealing cattle and wheat. But most of the Americans were too weak to move, and hundreds died of cold, dysentery, and malnutrition, while Wilkinson convalesced in a comfortable inn at Malone, New York.

Moral: "Don't get fancy against professionals on a level playing field."

The End of the Invasion

The U.S. expedition against Montreal in the fall of 1813 was the most magnificent fiasco of the War of 1812.

Neither army had enough strength to capture Montreal without the other's aid. The two commanders hated each other, and each suspected that the War Department was leaving them in the lurch. At first contact with the British, Hampton retreated. He later resigned his commission in disgust when Wilkinson blamed Hampton's "unwarrantable conduct" for the failure of the campaign.

The Battles at Chateauguay and Crysler's Farm left the British now firmly in control of both sides of the St. Lawrence.

The following March, Wilkinson was back in Canada, leading 4,000 men down the Richelieu River. This time he was stopped by 180 men defending a stone mill on the Lacolle River. He eventually faced a court of inquiry for his wartime conduct. He was exonerated on all counts, but later relieved of command.

Moral: When winter is coming, and you can't think of anything better to do, don't invade Canada. Chop wood instead.

BY FIRE AND SWORD

> "Let us retaliate by fire and sword."
> —*Colonel Murray to General Drummond*

War is a cruel sport. It can blaze up in glory, luring young men and old soldiers to taste the drug of victory. Then, when its participants are exhausted and spent by defeat and mayhem, degenerate into the ugliest debauchery and nightmarish suffering.

As the leaves turned to gold and red in the fall of 1813, most British and American regulars left Niagara for the eastern and of Lake Ontario and the north of Lake Champlain to fight each other in the campaign against Montreal. The Niagara frontier was left nearly empty of regular troops. Soon a mob of lawless militiamen started to roam across the border at will, raiding, looting, raping, and murdering civilians.

Were these raids of terror deliberate U.S. military policy? Was a promise of pillage the only way Ohio or New York state recruiting officers could keep their militia up to strength? Was the chance for booty the only way they could get demoralized civilians to sign up and cross state borders? Or was the American militia simply out of control?

WILLCOCKS' CANADIAN VOLUNTEERS

Even with the victories at Chrysler's Farm and Chateauguay that ended any threat to Quebec and Montreal, the British loss at the Battle of the Thames on October 5, 1813, left Niagara in a vulnerable state, and the Americans soon reoccupied Fort George, Queenston, and Chippawa. They were aided by a troop of so-called Canadian Volunteers, led by Joseph Willcocks, a former member of the Upper Canada legislature, who had gone over to the American side that year. Willcocks soon unleashed a reign of terror on his former neighbours, particularly those who had opposed him during his prewar political career in Niagara (the former Upper Canada capital of Newark), where he edited a radical newspaper for four years.

In late October, Sir George Prevost nervously ordered the evacuation of all of Upper Canada west of Kingston. But Major-General John Vincent called a council of officers, and to a man they resolved to disobey Prevost's order and not only hold the Niagara Peninsula, but try to recapture every British post.

Vincent was ill and was being posted back to Kingston, but before leaving in late November, he ordered Colonel John Murray to move to protect the inhabitants against further raids from Willcocks.

In early December, Murray led a force of 378 regulars of the 8th Regiment and some volunteers, including Merritt's Dragoons, to Forty Mile Creek, where they set up their base of operations. Captain William Hamilton Merritt first moved his troop east to hunt for Willcocks and the American raiders. A Mohawk scout found the tail end of the American column marching toward Twenty Mile Creek, and Merritt sent his dragoons after them to Twelve Mile Creek, forcing them back to Fort George.

The American commanding officer, Brigadier-General George McClure, was in a tough position. Most of his regular troops had gone east to reinforce Sackets Harbor, and his New York State militia force had started melting away as their contracts ended, and they went home to harvest their crops. With renewed British attacks, he decided to withdraw across the Niagara River to the American side and the safer confines of Fort Niagara.

Before the Americans left Upper Canada, McClure made a grave mistake and gave Joseph Willcocks permission to destroy the town of Niagara, on the pretext of following Armstrong's order to deny shelter to British troops.

WILLCOCKS BURNS NIAGARA

December 10, 1813, was a cold and blustery day with snow drifting up to five metres in places. Joseph Willcocks was furious at American plans to abandon the peninsula. He was determined to punish his former neighbours for slights, real and imaginary, that he had suffered since going over to the Americans.

Willcocks came home to Niagara-on-the-Lake with a vengeance that day, riding at the head of about 100 heavily armed members of his renegade unit, along with seventy U.S. militia. He proudly sported a green band and a white cockade hat identifying him as a Canadian Volunteer. He shouted threats at his former neighbours and other Tories as his men started looting and warning inhabitants to get out what they could. At dusk the destruction began.

Willcocks' militia then burned the town of Niagara to the ground, torching 149 houses and turning nearly 400 civilians (mostly women and children) out into the cold of winter. Only three buildings were left standing.

Willcocks then targeted the nearby house of an old rival, William Dickson, brother of the fur trader whose command of the Indians led to British victories at Michilimackinac and Detroit. Willcocks sent Dickson away in chains and ordered two soldiers to remove a woman who was ill in bed and place her in the snow. The two wrapped her in blankets and put her in a snow drift while Willcocks burned the house and its contents. He walked away, leaving Mrs. Dickson in the snow to watch her house burn to the ground.

As a witness wrote, "In the village, at least 130 buildings were consumed, and the miserable tenants of them, to the number of nearly 400, consisting mostly of women and children, were exposed to all the severities of deep snow and a frosty sky, almost in a state of nakedness. How many perished by the inclemency of the weather, it is, at present, impossible to ascertain."

Besides Dickson, Willcocks also arrested other Niagara loyalists and sent them back to New York State, declaring them "prisoners of war." Among them were Willcocks' successor as member of the legislative assembly for Lincoln, Ralfe Clench. Another was Thomas Merritt, William Hamilton Merritt's father, and eighty-year-old Peter McMicking of Stamford County, a coroner and a town warden.

Captain Merritt was so angry at the treatment of his father that he wrote in his journal of "having taken many long and weary ride, in the lonely hours of the night, in hope of catching Willcocks and making an example of him and all traitors."

When Captain Merritt and Colonel Murray saw the glow of the burning town in the eastern sky, they rode to the aid of the Niagara townspeople. They arrived in time to see the Americans pulling out. They attacked the rear guard of Canadian Volunteers, killing two and taking a number of prisoners.

Merritt and Murray found a scene of total destruction that morning. As Merritt wrote, "Nothing but heaps of boats, and streets full of furniture that the inhabitants were fortunate enough to get out of their houses, met our eyes. My old quarters, Gordon's house, was the only one standing."

The town was a pile of glowing embers, and people were desperately seeking shelter in the freezing cold. Some had moved into Fort George and Butlers Barracks, which the Americans had been unable to destroy before they fled, but when day broke, Merritt and Murray found a sight that melted their hearts — the many frozen bodies of women and children who could not find shelter in the bitter cold of that awful December night.

A burning farmhouse during the war.

FIRE AND THE SWORD

Willcocks' needless act of destruction infuriated the British commanders, and they retaliated swiftly, backed by the new provincial governor, General Gordon Drummond, who was sent to Upper Canada in late 1813, first to Kingston and then to York. In December he ordered a retaliatory campaign of fire and sword across the American frontier.

Drummond had brought with him General Phineas Riall, a feisty Irishman in his late thirties who had fought with Drummond in the West Indies and previously commanded the Montreal district. Canadian militia dragoon officer William Hamilton Merritt described him as "very brave, near sighted, rather short, but stout."

For their first move, Drummond, Riall and their officers pulled together a plan for surprise attack on Fort Niagara. On the moonless night of December 18, Colonel John Murray and 562 soldiers of the 100th and 41st Regiments, Royal Scots, Royal Artillery, and Canadian Militia were rapidly rowed across the Niagara River in boats with muffled oars. They landed upstream from the fort and moved quickly north, their steps muffled by a blanket of soft snow. They carefully silenced the advance guards, got the password to the fort, and in a pre-dawn bayonet attack surprised the sleeping garrison, took out eighty Americans, and captured 365 prisoners.[18]

While Murray started to repair Fort Niagara and inventory the booty — later valued at a million dollars — Riall took some regulars and a party of Mohawks, crossed to Lewiston, and burned down the town.

The news spread rapidly. At Buffalo, the inhabitants knew very well what vengeance awaited them. They jeered Brigadier-General George McClure in the streets, then started to flee eastward with their possessions.

On December 29, Riall started to move south, and in a two-week raid, methodically set fire to the American villages of Manchester, Fort Schlosser, Black Rock, and finally the town of Buffalo, where all 333 houses were burned. He stopped only at Tonawanda Creek, where the bridges had been destroyed by Willcocks and the Canadian volunteers.

Drummond had forbidden the troops from looting personal homes, under pain of death, but the Mohawks were harder to restrain, and several civilians who resisted were tomahawked. The British did capture some legitimate military targets, including the Buffalo navy yard, where they put three of Perry's schooners to the torch.

When Sir George Prevost got the news of these reprisals along the frontier, he professed himself dismayed to find this sort of warfare being practiced against civilians. On January 12, 1814, he wrote a letter to Armstrong, regretting that the British troops had been forced to take measures "so little congenial to the British character." He proclaimed to the American in his most pompous verbiage:

> To those possessions of the enemy along the whole line of frontier which have hitherto remained undisturbed, and which are now at the mercy of the troops under his command, his Excellency has determined to extend the same forbearance, and the same freedom from rapine and plunder

which they have hitherto experienced; and from this deter-
mination the future conduct of the American government
shall alone induce him to depart.

Meaning, from now on, we won't do it if you don't.

As for the villain McClure, who had fled Niagara, he claimed he had taken
a "liberal interpretation" of orders from Secretary of War John Armstrong when
he ordered Willcocks and his volunteers to burn the town of Niagara.

Armstrong was apoplectic. He deeply resented being blamed for the
burning of Niagara, officially repudiated McClure's act to the British, and
immediately removed him from command. Even so, Jacob Brown continued
militia raids on Upper Canadian civilians along the north shore of Lake Erie
and at Port Dover in the spring of 1814. To retaliate for these acts, Admiral
Alexander Cockburn was ordered to step up his raids in the Chesapeake Bay,
and eventually put fire to Washington, D.C.[19]

As for Joseph Willcocks, he was killed at the Siege of Fort Erie, and his
body was buried in Buffalo, NY.

Moral: Sometimes the only way to motivate your troops is to promise
them pillage.

So Injurious an Operation

> "Men do not change, they unmask themselves."
>
> *—Mme de Staël*

On May 24, 1813, Thomas Jefferson wrote a letter to his old Paris friend
Germaine de Staël. Mme de Staël was the daughter of Swiss banker and
statesman Jacques Necker, Director of Finance under Louis XVI. Mme de
Staël kept a famous Paris salon and was a sworn enemy of Napoleon. She
wrote a novel titled *Delphine*, in which she declared, "There is nothing real in
the world but love."

Jefferson felt the need to compose a *bon mot* comparing Napoleon, recently
shamed by his disastrous Russian invasion, to Robespierre, leader of the French
during the Reign of Terror. Robespierre, he wrote, went after the rich and killed
thousands, but "it is by millions that Bonaparte destroys the poor."

The day will come when a just posterity will give to their hero
the only pre-eminence he has earned, that of having been the
greatest of the destroyers of the human race. What year of his
military life has not consigned a million of human beings to
death, to poverty, and wretchedness? What field in Europe
may not raise a monument of the murders, the burnings, the
desolations, the famines, and miseries, it has witnessed from
him! And all this to acquire a reputation.

While Jefferson was writing charmingly to Mme de Staël about the dep-
redations of Bonaparte, unleashed U.S. militia were burning and looting York,
torching the Upper Canada Parliament Buildings, and then laying fiery waste to
the farms and villages of Upper Canada, from Niagara to Windsor.

As the 1813 season closed in North America, the Jeffersonian myth of the
citizen general had taken a significant beating. Wave after wave of Republican
lawyers and politicians, convinced they had what it took to lead the young
into battle, butted heads with the British professional opposites and lost badly,
sometimes at odds of ten to one.

On the American side that year, there were two very bright lights:
Commodore Isaac Chauncey and Oliver Hazard Perry. Harrison would have
failed in his invasion without Perry's victory (... and without Barclay's infatua-
tion with a pretty widow from Malden?). The rest of the American commanders,
from Armstrong and Dearborn down to Morgan Lewis, William Winder, John
Chandler, and Wade Hampton, were pretty much all Sunday soldiers and bumbling amateurs. James Wilkinson was an evil alcoholic.

America's younger soldiers, like Winfield Scott and Jacob Brown, were
rarely given enough lead to be able to perform. In many cases, their old fogey
generals singlehandedly lost battles through their stupidity, drunkenness, or
greed for glory.

On the British side, generals like Vincent and de Salaberry shone because
of their knowledge of the arts and artifices of war, often in spite of their own
vacuous old fogey, Sir George Prevost.

All this was about to change in what was to prove the final year of the war.

As for the victorious Duke of Wellington, now happily back in London,
he himself remained mystified about America, which he regarded as a jellyfish
that couldn't be attacked in one spot. Early in 1814, he wrote Lord Bathurst

that "I do not know where you could carry on an operation which would be so injurious to the Americans as to force them to sue for peace."

But he was open to releasing the best of his generals for service in North America. Perhaps four operations would work...?

FOUR

1814

THE EMPIRE STRIKES BACK

NAPOLEON'S LAST INNINGS

> "I grew up upon the field of battle and a man such as I cares
> little for the lives of a million men."
>
> *−Napoleon*

On March 31, 1814, the Allies entered Paris. A week later Napoleon I of France abdicated the French throne, bade farewell to his Old Guard, and went into exile on the Mediterranean island of Elba. The Allies in fact deeded him the small island as his own personal property, hoping that it might provide the monster with a satisfactory arena for his diminished ambitions.

At that time, Madison's newly retired Treasury Secretary Albert Gallatin was in London. He was trying without success to meet Foreign Secretary Lord Castlereagh when news of Napoleon's downfall reached the capital.

He saw citizens everywhere celebrating the end of twenty years of war against France, lighting bonfires, setting off fireworks, and pealing bells until their arms ached.

Not all the feelings Gallatin glimpsed were joyful; he also detected from the British "a strong expression of resentment against the United States." There was talk of chastising the Americans, of taking over the Great Lakes, of taking New England back into the Empire.

Ships carried the reports across the Atlantic. On May 14, 1814, the brig *Ida* returned at her home port of Boston, Massachusetts, with the news that Napoleon had been deposed.

On May 30, 1814, another ship arrived in the port city of Saint John, New Brunswick, with news that Bonaparte had abdicated. The residents of the port city roasted an ox in King's Square to celebrate the blessed event.

The British Are Coming

The news reached Washington and Montreal in early June. It was not unexpected. Madison's cabinet had been monitoring Bonaparte's reverses in France and Spain for months. Now, reports were coming in of Wellington's soldiers marching to boats at Bayonne, France, and fourteen British regiments bound for Quebec, Halifax, and Bermuda. Time was running out on the War Hawks' plans.

In Montreal, Sir George Prevost was eagerly putting together a four-part watery invasion of the United States, to knock the U.S. out of the war and grab territory that could be used to influence peace talks.

By that point, Prevost's reputation in the Canada's was starting to suffer at the hands of the elite and the military. Many were coming to agree with the Rev. John Strachan's comment on October 13, 1813, that:

> Our Commander-in-chief has produced all our defeats. If this country falls he only is to blame. Never was a country lost so shamefully as this one has been or will be. Not the smallest vigor has been displayed, there is no campaign plan, everything is left to chance and all our movements are directed not by us but by our enemy. General Prevost appears not only ignorant of the art of war but destitute of common sense.

Prevost desperately needed to restore his credibility with another hands-on campaign. The first blow, which he would personally command, was a strike down Lake Champlain and the Hudson Valley, to separate New England from the rest of the nation. Backed by the best battle-hardened regiments in the British army, he had no doubts regarding the strong possibility of a glorious outcome.

The second blow would be the capture of the territory of Maine by Sir John Sherbrooke.

The third blow would fall in the American heartland of Chesapeake Bay, where British sea power was now unchallenged. Capturing Baltimore would extinguish that nest of privateers.

The final blow would be at New Orleans, since losing control of the lower Mississippi would threaten America's westward expansion.

Then perhaps America would come to its senses and rejoin the British Empire.

Yeo Takes Command of the Lake

Over the winter of 1813–14, a lull descended on the Lake Ontario frontier. For a time, the swish of planes on oaken boards and the drumming of hammers on wooden plugs replaced the crack of musket fire and the boom of cannons, as the arms race continued apace in the stocks of Kingston and Sackets Harbor.

Sir James Yeo of the Royal Navy and Lieutenant-General Gordon Drummond had spent the winter planning on taking back control of the lake from Isaac Chauncey by hitting him where it would hurt — at his main supply depot at Oswego.

On April 15, with the ice barely gone out of the lake, Kingston Navy Dockyard launched two ocean-sized frigates, the fifty-six-gun *Prince Regent* and the forty-two-gun *Princess Charlotte*. Yeo still had the advantage in short range carronades, but he could now bring eighty-seven long guns to bear against Chauncey's reputed sixty-one.

The Capture of Oswego

On May 5, after quick sea trials of the new ships, Drummond loaded his troops and cannon, and Yeo sailed the fleet across the Lake to Oswego to attack Fort Ontario and capture its wealth of supplies and schooners. The harbour was an important military depot at the head of the road from Albany, although its waters were too shallow to accommodate the bigger ships. Most American freight bound for Sackets went through Oswego.

While Yeo bombarded the fort at a safe distance offshore, Drummond landed 1,100 troops and six field pieces on the shore, and ordered Colonel Fisher and Captain Mulcaster to attack the fort and its 500 defenders. They took it the following day, held it against counterattack, and before they left, burned it and all the surrounding warehouses to the ground, thus depriving Chauncey and the Americans at Niagara of much-needed supplies by lake.

Yeo then sailed on to Sackets Harbor, where *Prince Regent* and *Princess Charlotte* began bottling up Chauncey's fleet. General Drummond got a sailor to paddle him closer to the shipyard to see for himself the commodore's progress in building his own big frigate, the sixty-four-gun *Superior*. It was not yet rigged, but the shipyard was bustling with men. From a spy he learned that *Superior* was still missing heavy guns, cable, and rigging. They broke off the blockade on June 6 for other supply duties and to prepare for an expected showdown with Chauncey's new ships.

On August 9, as expected, Isaac Chauncey appeared off Fort Henry proudly showing off his new frigates, the forty-two-gun *Mohawk* and the sixty-four-gun *Superior*, which also sported thirty forty-two-pounder carronades.

Sir James Yeo knew how to count guns, but if there was any question of which side was most determined to win, Yeo's shipyard had nearly finished building a colossal lake frigate, the *St. Lawrence*. Bristling with 112 long-range guns, half of which were big twenty-four- and thirty-two-pounders, it was in fact the largest ship in the Royal Navy. It cost over two hundred thousand pounds to build and would be manned by hundreds of sailors from the Royal Navy's Halifax fleet.

After some friendly target practice, Chauncey sailed away on September 1, but Sir James cautiously stayed in port until mid-September, when the *St. Lawrence* was launched and outfitted, just in time to get supplies to refugees at Burlington and to Drummond's army on the Niagara peninsula, desperately in need of reinforcements, by mid-October.

The British attack on Fort Oswego.

As for Isaac Chauncey, he remained discreetly at Sackets Harbor, taking a few tentative sails in his schooners to keep his tars in trim. He was ill, and the loss of Fort Ontario meant his war was effectively over.

The Americans' only hope of victory this year was over the Niagara River by land. But Drummond's one smart strategic move against Oswego would turn the tide firmly against the U.S. invaders.

Moral: With 112 guns, you can easily beat an enemy vessel with sixty-four. Believe it.

STALEMATE AT LUNDY'S LANE

"A soldier will fight long and hard for a bit of colored ribbon."
—Napoleon

Last Campaign in Niagara

The war was clearly winding down, and Britain was accepting peace feelers through the czar of Russia and John Jacob Astor's agents. But neither side wanted to quit just yet. The campaign of 1814 on both sides was marked by last desperate attempts to gain territory that could be swapped during peace talks.

Chauncey had on his stocks an even bigger ship than the *St. Lawrence*, but the destruction of his supply depot at Oswego bit deeply, and there was no guarantee he could win the arms race. Never mind. The War Hawks in Congress convinced Madison there was time to make one more stab against the Niagara frontier before peace was declared.

Early in the year the War Hawks got Congress to increase the army to forty-five infantry regiments, four regiments of riflemen, three of artillery, two of light dragoons, and one of light artillery.

Secretary of War Armstrong finally rooted out all the old generals and replaced them with young, athletic officers. In 1812, the average age of the eight generals had been sixty. By the summer of 1814 the average age of his nine new generals was an astonishing thirty-six. They were certainly braver and more aggressive than old warhorses like Granny Dearborn. He was convinced they had the stamina to get the job done.

Armstrong promoted Chateauguay veteran George Izard to major general and gave him command of the Lake Champlain army with Alexander Macomb as his brigadier. Andrew Jackson, finally a major general, was given the south. Jacob Brown, also now a major general, was put in command of "the Army of the North" at Niagara. Brown was a Quaker-educated militiaman from Sackets Harbor whose family members were well-respected smugglers of potash from Canada before the war. In fact, his nickname was "Potash." A touch pig-headed, he possessed some imagination and knew how to get the best from his men.

Potash Brown's second-in-command was twenty-eight-year-old Winfield Scott, who had taken control at Queenston Heights, and did a good job of planning and leading the capture of Fort George the year before. His rank was boosted to brigadier, and to his delight he was put in charge at Buffalo. Scott had been critical of the old fogey generals for the past two years, calling them "imbeciles and ignoramuses." Now, blessed with command, he threw himself into planning the coming invasion with the focus of an eagle, studying maps of the Niagara topography, finding out exact British troop placements from his network of spies.

Scott's troops nicknamed him "Old Fuss 'n Feathers" because he insisted on military appearance and discipline. Towering over his troops at six-foot-five-inches (1.95 metres), he loved to sport uniforms dripping with gold braid and tricorne hats topped with an ostrich feather. Scott was a Virginia plantation squire like his president. He studied law at the College of William & Mary but never received any formal military education. He studied the classics to learn the lessons of war and pored over old French infantry manuals. He found out how to train his men to wheel on a battlefield, and to face redcoats without flinching, and he drilled them for ten hours a day at the Buffalo parade grounds. Deserters he shot without mercy.

The militia of New Yorkers[1] was headed by veteran War Hawk Peter B. Porter, Henry Clay's congressional comrade and former quartermaster general. Porter was there for pure revenge. Back in December, Riall's regulars had entered Porter's home, forced his family into the snow, clad only in their nightshirts, and proceeded to burn their Black Rock house and all its contents.

Armstrong's only holdout was William Henry Harrison, who saw nothing but trouble ahead, refused point blank to serve under the secretary of war's interfering hand, and resigned from the field.

Armstrong expected Chauncey's naval force at Sackets Harbor to be strong enough to supply Brown's army by the summer and decided upon a repeat of last year's coordinated navy and army attack. For the moment, he offered this to the frustrated commanders at Buffalo. It was more in the way of a suggestion than an order:

"To give immediate occupation to your troops, and to prevent their blood from stagnating, why not take Fort Erie?"

Armstrong found his generals were amenable to the suggestion. He then gave Brown more detailed orders: Brown was to assault and capture Fort Erie, then march north and seize and hold a bridge over the Chippewa River. All being well, he would move to recapture Fort George, and then root the British out of Burlington Heights. If that was successful, Brown's army could board Chauncey's ships for an attack on Kingston.[2]

THE BRITISH COMMANDER

The British were not quite as blessed with the same youthful leadership as the Americans, but the British army field commanders were all equally well-trained and warlike. And more were on the way. Sixteen thousand British veterans, fresh from Wellington's victories over the French, arrived in Canada that June, so Prevost relaxed his grip slightly and let 1,000 regulars that had been defending the upper St. Lawrence move west to York to reinforce General Sir Gordon Drummond. The rest he kept for his own glorification.

Forty-two-year-old Gordon Drummond was the first Canadian-born officer to command a military and the civil government in Canada. In 1794, he served as a junior lieutenant-colonel in the Netherlands under the Duke of York, and then was posted to the Mediterranean and West Indies.

An aggressive officer in the mold of Isaac Brock, Drummond was sent to Upper Canada as lieutenant governor to replace the unpopular and inoffensive Francis de Rottenburg. Unlike Brock, Drummond was a stern ruler who declared martial law for the first time in the war. He relied on decrees to control price gouging, and public executions to deter traitors. As the war got nastier and civilians began to suffer from enemy brutality, Drummond believed a hard line was the only course to take.

THE RAIDING CONTINUES

To kick things off, and get the bluecoats riled up, Drummond had already captured Fort Niagara and sent General Phineas Riall to give the Americans a taste of "hard war" to retaliate for the burning of Niagara-on-the-Lake.

Meanwhile, the guerilla raids against civilians continued, as both sides lit fires along the frontier from Tonawanda, New York to Windsor, Upper Canada, causing total desolation in village and farms.

On January 16, British troops from Kingston mounted a week-long raid on the towns of Madrid, Salmon River, Malone, and Four Corners in northern New York State. On St. Valentine's Day, an American force from Detroit raided and burned the Lake Erie settlement of Port Talbot, where old Tory Thomas Talbot still ruled his little demesne.

The worst raiding occurred in mid-May, when Abraham Markle, Willcocks' successor as head of the Canadian Volunteers, led a party of 600 across the lake from Erie, Pennsylvania. His militia burned and looted every privately owned building between Turkey Point and Port Dover, which was at the head of a strategic road leading to Burlington Heights.

As sixteen-year-old farm girl Amelia Ryerse wrote,

> I looked up I saw the hillside and the fields as far as the eye could reach covered with American soldiers... My mother knew instinctively what they were going to do. She entreated the commanding officer to spare her property and said that she was a widow with a young family. He answered her civilly and respectfully and regretted that his orders were to burn... Very soon we saw a column of dark smoke rise from every building and what at early morn had been a prosperous homestead, at noon there were only smoldering ruins.[3]

Prevost petitioned the Royal Navy to retaliate with its own raids along the Atlantic coast, and "destroy and lay waste to such towns and districts as you may find assailable." After the raid on Port Dover, the firing of private American property was now official British policy.

Retreat at Chippawa

Potash Brown had finished assembling a 5,000-man invasion force at a camp outside Buffalo, and now it was the turn of Armstrong's young generals to show that they were made of. Winfield Scott commanded the 1st Brigade with 1,377 men, and Brigadier Elzear Ripley the 2nd Brigade with 1,082 men, and they had four companies of artillery numbering 327 men under Major Jacob Hindman. While officers at Winfield Scott's "Camp of Instruction" waited for orders to proceed, they kept up his brutal regimen of ten hours a day of drill, using a new translation of Napoleon's *Manual of the French Revolutionary Army*. He insisted on proper camp discipline, clean water, daily washing, cleaning the chamber pots three times a day and lining them with charcoal, changing the straw bedding every few weeks. This cut rates of debilitating diseases that were far more fatal than musket or cannon balls. In fact, of the 20,000 people who perished during this war, three quarters died from dysentery, typhus, influenza, malaria, measles, syphilis, and smallpox.

In late June, Jacob Brown returned from Sackets Harbor with the news that they might have to operate without help from Isaac Chauncey, who was in his sickbed and low on supplies due to the British raid on Oswego.

It was time to move. Brown could not yet afford a direct attack on Fort George. He moved instead to take Fort Erie, crossing the river on the dark rainy night of July 2. The Americans easily surrounded and captured the fort, defended by two weak companies under Major Thomas Buck. American engineers were then put to work, rebuilding and buttressing the old structure, turning it into a two-sided complex of earthworks, trenches, and batteries.

On July 4, the clouds blew away and a glorious summer's day dawned over Scott's camp. Later that morning, Peter B. Porter joined them, leading a brigade of 753 volunteer militia and 400 Seneca warriors led by Red Jacket — almost the entire military force of the Six Nations then remaining in the U.S. They were not entirely pleased with having to fight other Iroquois, John Norton's Grand River Mohawks.

Scott didn't dawdle. He quickly led the way north along the Niagara portage road toward Chippawa, driving back a British covering force under Lieutenant-Colonel Thomas Pearson before they could block the roads with trees or burn any of the bridges. That afternoon, his advance troops came upon Major General Phineas Riall's 2,000 defenders digging in on the far bank of Chippawa Creek.[4] The two armies swapped artillery fire before Scott retired for the night back at Street's Creek.

Phineas Riall had chosen a good defensive position, because the sluggish Chippawa had no ford for an army to bring across artillery, and his sappers were ready to blow up the only bridge. With the Royal Scots under

Lieutenant-Colonel John Gordon and the 100th under its eccentric leader the Marquis of Tweeddale, and 300 newly arrived regulars of the King's Regiment, Riall though he had enough men to face the Americans.

Here Riall made the first of several errors. As the battle was brewing, he failed to send out enough scouts to properly gauge American strength. He thought that Fort Erie was still holding out, and the Americans he faced were not a full army. So he failed to bring in the 103rd Regiment from Burlington Heights and did not bother to muster the local militia. He also ordered a regiment back to Fort George, thinking that Chauncey was going to bombard the lakeshore at Niagara, in a repeat of last year's battle.

New to command in Canada, Riall also shared the prejudices of his officer class that U.S. regulars were poorly trained and not much better than militia. His brain was marinated with this mindset, and he planned his attack accordingly.

In actual fact, Riall was facing the best force ever to invade Canada, a well-drilled army of 5,000 regulars and militia.

THE BATTLE BEGINS

> "Men of the eleventh! The enemy say we are good at a long shot, but cannot stand the cold iron. I call on you to give the lie to that slander. Charge!"
> —*Winfield Scott to the 11th Infantry Regiment before the Battle of Chippawa*

Very early on July 5, Riall ordered his light infantry, militia, and Indians to cross the Chippawa and start sniping at Scott's outposts from the woods to their west. Some of them nearly captured Scott, who was having breakfast in a farmhouse. Brown quickly sent Porter's brigade and the New York Mohawks to look for a ford and clear the woods on the British right. They did so, but Riall's regulars were now on the move and firing at them with muskets, backed by nine field guns protecting the bridge.

Meanwhile, Scott was already advancing from Street's Creek. Captain Nathaniel Towson's company, with three twelve-pounder guns, soon opened fire on Riall's regulars. At this point early in the battle, the Gods of War decided to smile on Winfield Scott, and a lucky American shot blew up the British ammunition wagon, putting most of their artillery out of action. It would have been a good time to fall back, but Riall foolishly kept on going.

Scott's troops soon deployed into line, with the 25th U.S. Infantry on the left near the woods, the 11th U.S. Infantry and 9th U.S. Infantry in the centre, and the 22nd U.S. Infantry on the right with Captain Towson's guns. When the American line held steady under heavy British fire, it dawned on the nearsighted Riall that he was up against some professionals. One tale from the battle says that when he looked through his telescope and saw that the American soldiers were clad in grey, Riall joked that they were really "nothing but a body of Buffalo militia!" He reckoned it would take only a few musket volleys to drive them back. But when they held and advanced, he realized he was mistaken and cursed, "Why, those are regulars, by God!"

Perhaps changing his tactics, Riall then made a move that made matters far worse. He formed his regulars into line to increase their firepower instead of keeping them in column, where they could have moved ahead more rapidly. Because they moved at a slower pace, they stayed under fire from the American artillery for longer, and Riall's remaining field guns had to stop firing in order to avoid hitting them. Perhaps panicking, Riall ordered his infantry to fire only one volley before they closed with the bayonet. By that time the American gunners had switched to firing canister shot, and the big iron balls flew in all directions, knocking down the redcoats like bowling pins. Finally, when the two forces were less than 100 metres apart, Scott wheeled his wings around the British and subjected them to a deadly crossfire.

After twenty-five long minutes of punishment, Riall sounded the retreat. As they fell back, three British six-pounder guns, finally supplied with ammunition, covered their withdrawal, joined by two more six-pounders firing from the bluff north of the river. Riall ordered the King's Regiment to fire Chippawa Bridge as they went, so Scott wisely declined to pursue.

Two days later, Winfield Scott went west through the woods, waded across the Chippawa upstream, outflanked the British, and captured Riall's camp, forcing him to fall back to Fort George. Since Chauncey was still failing to support his army, in spite of his pleas, Brown lacked manpower and artillery to attack the fort.

Relying on lakeside protection from Yeo and fresh troops from Kingston, Drummond was able to rush several units of regulars across the lake from York. He and Riall then forced Brown back from Fort George to Queenston, just a few miles away. The British now had about 2,200 men near Burlington Heights, plus another 1,500 troops at Fort George and across the river at Fort Niagara, which they had held since December 1813. The British had evened the odds against Potash Brown.

The Battle of Chippawa left 137 British killed, 304 wounded, and forty-six missing in action; the Americans lost forty-eight killed, 227 wounded, and nineteen missing. The action was proof positive that American regulars could hold their own against British regulars if properly trained and well led. Riall's tactics might have worked with U.S. militia but were disastrous against Scott's well-disciplined units. In the fog of war, Riall also failed to change his tactics to deal with the new reality. Lacking artillery, he should have retreated instead of advancing.

Moral: If your ammunition wagon blows up in your face, retreat.

BLOODBATH AT LUNDY'S LANE

"Pyrrhus, when his friends congratulated to him his victory over the Romans under Fabricius, but with great slaughter of his own side, said to them, 'Yes; but if we have such another victory, we are undone.'"

−Francis Bacon

Drummond and his officers correctly reckoned that without Chauncey's supplies from Sackets Harbor, the Americans were starting to run out of powder and shot. So they tried to lure them into battle before the balance of power on the lake changed again. Unknown to them, Chauncey had launched two new warships but was missing cannon and supplies. He was still knocked out by sickness and couldn't or wouldn't move. In reply to another desperate plea from Brown for supplies, or at least some news, Chauncey replied on the 23rd that his business was to engage enemy ships, not serve as a ferry service, an "agreeable appendage" for Brown's army.

Huddling with his offers, Brown was now caught between the gung-ho aggression of Winfield Scott, who was dying to get at the British, and the caution of Elzear Ripley, who argued that without Chauncey's supplies and reinforcements, they could be headed for a bloodbath.

The British were starting to move. Riall wanted to get back onto on the escarpment, so he ordered the Canadian militia and Mohawks to harass the Americans at Queenston with sniper fire. On July 24, Brown decided to fall back to the Chippawa River to wait for supplies. Riall dogged his heels with his light infantry and militia and advanced to Lundy's Lane, a dusty cart track that ran west of the portage road four miles (6.4 kilometres) north of the Chippawa, within hearing distance of the boom of Niagara Falls. It could be a good fallback route if needed. Lundy's Lane was the most direct road to Burlington Heights and the new British camp at Ancaster.

Early on July 25, Drummond arrived from York to take command of the developing battle. At that point British unity broke down on the chessboard.

Drummond ordered a force under Lieutenant-Colonel John Tucker to advance south from Fort Niagara along the east bank of the Niagara River, hoping to force Brown to evacuate the west.

Watching from the west bank, Brown did not fall for the ruse, but he was worried about the British cutting his lines of communication. He ordered Winfield Scott to advance north toward Fort George so the British would have to recall Tucker's column. But Brown did not know that Riall was now holding the heights of Lundy's Lane in strength.

At about 5:00 p.m., Riall was reoccupying his position when he was surprised to see Winfield Scott's first units come into view. Without news from Drummond, he ordered his troops to prepare a fall back to Fort George and sent word to Colonel Hercules Scott to move from St. David's to Queenston to cover them. Drummond was already force-marching from Fort George to Lundy's Lane. He moved urgently to countermand Riall's orders. And just in time. Riall was just starting his retreat when Drummond arrived on the field.

The two British generals now held a strong position along some rising ground twenty-five feet higher than the surrounding area. They had brought up two twenty-four-pounders, two six-pounders and one 5.5-inch howitzer, as well as a good brace of Congreve rockets. They placed the guns in a crescent among the gravestones of a cemetery next to a red-painted Presbyterian church and above a small apple orchard. It was a hot and humid evening as the British awaited the oncoming American attack. They knew things were about to get a lot hotter.

When Winfield Scott's 1st Brigade of regulars emerged from the chestnut woods into an open field, they immediately came under fire from British artillery as they waded through waist-high crops and over chest-high split rail fences.

Scott reported back to Brown that the fighting was "close and desperate." His battalions were being torn apart by British fire. As John Norton later described it, Scott "remained firm in the position which he had first assumed, exposed to a galling fire in front and flank — dread seemed to forbid his advance and shame to restrain his flight."

For two hours Scott attacked and beat back the larger British force, which had the advantage of position. He also made a smart move, sending the 25th U.S. Infantry under Major Thomas Jesup to outflank the British left. They found a narrow, overgrown trail leading to the river, and used it to pass round the British left flank. They surprised the light company of the 1st Battalion of the 8th (King's) Regiment and the Upper Canada Incorporated Militia, who mistook them for British regulars and drove them off the Portage Road. Jesup then sent Captain Ketcham's light infantry company to the junction of Lundy's Lane, just down the hill from the British cannon, where they surprised a party of British, including General Riall, who had been shot badly in the arm, and militia cavalry leader Captain William Hamilton Merritt.

"What does all this mean?" asked the astonished General Riall.

"You are prisoners, sir," Ketcham answered.

"But I am General Riall."

"There is no doubt on that point; and I, sir, am Captain Ketchum of the United States Army."

"Captain Ketcham! Ketcham! Well, you have caught us, sure enough."

American attack at Lundy's Lane.

As night fell, Drummond responded by instinct to the weakness on his left flank, by pulling back his centre and the Glengarry Light Infantry on the right to maintain alignment. This left his artillerymen in the graveyard dangerously exposed to the American infantry. At that point, Brown arrived with Brigadier Ripley's 2nd Brigade of regulars and Peter B. Porter's militia. At about 9:00 p.m., he ordered the 21st U.S. Infantry under Lieutenant-Colonel James Miller to capture the British guns, Miller famously responded, "I'll try, sir," and charged up the hill.[5]

Pennsylvania Militia private Alexander McMullen recalled that they had to "pass over the dead and dying, who were literally in heaps." The Americans quickly stormed the heights and fired a volley of musketry, which killed most of the gunners, and bayonetted the rest as they struggled to reload. Another bayonet charge drove the British centre from the hill. A British counter-attack was driven back by Miller and Ripley. Then a British column under Colonel Hercules Scott blundered into Ripley's brigade. They were also driven back in disorder, leaving three six-pounders behind.

After 10:00 p.m. the moon went down. Drummond, bleeding from a wound in the neck, tried to retake his own cannon by launching an attack in line. In the heat of battle he failed to use his light infantry to harass or disorder the American line. The attack was beaten back after a brutal short-range musketry duel, and bodies began to pile up in the graveyard.

With no breath of wind, the battlefield was by now completely enveloped with smoke from the black powder, and all was chaos. There was no water to be had, and soldiers were getting delirious with thirst. Some of the British regulars mistakenly fired on their own Glengarry Light Infantry, mistaking them for Americans, and the Glengarries had to withdraw. Drummond again lost a chance to win the battle. With any kind of battlefield scouting, he would have learned the Glengarries had pushed back the American left, and were threatening to outflank Brown.

Without learning from his first mistake, Drummond stubbornly launched a second mass attack in line, without light infantry support, and was stopped by Ripley. Winfield Scott then led his depleted brigade against Drummond's centre, but ran into friendly fire from units of Ripley's brigade. Scott's men broke in disorder and retreated. Just as he was riding off to join Jesup on the right, Scott was severely wounded by a bullet that could have come from anywhere.

Midnight in the Graveyard

Shortly before midnight, Drummond was still obsessed with straightforward victory and ordered a third brute force counter-attack, using every man he could find from a jumble of mixed-up units. They nearly reached the lost artillery before they too were driven back again.

After midnight, Brown, badly wounded himself, found only 700 of his men were still standing. He was out of water and ammunition, and the battlefield was loud with the cries and moans of the wounded and dying. Winfield Scott was in the field hospital, out of action for the rest of the war.

Brown had Ripley's bugler sound the retreat. Some of his officers protested against leaving the captured guns and wounded behind, but they soon complied. Wagons could not be pulled, since most of the horses were dead.

When Ripley's surviving soldiers got back to camp in Chippawa, they were so maddened with thirst, they leaped into the muddy river and drank the water.

Drummond still had 1,400 men on the field, but they were too exhausted to chase the Americans. Most of them had marched twenty miles on a hot July day. He simply ordered some units to hold the Portage Road and watch the Americans, and withdrew the rest a short distance west along Lundy's Lane.

During the night, Brown's Artillery Major Hyndman found a few surviving horses and sent a team to drag away one of the big British twenty-four-pounders, but they were captured by some exhausted redcoats wandering around the battlefield in a daze.

Many British troops simply slumped to the ground and went into a dead sleep on the hillside, not caring whether they were next to a corpse or not.

Lieutenant John Le Couteur of the 104th Foot was on duty that night: "What a dismal night. There were three hundred American dead on the Niagara side of the hillock, and about a hundred of ours, besides several hundred wounded. The miserable badly-wounded were groaning and imploring for water.... Our Men's heads and those of the Americans were within a few yards of each other at this spot, so close had been the deadly strife."

By dawn all the smoke had cleared, and British scouts found a scene of utter carnage. But the guns were unharmed, and Drummond wasted no time bringing them back to their original positions on the hill. When U.S. General Ripley arrived on the scene with 1,200 soldiers, he found the British drawn up on the height and ready to resume the fight. Ripley realized the battle was over and withdrew slowly toward Fort Erie, his wagons packed with the wounded, and with General Riall as his prisoner.

Drummond did not mount a pursuit, and later in the morning, ordered his soldiers to separate the dead from the dying, and the American corpses from the British. They excavated a mass grave and gave the British a Christian burial. Then, as local militiaman Christopher Buchner watched, they tore apart a cedar rail fence from his own farm, and started burning the American corpses and parts of corpses on a large funeral pyre. Soon the hot flames licked skyward and the black smoke of death enveloped the Niagara frontier, until thunderstorms rolled in, blowing it all away.

So ended the harshest, hardest-fought, and bloodiest battle of the War of 1812. The British and Canadians took 643 casualties, with eighty-four killed, out of 3,000 men; 169 were captured and fifty-five missing. The Americans reported 746 casualties, including 174 killed; seventy-nine were captured and twenty-eight missing.

The carnage was dreadful. Lieutenant-Colonel James Miller of the 21st U.S. Infantry wrote to a friend that "Since I came to Canada this time, every major save one, every lieutenant colonel, every colonel that was here when I came and has remained here has been killed or wounded. I am now the only general officer out of seven that has escaped."

For two days and nights, British surgeon Tiger Dunlop sewed up ugly wounds and sawed off the shattered limbs of British and American alike. Wounded soldiers either got drunk or "bit the bullet" to handle the pain. Some tough ones sang or joked during the operation. It was worth it; if you had a bad arm or leg wound below the elbow or knee, you had an 85 percent chance of survival if it was amputated and quickly cauterized with a red-hot iron.

On the second morning, an older American woman came across the river to find her husband, a militiaman, with a shattered leg and internal bleeding. She found him moaning in agony, clearly dying, and she clasped her hands, and looked wildly around, exclaiming, "O that the King and the President were both here this moment to see the misery their quarrels lead to — they surely would never go to war without a cause that they could give as a reason to God at the last day, for thus destroying the creatures that He hath made in his own image." Half an hour later her husband was dead.

Drummond reported victory to Lord Bathurst but said the attacks against his troops were so ferocious "that our Artillery Men were bayonetted by the enemy in the Act of loading, and the muzzles of the Enemy's Guns were advanced within a few Yards of ours".

One British veteran said the carnage he saw at Lundy's Lane was far worse than any bloody battle he'd witnessed in the Peninsular War.[6]

Moral: It's one thing to capture the cannon; it's another thing to keep it.

END GAME AT FORT ERIE

The implacable Drummond was not through yet. He followed Brown to Fort Erie, with the 41st Foot and the De Watteville regiment of Polish, German, and Spanish mercenaries making up his losses from Lundy's Lane. For seven weeks he tried obsessively to besiege and dislodge the Americans from the rebuilt and heavily reinforced fortress.

By this point, Prevost was hearing rumours from Drummond's officers about his poor generalship at Lundy's Lane, and complaints that his attack on Fort Erie was too risky and overly complicated.

On August 14, his first attempt to storm the fort failed utterly when the fort's magazine exploded, wiping out an entire arm of his attack force and causing over 900 casualties, more than one third of his force. His own nephew, Lieutenant-Colonel William Drummond, was killed in the blast.

On September 4, Drummond was taken by surprise by an American sortie, which destroyed two out of the three siege batteries and inflicted heavy casualties. One of the dead on the American side was Canadian turncoat Joseph Willcocks, the head of the Canadian Volunteers.[7]

Shortly afterward, American General Izard finally arrived with his army from Plattsburg, drove Drummond back to Chippewa and then destroyed his siege works at Fort Erie.

Most members of Drummond's staff were sick or wounded; his siege guns were out of action; the weather was getting worse; and his food supplies were diminishing. Blaming his senior officers, many of whom were dead, for the debacle, Drummond abandoned Niagara, declaring the operation a complete failure.

That November, Izard and Brown took the opportunity to retreat back across the river to Black Rock.

So ended the 1814 American invasion of the Niagara Peninsula. It was Drummond's last major military campaign. When Sir George Prevost was recalled to Britain, he took over as governor-general and administrator of Canada. Many of the Duke of Wellington's veterans were arriving to replace the exhausted regulars in Canada, although the duke himself wisely stayed behind in England in case Bonaparte got up to any more wickedness.

As for General Riall, his wounds healed well, and he was allowed to sail for England on parole that December, and served for a time as governor of the delightful West Indies island of Grenada.

Winfield Scott was out of this war, but he went on to fight for his country for another half century. In 1830 he published Abstract of Infantry Tactics, Including Exercises and Maneuvers of Light-Infantry and Riflemen, for the Use of the Militia of the United States. In 1838, he gladly served when called upon to prevent republican raiders from invading Upper Canada. Go figure. In 1854 he won the Mexican–American war.

Jacob Brown's last battle of the war was the Siege of Fort Erie. On November 3, 1814, he was awarded the Congressional Gold Medal.

Moral: The enemy is not an inanimate object. The enemy is an independent and animate force.

McArthur's Raid and Malcolm's Mills

Six months after the Port Dover raid, the Americans again invaded Upper Canada, this time from Detroit.

Brigadier-General Duncan McArthur set out on October 22, 1814, with a long line of 650 mounted volunteers and seventy Native allies. His orders were to attack Native territory in the Grand River, destroy homes, barns, and mills, demoralize the military and civilian populations, and make it hard for the British to defend the territory and make an attack on Detroit in winter.

The cavalry moved quickly along the rough roads, taking the Canadians by surprise. They burned barns and houses and carried off 250 horses, 200 sheep, 100 oxen, and 100 hogs, along with 200 barrels of flour, 400 blankets, and large quantities of whiskey, salt, cloth, and arms.

The local militia, 500 poorly armed and equipped men from the 1st Middlesex, 1st Oxford, and Norfolk regiments, withdrew east toward a defensible position at Malcolm's Mills. One contingent of militia, regulars, and Six Nations warriors led by John Norton assembled at Brant's Ford on the Grand

River to stop McArthur from crossing the river. They sank the ferry and took up a defensive position on the east bank. When McArthur reached the ford on November 5, they started firing on the cavalry, and the Americans replied. After a hot skirmish, McArthur drew back, and decided it would be too dangerous to cross. Besides, the river was swollen with fall rains, and scouts reported that British regulars were on the way south from Burlington Heights.

McArthur moved toward Lake Erie the next day, burning the Perrin Mill and other buildings in Mount Pleasant en route. At Malcolm's Mills, the Canadians were waiting, led by Lieutenant-Colonel Bostwick of the 1st Oxford Militia. McArthur's troops attacked them on two fronts, easily outflanking them and forcing a retreat. In the last land battle on Upper Canadian soil during the war, the defenders lost eighteen killed and nine wounded, while McArthur's losses were one killed and six wounded.

On November 7, the Americans burned Malcolm's Mills to the ground then rode south to Port Dover, torching any buildings they could find still standing. When McArthur found the Americans had abandoned Fort Erie, he turned back for home, reaching Detroit on November 17, after 800 kilometres in twenty-seven days.

THE BATTLE OF WASHINGTON

T HE BRITISH BURNING OF WASHINGTON, DESIGNED TO WEAKEN AMERICAN morale, was the 9/11 of its generation.

COCHRANE AND COCKBURN

It's early August 1814, and a heavy heat has settled over the Atlantic coast of America. At the Royal Naval Dockyard in Bermuda, a ship arrives from Spain, with orders for Vice Admiral Sir Alexander Cochrane, new commander-in-chief of the North American Station.[8]

He is to proceed to Tangier Island in the Chesapeake Bay and rendezvous with Rear Admiral George Cockburn. They are to await troop ships, then mount an attack on the U.S. capital of Washington and capture the port of Baltimore.

Cochrane is the ninth son of an impoverished Scottish lord, Thomas, eighth Earl of Dundonald. He joined the Royal Navy as a boy and served during the American Revolutionary War. In 1801, he sailed with Horatio Nelson's expedition against Napoleon in Egypt, when the British defeated the demoralized remains of the French army. In 1806 he moved to the Caribbean to chase the remains of the French navy after Trafalgar, and fought bravely with Duckworth at the Battle of San Domingo. While on the deck of his ship, HMS *Northumberland*, he narrowly escaped a gory death when a piece of French grapeshot whistled past his ear, whipping the hat off his head. Then, from 1810 to 1813, he was governor of the rich French sugar island of Guadeloupe.

Waiting for Cochrane at the mouth of Chesapeake Bay is George Cockburn, on board HMS *Marlborough*. Cockburn, who fought with Nelson at the Battle of Cape St. Vincent and the blockade of Toulon, had been attacking American shipping, disrupting commerce, and raiding coastal towns in Delaware Bay and the Chesapeake since 1812. He had been increasingly effective, and American merchant tonnage had dropped to 60,000 tons from almost a million tons in 1812. Despite doubling customs revenue, Cockburn had cut Madison's revenue in half, to only $6 million in 1813.

This year Cockburn was continuing to smother the entire United States coastline, chasing and boarding merchant ships to stop them from sailing into U.S. seaports. He was also trying to collar U.S. Commodore Joshua Barney, king of the Baltimore privateers, a Revolutionary War hero who was now holed up in Chesapeake Bay.

Cockburn's captains had been busily hauling off tons of tobacco, deer-skins, cotton, and other goods from coastal warehouses before burning them to the ground. The admiral became notorious to the American merchants, and journalists accused him of turning a blind eye while his sailors looted private property and even committed rape. This demonization infuriated him. He was man of honour, and in his own way, a lover of liberty.

One of Cockburn's special instructions was to recruit a corps of black Colonial Marines, and encourage black American slaves to liberate themselves. In April of that year, he issued a proclamation that:

> All those who may be disposed to emigrate from the United States, will, with their Families, be received on board of His Majesty's Ships.... They will have their choice of either entering into His Majesty's Forces, or of being sent as FREE Settlers to British possessions ... where they will meet with all due encouragement.[9]

More than 4,000 people took up the offer, with entire families fleeing by canoe to the British ships.

Cockburn formed three companies of Colonial Marines that would take part in the entire campaign before them, against Washington and Baltimore. Admiral Cochrane later said they were "infinitely more dreaded by the Americans than the British troops."

Now, along the Chesapeake, Cochrane and Cockburn felt the winds of war changing. They had just received an urgent dispatch from Montreal, where Commander-in-Chief Sir George Prevost urged them immediately to step up attacks on the Americans, to relieve the pressure on Canada, avenge the cruel burning and looting of York and Port Dover, and "deter the enemy from the repetition of similar outrages."

They had some leeway for action, but they ignored the officious general in Montreal for the moment. It was not yet time to move. They had to wait for their reinforcements.

The bay was hot and muggy, the sailors always in a sweat, the sails flapping listlessly on the booms. Sometimes raging thunderstorms blew in from the west, forcing the men to take down the sails and either run or head into the wind. On good days, when the breeze freshened, the oppressive humidity lifted, and they tacked back and forth up the bay, sending in boats to steal food from farmers — that was the way of war, and not a pleasant task.

The two commanders had happily read the dispatches from Europe that spring: the fall of Bonaparte, the burning of the pride of the French navy at Toulon. All this satisfied the souls of sailor Cochrane and sailor Cockburn. But now they were growing weary of this waiting. It would be a fine thing to get the fireworks under way, to let loose the power of the Royal Navy, seize some rich booty in Baltimore, and demoralize the Americans into suing for peace.

When news came about the opening of peace talks in Europe, their game suddenly changed to offence. The main goal now was to get some advantage over the Americans that the negotiators could use. The promised troop reinforcements soon arrived in the Chesapeake Bay — a small flotilla of troopships, with 4,000 battle-hardened infantrymen from the Peninsular War. They were commended by Major General Robert Ross of the 20th Regiment of Foot, one of the stars of Sir Arthur Wellesley's army. With Napoleon safely in exile in Elba, Wellesley — soon to be granted the title Duke of Wellington — had ordered Ross to march north from Spain to Bordeaux and proceed immediately to join Cochrane and Cockburn in America.

For Cochrane, the mission was personal. He knew Chesapeake Bay well. A generation earlier he was a boy serving on a Royal Navy frigate and felt first-hand the British humiliation at Yorktown. Britain's navy lost the last battle of the American Revolution, all because the French West Indies fleet of the Comte de Grasse had been able to hold off a relief squadron from New York. After the battle, when the British ships took away the last of the beaten British soldiers, young Cochrane found to his dismay that his brother Charles was one of those killed by American and French artillery at Yorktown.

This time there were no French warships to help the Americans. Cochrane had a debt to pay, and the enemy were pretty much at his mercy.

Mister Madison's Washington

James Madison.

Washington in those days was no more than a dusty rustic backwater with 16,000 residents, one-sixth of them slaves. The seat of United States government since 1800, the town sported a few elegant federal buildings, but there was more swamp than settlement, and the place had scant strategic significance. The nearby port of Baltimore was fat and wealthy and was protected by the impressive fortress of Fort McHenry. It was Baltimore and its prize money that Cochrane and Cockburn lusted after, not sleepy little Washington.

Sixty-one-year-old James Madison presided over the business of Washington. A painfully shy hypochondriac with a frost-bitten nose, just under five-foot-four, Madison was at the same time a brainiac, an intellectual dynamo. Drilled in Latin, Greek, and politics, taught first by a Scottish tutor and then by Princeton professors, he became a delegate to the Continental Congress, Jefferson's secretary of state, and an impressive drafter of laws.

Madison was the main author of the United States Constitution and Bill of Rights. In 1787, he persuaded the Convention at Philadelphia to dismantle the malfunctioning infrastructure of the Articles of Confederation, and convinced the delegates to adopt a system of checks and balances to protect individual rights from the tyranny of the majority. More than anyone else, James Madison put in place the real cornerstones of the American republic.[10]

Some have portrayed James Madison as a weak president, but he was the chief draftsman of the Louisiana Purchase, meant to hold off any other claimants, including the French, to break the power of the Native Americans, and to open the west to settlers. While supremely annoyed by the cares of this infernal war, he knew, like Jefferson, that their republic needed a little bloodshed to fertilize its growth.

The war had been necessary, he knew, and by 1813, the main Indian threats in the south and west were being dashed by Andrew Jackson and William Henry Harrison. The main goal of the president had been achieved by all this fighting. It was not called "Mr. Madison's War" for nothing.

Like Jefferson, Madison was the son of a wealthy tobacco grower. He owned about 100 slaves and by all accounts was a kind and fair man. He dressed always in black, rarely drank to excess, and never beat his slaves. He chopped his own wood at his farm, loved horses, and was never cheated by his jockeys. Where he was severe, his First Lady, the marvellous Dolley Payne Madison, was a *bon vivant* who loved to entertain. When her husband won the election, she moved into the White House joyously and began to entertain the world.

Dolley Madison was a vivacious woman of Quaker extraction who had served as White House hostess to their friend Thomas Jefferson. Dolley could work a room better than anyone. She usually carried around a copy of Homer's *Iliad*, clasped to her ample bosom, and used it as an ice-breaker, telling guests she was just starting to read it, and did they know the plot? If Dolley Madison had been able to get all of Madison's old generals in one room for some friendly advice, she would have won the war single-handedly.

Dolley Madison.

Like Jefferson, her husband was a farmer/philosopher who liked nothing better than retreating to his plantation at Montpelier to evade the affairs of state. Dolley humanized him and nudged him into putting up with social duties and presidential occasions. And she clearly stiffened his spine as the war spun closer to Washington.

When news came of the British troops massing in Chesapeake Bay, Madison's Secretary of War John Armstrong, a proud peacock of a man, scoffed at all talk of the capital being attacked. "They certainly will not come here," he told an audience in Dolley's sitting room. "What the devil will they do here? No! No! Baltimore is the place ... that is of so much more consequence." He was right to a point. The capture of Baltimore would make Cockburn and Cochrane and their officers as rich as lords, as well as restoring the Cochrane family fortune.

Secretary of State James Monroe was not so sure Washington was safe. Madison — not a military man — shrugged. He had other problems to face. His agents were telling him that the New England states were holding a secret convention at Hartford to discuss leaving the union. His cupboard was bare, and northerners were refusing to provide financial support for the war. Treasury Secretary Albert Gallatin was having to tap into loans from John Jacob Astor and David Parish, an agent of the Rothschilds with major land holdings in upstate New York.

While Armstrong bustled about preparing the defenses of the region, particularly at Baltimore, the new American capital was left virtually undefended. Cochrane and Cockburn knew this from their spies, and while they were tempted to mount a quick attack on Baltimore, they decided that an easy dash to Washington and its port of Alexandria would be the first order of business. As Cockburn quipped, the fall of a capital is "always so great a blow to the government of a country."

It was a mistake that would prove costly to the British.

In early August 1814, they put the game in motion. To protect their rear, Cockburn rapidly cornered Commodore Joshua Barney's fleet of shallow draft gunboats up the Patuxent River, but Barney scuttled his own boats and blew up his ammunition before Cockburn could catch them.

By the 19th, the British ships had landed General Robert Ross and his force of 4,500 soldiers at Benedict, Maryland, down the Patuxent, and they started their sixty-mile march towards Washington. Ross didn't push his men in the furnace heat, lest they became exhausted. It took them five days to reach

Bladensburg, ten miles outside the capital, where the American militiamen were waiting.

At this point, Cochrane began to get itchy, and wanted to wheel off and head north toward Baltimore instead, but Cockburn and Ross prevailed. The going was easy, and they found all the bridges intact. This meant there was no real leader directing the defenders. Their first mission was to humiliate Madison and retaliate for the burning and pillaging of Upper Canada. An easy capture of their capital, and the very heart of their government, would be terrible for American morale. But they also intended to behave as gentlemanly as possible, unlike the Yankee barbarians who had torched York and Niagara.

SIDELIGHT: WHY WASHINGTON?

Why, in 1790, did George Washington choose what is now Washington, D.C., to be the new United States capitol? The district, a 100-square-mile diamond of land, was swampy, and for six months of the year the heat was absolutely stifling. The city today could simply not exist without air conditioning.

Washington was placed there for political reasons. Jefferson and Madison would only agree to Alexander Hamilton's banking schemes if the capital were moved south from Philadelphia.

The Jeffersonians planned Washington to serve as a grand backdrop for the romance of the new American state, a republic that would rival Rome. The site also had some good Roman-style hills; planner Pierre (Peter) Charles L'Enfant chose Jenkins Hill as the site for the Capitol building, with a grand boulevard connecting it with the president's house, a public space stretching westward to the Potomac River, and streets laid out in various iterations of the angles so beloved by members of the Masonic order. A canal was dug to drain the swamps, and it was grandly called the Tiber, after the river that ran through Rome.

Philosopher President Thomas Jefferson insisted the legislative building be called the "Capitol" rather than "Congress House." The Latin word "Capitol" means city on a hill and is associated with the Roman temple to Jupiter Optimus Maximus on Capitoline Hill.

The keys to these new republican ideals were land and liberty. Washington himself came from a family of property developers and land dealers. His father was a founder of the Virginia Company, and before the American Revolution, he had applied himself to military pursuits in order to drive the French out of the Ohio Valley, free it for settlement, and reap a good profit from land sales. After his death, it was up to his successors to do the same to the British and drive them out of the huge territory America had acquired from Napoleon: the 1808 Louisiana Purchase, negotiated by James Madison.

Bumbling at Bladensburg

The U.S. military response to the British threat was pathetic, as the heirs of George Washington fumbled and bumbled like rank amateurs. President Madison was highly annoyed at his war secretary, John Armstrong, for not taking the threat to Washington seriously. So when Armstrong chose veteran artillery officer Moses Porter, who commanded the bombardment of Fort George in May 1813, to lead the defence of the town, Madison overruled him. He personally gave the job to William Winder, a Baltimore lawyer, Republican stalwart and cousin of his good friend, the governor of Maryland, who was co-commander with Chandler in the American defeat at Stoney Creek a year earlier.

Armstrong was stung by Madison's actions. When Winder asked to call up at least 4,000 militia troops, Armstrong refused him point blank, insisting that they would only need to be mustered "once there is evidence of clear and present danger."

When news of the British landing at Benedict arrived, it suddenly put a fire under the tails of the Cabinet. While Armstrong finally fessed that he was wrong, a disgusted Secretary of State James Monroe galloped off with an escort of cavalrymen to evaluate the threat. Afraid to get within three miles of Benedict, and lacking a telescope, he guessed that 6,000 British troops had landed (there were only about 4,500). He then raced back up the road to Washington to brief his colleagues, not thinking to get the cavalry to burn a few bridges on his return trip.

When the British started to move after two days of landings, Armstrong finally allowed Winder to muster the militia, and by August 20, he had 9,000 men under arms, but no real strategy. Were the British going to attack Washington or march east of the town and wheel north toward Baltimore? To play it safe,

Winder divided his force. He deployed 5,000 soldiers in the Baltimore area and split the rest into two separate detachments. He kept Samuel Smith in Washington and led Tobias Stansbury off toward Benedict with Madison and Monroe. When they bumped into an advance party of British regulars, Winder ordered a retreat to Battalion Old Fields, about five miles south of Washington.

With Madison and Monroe looking over his shoulder and advising his every move, Winder ordered Stansbury to deploy his troops to the east of the village of Bladensburg in the best possible defensive position. But on August 23, Stansbury received a false report that the British were a mere six miles away and heading straight for Bladensburg. He was clearly terrified at the prospect of going up against British regulars and ordered an immediate retreat all the way back to Washington. Winder countermanded the order and sent Smith's force to join him at Bladensburg.

While Madison hurried back to Washington to salvage all the documents he could and take them into safe custody in the Virginia hills, the secretary of state was already at Bladensburg directing traffic. He mistakenly ordered one regiment to fall back a quarter mile from the front line, leaving the forward guns and rifles without support. By the time Winder got there, it was too late to change any plans.[11]

THE BRITISH MOVE ON WASHINGTON

British General Ross was clearly delighted by the easy going. The Americans didn't appear inclined to defend their capital; the only enemy they met had run away. The villages they passed through were ghostly and abandoned, all the bridges were intact, and by mid-day on August 24, they found Bladensburg empty of American soldiers; no need for street fighting. Across the bridge over the east branch of the Potomac, they saw clouds of dust and realized the Americans were waiting for them there.

At noon, an overconfident Colonel William Thornton and the 85th Regiment led the charge across the bridge without waiting for the rest of the British force. They quickly captured the forward guns and drove off the American riflemen, but had to retreat sharply back to the river when the Baltimore 5th Regiment of Militia counterattacked, killing or wounding many of Thornton's officers.

Ross then ordered out the Congreve rockets. Extremely inaccurate but terrifying to behold, they whistled and crackled over the heads of the raw American militiamen, who dropped their weapons and fled in terror. The American rear line, made up partly of Commodore Joshua Barney's sailors, was still forming up when the panicked militia arrived, with the British in hot pursuit. Barney and his men were swept along in the rout.

Since Winder failed to designate a rallying point in the case of defeat, all was confusion. He simply abandoned any pretense of defence, and the so-called "Bladensburg Races" didn't stop until he called a halt at the Montgomery Court House, eighteen miles beyond Washington.

With nothing blocking their path, the British 3rd Brigade, with General Ross and Rear Admiral Cockburn at its head, entered the town of Washington at eight in the evening, carrying a flag of truce. They could hear retreating Americans blowing up the Washington Navy Yard, founded by Thomas Jefferson and the first federal installation in the United States, to prevent capture of stores and ammunition.

Dolley Madison Takes Charge

"Four things greater than all things are / Women and Horses
and Power and War."

–Rudyard Kipling

Earlier that morning of August 24, John Armstrong had assured Dolley Madison that there was no danger from the British. Her husband had gone up to Georgetown, but Dolley had planned a victory supper for forty people in the White House. Above all, Dolley knew how to keep up appearances. Unfortunately, at 3:00 in the afternoon, the White House servants had just prepared the table when Armstrong strode into the White House and ordered a retreat.

Outside, people were now running about in all directions. Dolley and her servant girl Sukey jumped in her carriage and prepared to flee over the Georgetown ferry to join her husband. Dolley couldn't take Gilbert Sullivan's full-length portrait of George Washington, just her personal silver. As her husband's black valet, fifteen-year-old Paul Jennings, later recalled,

"She had no time to do it. It would have required a ladder to get it down. All she carried off was the silver in her reticule, as the British were thought to be a few squares off."

Before leaving, Dolley ordered a few important things saved. Madison's French butler and the White House gardener got a ladder, cut the Washington portrait out of its frame and rolled up the canvas; two visiting New Yorkers took it off in a wagon along with several large silver urns, which they hid in some farm buildings outside the city. As for the precious Declaration of Independence and George Washington's correspondence, senior clerk Stephen Pleasonton packed them in saddlebags and delivered them on horseback to an old grist mill two miles above Georgetown, where the miller covered them with sacks of flour.

Dolley Madison didn't realize it, but the main British force was still a few hours away, and the minute the White House was empty, a gang of local looters scrambled in and stole the rest of the silver and anything else they could lay their hands on.

As for Dolley, she found a house across the river a few miles on and asked for lodgings. The woman of the house, a Mrs. Love, was furious at the government for taking her husband into the militia, and shouted at Dolley, "Your husband has got mine out fighting, and damn you, you shan't stay in my house, so get out!" Dolley complied and soon found a more congenial refuge when some women took pity on her.[12]

The Gentlemanly Burning of Washington

That evening, as General Ross led his victorious troops up Capitol Hill under a white flag of truce, looking for someone to take the surrender, a sniper in a house shot at Ross but only killed his horse. A second shot killed a soldier. At this lack of respect, the enraged Britons set fire to the house, whose sharp-shooter, it is said, was a club-footed barber from Ireland. The troops then fired a volley into the windows of the Capitol and stormed the building to prepare it for destruction. Admiral Cockburn, realizing that there was nobody in Washington ready to negotiate a truce, mounted the Speaker's chair and shouted to the troops: "Shall this harbour of Yankee Democracy be burned? All for it say Aye!'" It was carried unanimously, and the buildings set ablaze.

When the Capitol building was truly aflame, Ross and Cockburn and their aides rode down the Mall to the White House. They discovered the sumptuous supper that the First Lady had prepared, happily ate it up, and drank up all the beer, cider, and wine from her coolers. After some final tipsy toasts to "President Jemmy" and the Prince Regent, Cockburn ordered the mansion put to the torch.[13]

All that day and the next, the British set to work pillaging government property and burning buildings. In the Senate, made almost entirely of stone, the troops had to chop up shutters and doors and then add rocket powder to make the fire burn hot enough. The first Library of Congress, located in the Senate majority leader's suite, was easier to put to the torch. The large, heavily timbered room had a double row of windows, and shelves laden with 3,000 books, many of them from Thomas Jefferson's personal collection. It burned to ashes, along with huge oil portraits of Louis XVI and Marie Antoinette, sent to the U.S. government in Philadelphia by the French king himself. The House of Representatives was easier to set ablaze, and the fire raged so hotly that glass melted, limestone burned into lime and the huge marble eagle over the speaker's canopy crumbled into dust.

Throughout the city, clouds and columns of fire and smoke rose from the president's house and all the other public buildings, and black ash rained down everywhere.

The shell of the White House, September 1814, by George Munger.

Unfortunately, against the orders of Ross, a number of private homes also went up in smoke, so discipline was tightened. On the second day, Admiral Cockburn, still stung by newspaper reports questioning his honor, marched up to the office of the anti-British National Intelligencer, intending to burn it to the ground. Waiting in the street was a gaggle of local women who begged him not to torch the building, because they feared the flames would spread to their neighbouring homes. Cockburn relented but ordered his marines to throw all the wooden presses and lead type out onto the street to be burned. "Make sure that all the C's are destroyed," he told his soldiers, "so that the rascals can have no further means of abusing my name."

The British also set fire to the U.S. Treasury and all the other public buildings. Only the U.S. Patent Office was saved by the efforts of William Thornton, architect of the Capitol and then superintendent of patents, who convinced Ross of the importance of its preservation.[14]

In the afternoon of the second day, a severe thunderstorm rumbled in and a tornado roared through the town. It doused the flames, dampened black ashes, and blew away the oppressive heat and the stench of ruined basements.

As if it was a signal after twenty-six hours of occupation, Ross knew it was time for the British to leave. He ordered the good people of Washington to remain inside their homes to avoid the risk of death, while his soldiers added new fuel to the fires to make sure they burned through the night. Then the troops quietly made their way by twos and threes to the outskirts of the town, where they formed up and quickly marched away.

Four days later, they were back on board ship and within a week they were dispatched to their next target, Baltimore. Madison and the rest of the government returned to the city, but all was in such disarray that they were unable to manage the war with any effect. Peace could not come too soon.

So ended a most humiliating episode in U.S. history. However, war has a tendency to humble the victors, and the American defence of Baltimore was a different story altogether.

THE STAR-SPANGLED BANNER

The British did take back some unexpected booty from Washington. While Ross had been busy at Bladensburg, Royal Navy Captain James Gordon had sailed up the Potomac with two frigates and four ships stuffed with bombs and rockets. His orders were to stand by if Ross needed to be evacuated by water. He was also to attack Fort Warburton, a small gun emplacement set up to guard the Washington naval yard. Approaching the fort on the evening of August 27, Gordon could only lob off a few shots before the defenders suddenly fled, blowing up the fort as they left. This was the sound heard by Cockburn and Ross as they entered Washington by road.

Hardly believing his luck, Gordon sailed farther upriver to Alexandria, and for several days his sailors looted hundreds of tons of merchandise from city merchants, loading them on captured American ships. On August 31, he got orders to return downriver, taking care to avoid or if necessary destroy two makeshift gun emplacements erected along the shore. Gordon's accurate cannon fire made short work of two of the batteries. The third crew, led by Oliver Hazard Perry, the hero of the Battle of Lake Erie, mounted a good fight, but they ran out of ammunition, leaving Gordon to cruise back to his fleet, happily laden with the spoils of war.

Cochrane and Cockburn were already mounting the second stage of the invasion, the attack on Baltimore, not by marching north from Washington, but by a combined land and sea invasion up the bay. They fully expected to strike a knockout blow against the demoralized Americans. Plus, Baltimore was a prize port, a city of 50,000 and home to many of the privateers who were raiding British shipping. To the British, it was a "nest of pirates."

Over two weeks in early September, Cochrane had moved the British frigates and supply ships up the Chesapeake. On the morning of September 12, he landed Cockburn, Ross, and the army of 3,700 troops and 1,000 marines at the southern tip of the Patapsco Neck peninsula at North Point, eleven miles south east of Baltimore. Then he ordered his captains to prepare for the bombardment of star-shaped Fort McHenry, the last American defense before the harbor. Once they neutralized the fort, then HMS *Volcano* would sail close to the wharves to begin the burning of Baltimore. *Volcano* carried special incendiary bombs called carcass shells, full of phosphorus that burned for fifteen minutes when they landed.

One of the ships held a young Baltimore lawyer Francis Scott Key, who was petitioning the British attackers to release a doctor friend held for unfriendly acts toward the British. Key himself was detained overnight on the truce ship and witnessed the bombardment of Fort McHenry from the British vessel.

On the morning of September 13, as the sun rose, Key was amazed to see the American flag still flying over the battered fort, and its cannons still firing back, as the British finished throwing 1,500 to 1,800 mortar shells and Congreve rockets at the fort. Key was inspired to write the lyrics of a poem, "The Defense of Fort McHenry," which later appeared in the Baltimore *Patriot* newspaper. His brother also printed handbills of the poem and gave them to every man who was at Fort McHenry during the bombardment. Key adapted his verses to the tune of a well-known British drinking song, "To Anacreon in Heaven." With its stirring words about of the "rockets' red glare," and "shells bursting in air," it soon became known as "The Star-Spangled Banner."[15]

THE DEATH OF ROSS

The British landing place, a narrow peninsula with swamps and tidal inlets, was probably ill chosen. Major General Samuel Smith of the Maryland militia anticipated the British move and sent Brigadier-General John Stricker to meet them with five regiments of Maryland militia, a small militia cavalry regiment, a battalion of three volunteer rifle companies, and a battery of six four-pounder field guns.

As the troops continued landing, Ross ordered them to move at once up the peninsula toward the city, but he soon encountered well dug-in American skirmishers. At noon, Stricker sent 250 sharpshooters and a cannon to further provoke the British. Cockburn argued caution about advancing without more support, then, just as Ross was going back to the landing site to call up the main army, an eighteen-year-old American sniper shot him through the right arm into the chest. He died while being transported back to the fleet.[16]

Colonel Arthur Brooke reorganized the British troops and started his assault on the American positions at 3:00 pm. It was bloody going, but the British fought their way up the peninsula all that day, with Stricker ensuring an orderly retreat. Brook advanced to within a mile of the main American position outside Baltimore. It was getting dark, and he chose to wait until he got word that Fort McHenry was neutralized. British losses that day were forty-six killed and 295 wounded. The Americans had twenty-four killed, with 139 wounded and fifty taken prisoner.

The Battle of North Point had been costly for the British. Losing a respected leader like General Ross was a critical blow to the invaders and damaged British morale. The combined effect of the blow suffered at North Point and the failure of the Royal Navy to capture or get past Fort McHenry, despite a twenty-five-hour bombardment, proved to be the turning point of the Battle of Baltimore.

The next day, Brooke advanced cautiously toward the city. He was dismayed to learn that the new earthwork defences were manned by almost 22,000 militia and bristled with 100 cannon. Preparing to attack at night, he first asked Cochrane to silence an American battery, "Roger's Bastion," on the flank of his proposed attack. Despite a stiff fight by Captain Charles John Napier, the attack failed, the Bastion stood, and Brooke, mindful of the potential slaughter of his troops, prudently called off the attack. The British backed down the peninsula before dawn and re-embarked at North Point.

With the loss of Ross, and the failure of the Royal Navy to knock out Fort McHenry, and with no sign from the citizens of Baltimore that they were prepared to pay the British a handsome ransom to sail away, the heart went out of the British attackers, and they slipped back down the Chesapeake to Tangier Island and then Bermuda, to ride out hurricane season.

New orders awaited them at Bermuda, and three months later, on December 12, 1814, Admiral Cochrane and his flotilla, with more than 10,000 soldiers and sailors, lay at anchor in the Gulf of Mexico, just to the east of Lake Pontchartrain and the city of New Orleans.

Moral: Keep politicians away from the battlefield, and snipers away from your best general.

LAKE CHAMPLAIN

> "I believe one bad general to be worth two good ones."
>
> *–Napoleon Bonaparte*

Sir George Prevost still felt the sting of his defeat at Sackets Harbor and was determined to redeem himself. Perhaps it was a reward for the victory he claimed to have won at Chateauguay. Perhaps he was just too annoyingly insistent. At any rate, it was Prevost himself that Lord Bathurst chose to lead a British campaign to capture Plattsburg, New York, there to await a signal to move down Lake Champlain.

The intent of this British invasion was to split Vermont and New England away from the rest of the country. The Federalists of the north supported peace with Britain, unlike the Republicans from James Madison's "United States of Virginia."

The proposed attack on Plattsburgh was coordinated with the campaign in Chesapeake Bay and got under way just as General Ross was landing in Maryland with his troops. The third thrust was to be the capture of New Orleans.

In mid-August, spies reported to Prevost that General George Izard's main U.S. force of 6,000 men was gone from Lake Champlain, called away by Armstrong on August 29 to relieve Jacob Brown at Fort Erie. Prevost was delighted and sped up preparations. He had spent his entire military career waiting for a chance like this, and he was determined to cover himself with glory, so his name would be forever talked about in drawing rooms and clubs throughout the Empire.

Prevost's splendid army of 10,531 regulars and militia began their march up the Richelieu Valley at the end of August, along the same route General John Burgoyne had taken thirty-seven years before. But they were larger than the army of Burgoyne, and the most lethal force ever assembled by the British in

North America. A third of them were seasoned veterans recently arrived from Spain and France.

Prevost appointed his friend the Polish baron Major-General Francis de Rottenburg to lead the parade. But the real working soldiers were three highly seasoned Peninsular War brigade commanders, Manley Power, Thomas Brisbane, and Frederick Philipse Robinson, all Wellington favourites carefully chosen to stiffen the spine of the British forces at Montreal.[17]

On their arrival, wearied from thrashing Bonaparte, half sick from the ocean voyage and with their red tunics and grey trousers very much the worse for wear, Prevost immediately told the trio that the dress standard of their Peninsular troops was not up to snuff, and was "a fanciful variety inconsistent with the rules of the service."

Prevost had shown who was boss, but it was not a good beginning. The brigadiers were not amused by this charlatan of a desk general. Besides, the Duke had always emphasized musketry and aggression above turnout. They were also concerned about the lack of intelligence they were given about the enemy and the lack of planning for the campaign. In fact, Prevost had a large intelligence budget but wished to keep control of the knowledge for himself.

Prevost happily assured the brigadiers that victory was in sight and that they were bound for certain glory.

The timing, he felt, was perfect. Unlike in most battles of this devilish war, they faced only 2,500 American regulars and at most a couple of thousand New York state citizen militia led by General Alexander Macomb. Plus they were going to be well supported by a lake fleet, at least if his Royal Navy colleague Sir James Yeo could speed up his ship building efforts.

In the dark back recesses of his mind, Prevost worried about facing Macomb again. More than a year before, the American had beaten Prevost badly at Sackets Harbor and tarnished his honour. No matter, he had Wellington's finest to command, and General Izard was away at Sackets. (At least he hoped so, and please God the report was not a ruse.)

Still, Prevost continued to feel pushed, and here he made the first of many major errors. While his magnificent army was quite capable of taking and holding Plattsburgh on its own, he couldn't resist sticking to his original plan and mounting a complete extravaganza, complete with naval support. But now his invasion fleet was lagging behind. In the last two weeks he had browbeaten Sir James Yeo's deputy at Île aux Noix, Captain George Downie, to get a move on. Downie had already complained to Yeo that Prevost was forcing him into premature action, which could lead to disaster.

Clearly Prevost was too thick-headed to alter his juvenile vision of how the battle should be fought. As his army continued its march toward Plattsburgh, he knew perfectly well that Downie's new ship the *Confiance* was not yet fully equipped to fight, but no matter; *Confiance* had lots of armament, and they needed to act fast in case Izard returned.

Downie's American counterpart, Captain Thomas Macdonough, had scrambled to build enough craft to meet the expected invasion. He now had ten gunboats and four larger vessels in the harbour at Plattsburgh, protected by the guns of the fort. Like Oliver Perry, he was another Chauncey protégé in his late twenties. He knew how to sail big ships and he especially knew how winds on this lake behaved. He was determined that seamanship would make the difference, as it did at Lake Erie.

In his rush to glory, Prevost had timed his campaign badly, arriving in the town of Plattsburgh on September 6. There he had to wait for almost a week, angry and frustrated, until Captain Downie had moved his four armed ships and twelve barges up the Richelieu to the lake. Downie's orders were to join the attack on Plattsburgh and then ferry the troops to the far end of Lake Champlain because the roads were so bad. And Macomb had made roads worse, far worse, with booby traps and abates. Knowing they would be heavily outnumbered, his engineers created fake roads to hide the genuine ones, and led the British into dead-end traps far from his three main forts. As Prevost advanced towards the American defensive works, his anger increased as his army's progress slowed, as long lines of marching soldiers got tangled up in the mazes. Many were picked off by snipers and skirmishers. But the main force advanced steadily.

Prevost's delay gave Macomb time to reinforce and strengthen Izard's line of redoubts and blockhouses on the south bank of the Saranac River. Macdonough was ready to help him resist the British assault, anchoring his vessels out of range of Downie's guns but near enough to bombard Prevost.

It took Downie's men two days to tow the unfinished frigate *Confiance* up the Richelieu River from Île aux Noix, against wind and current. Finally, on September 9, Downie's flotilla appeared. Carpenters and riggers were still at work on the frigate, but the wind was coming from the wrong direction to proceed. Before dawn on September 11, Downie reconnoitered the American line from a rowboat, then ordered his squadron to attack.

Moral: He who hesitates is lost, or, your dithering commander can ruin everything.

Debacle at Plattsburgh

"The transition from the defensive to the offensive is one of the most delicate operations in war."

–Napoleon

As Downie's flotilla rounded Cumberland Head to bombard the American ships in the harbour, Prevost ordered his three brigadiers to take Macomb's main fort from the rear, across the Saranac River. Unfortunately, Prevost's agents had failed to ascertain the whereabouts of the ford across the Saranac. Robinson's scouts finally found a good crossing three miles above Macomb's defences.

Macdonough knew the British would have more long-range guns, and to counter this he lined up his fleet inside Plattsburgh Bay, where the British would be forced to engage at close range and he could employ his carronades. His four warships lay across the harbour mouth, with the smaller gunboats inside and spaced in between the larger vessels. As Downie rounded the head, the wind lightened, as Macdonough knew it would, and Downie's sails started flapping. Losing headway, he had to anchor his flagship to start firing. Most of the naval action was between his 1,200-ton frigate *Confiance* and the 734-ton American vessel *Saratoga*. Downie's first broadside struck down forty men on the *Saratoga*, and the British soon disabled every gun on her starboard side. But Macdonough had cleverly laid out kedge anchors, and he suddenly spun *Saratoga* around and began firing at *Confiance* from the port guns.

At the fifteen-minute mark of the battle, the Gods of War smiled on Macdonough. A cannonball from *Saratoga* directly struck the muzzle of a cannon on the *Confiance*. The twenty-four-pound naval gun flew up off its mount and a piece slammed into Downie, crushing him instantly. An eyewitness later recorded: "His skin was not broken, a black mark about the size of a small plate was the only visible injury. His watch was found flattened, with its hands pointing to the very second at which he received the fatal blow."[18]

Downie's lieutenant tried to attempt the same manoeuvre as Macdonough, but the wind had died down completely, and *Confiance*'s untrained crew failed to turn her around, exposing her to even worse heavy raking fire from *Saratoga*.

After *Confiance* struck her colours, Macdonough easily rounded up the rest of Downie's leaderless flotilla, although many of the barges got away and rowed downstream to Île aux Noix. One of Downie's surviving officers, who had fought with Nelson, later said that the battle of Trafalgar was "child's play" compared to Lake Champlain.[19]

Back on land, Prevost's attack was slow to get going, and he didn't order an advance until 10:00 a.m., when the lake battle had been under way for more than an hour. When a messenger arrived and told him that *Confiance* had been defeated and Downie was dead, Prevost professed to be horrified by the news, but then resigned, even relieved. It was time to wrap things up before any more damage was done. He quickly called a conference with de Rottenburg, Power, and Brisbane, sent off orders to Robinson to retreat from the ford, and told them he was calling off the invasion. Without naval support, he said, they simply could not proceed with the campaign.

Power, Brisbane, and Robinson were furious, arguing that combat losses were less than 260 and that with a little valour they could take Macomb's position. Still nervous that Izard would return, Prevost would not hear of it, and

An engraving of the Battle of Lake Champlain.

ordered his buglers to blow a retreat. Clearly feeling a great sense of relief, he raced back to his desk in Montreal to spin his version of events to Lord Bathurst.

Macdonough's quick victory ended the danger of British invasion from the north. A young sailor's savvy and Prevost's bumbling were the keys to the American victory, but General Macomb got all the kudos. The press showered him with praise and dubbed him "The Hero of Plattsburgh." The War Department promoted him to major general, he received the thanks of Congress and a Congressional Gold Medal, and the state of New York gave him a thousand acres of land.

As for Prevost's daughter Anne in Montreal, the defeat was a terrible blow to her father's honour:

> I never was given to shedding tears, far from it but I now wept bitter tears not for poor Captain Downie or his Squadron, but because the Army was to retreat without having first destroyed Plattsburg! I felt certain that however necessary this determination might be, it would bring the greatest odium on my Father; it would not be tolerated at a period especially when our troops were so perpetually victorious. That my Father acted from the purest motives, who can doubt.[20]

Moral: Never let a weak commander say never.

GHENT

"Reconciliation with our enemies is but a desire to better our condition, a weariness of war, or the fear of some unlucky accident."

–La Rochefoucauld

Thomas Jefferson originally admired Bonaparte, who as First Consul had stabilized France. Now he was having to change his tune as French armies went from defeat to defeat, leaving Britain in command. On July 5, 1814, Jefferson wrote his old enemy John Adams that

> While I rejoice, for the good of mankind, in the deliverance of Europe from the havoc which would have never ceased while Bonaparte should have lived in power, I see with anxiety the tyrant of the ocean remaining in vigor, and even participating in the merit of crushing his brother tyrant. While the world is thus turned upside down, on which side of it are we? All the strong reasons, indeed, place us on the side of peace; the interests of the continent, their friendly dispositions, and even the interests of England. Her passions alone are opposed to it. Peace would seem now to be an easy work, the causes of the war being removed. Her orders of council will no doubt be taken care of by the allied powers, and, war ceasing, her impressment of our seamen ceases of course.[21]

Jefferson's "tyrant of the ocean" was still in a position to make Madison's nightmare come true. One or two major defeats, such as the capture of a city like Baltimore or Boston, could bring the whole edifice of the Republic down to its knees.

In 1813, President James Madison had sent Albert Gallatin as the U.S. representative to a Russian-brokered peace talk, which Britain ultimately refused, preferring direct negotiations. On November 4, 1813, Foreign Secretary Lord Castlereagh had offered to begin peace negotiations on the basis of *Uti possidetis*, or holding territory possessed at the end of hostilities. The Americans managed several confused missions, including one where Henry Clay cooled his heels in Sweden for several months. But nothing was done in 1813, and hundreds of innocent civilians and young soldiers suffered and died as the two sides dithered in the courts and meeting rooms of Europe. Only in January of 1814, after a disastrous invasion season in Canada and a warning from Gallatin that the U.S. was in debt to the hilt, did Madison agree to begin talks in the old Belgian city of Ghent.

THE GOOD NEWS FROM GHENT

> "War is God's way of teaching Americans geography."
> —*Ambrose Bierce*

On August 8, 1814, the two sides sat down to make a peace. Gallatin, who had resigned as secretary of the treasury, headed the U.S. delegation, along with Henry Clay and John Quincy Adams. Three superstars. The British were represented by three non-entities: Admiral Lord Gambier, MP Henry Goulburn, under-secretary of state for war and the Colonies, and maritime law expert William Adams. The real negotiators in the background were Colonial Secretary Lord Bathurst and Foreign Secretary Lord Castlereagh. Castlereagh and Wellington were already deeply involved in sorting out Europe post-Napoleon at the Congress of Vienna, and Ghent was very much a sideshow.

After the preliminaries were over, the straw dog of impressment was waved away, since the Royal Navy had no further need to impress sailors. Another non-starter was Gallatin's motion that the British might turn over Canada to the United States as a form of reparation for damages caused to American trade.

Early on in the negotiations, Henry Clay suggested to his colleagues that Britain was bluffing with its demands for an Indian homeland and peace on the basis of *Uti possidetis,* and that each side would keep what it had won. The timid Adams called his idea "inconceivable." Clay laughed and asked him if he knew how to play brag, a form of poker where you hold your hand with a solemn and confident face and simply outbluff your adversary.

The Americans got little chance to bluff the British, except for Henry Clay's flat-out refusal to cede any territory to the Native people. This shocked Goulburn, who wrote his boss Bathurst that he had no idea the Americans were so determined to "extirpate the Indians and appropriate their territory."

The shocking news of their defeats at Baltimore and Lake Champlain soon took away any leverage the British negotiators hoped for and bolstered Gallatin's efforts to get better terms.

British leaders were growing tired of the whole affair, and Wellington growled to Castlereagh that they should take the *status quo ante bellum* and have done with it. In fact, Wellington and Castlereagh were still focused very much on Europe and wanted the American problem mopped up.

On October 22, the two sides signed a Treaty of Commerce to normalize trade relations. On November 27, Britain dropped the *Uti possidetis* offer and its proposal to create an Indian buffer zone in Ohio and Michigan, and finally agreed to *status quo ante bellum,* or the way matters stood before the war began.

Commissioners of the Treaty of Ghent.

On December 14, the two negotiating teams signed the Treaty of Ghent, turning the clock back to June of 1812. Neither side gained or lost territory. Essentially, they called the whole thing off. As John Quincy Adams wearily put it, "Nothing was adjusted, nothing was settled."

However, the treaty released all prisoners of war, including more than 20,000 American sailors and privateers captured during the war, and in prisons in Canada, England, and South Africa. Returned to the United States were approximately 10,000,000 acres (40,000 km²) of territory near Lakes Superior and Michigan, in Maine, and on the Pacific coast (important for John Jacob Astor's Fort Astoria). American-held areas of Upper Canada (present-day Ontario) were also returned to British control.

Finally, on the day before Christmas, the Treaty of Ghent went into effect, officially bringing the war to an end.

Gallatin's patience and skill in dealing with the parties led Adams to call the treaty "the special and peculiar triumph of Mr. Gallatin."

On February 17, 1815, the U.S. Congress, forced to meet at Blodgett's Hotel because the Capitol lay in blackened ruins, ratified the Treaty of Ghent. Notes were exchanged to that effect with the British Ambassador, at which point President Madison declared his war to be at an end.

WHO WON THE PEACE?

U.S strategy had centred on the conquest of Canada, but the U.S. land campaign met with few successes. For most of the war, America's tiny navy stayed bottled up behind a tight British blockade, and only the speedy privateers had any effect on the British. Yet glittering victories at Lake Champlain, Baltimore, and New Orleans against the best army in the world made most Americans regard the war as a great victory for the United States. And with Ghent, Great Britain was at last treating the United Sates as a legitimate nation.

For British North Americans, the war showed them they could survive and thrive under their own institutions and laws, and under the British Crown. They had repelled three American invasions and now had their own homemade heroes, Isaac Brock, de Salaberry, Laura Secord, and Tecumseh, and a growing sense of unity and nationhood, which let them forge their own northern "Manifest Destiny" across the continent.

For Native Americans, the U.S. promise in Article IX of the Treaty, "to restore to such tribes or nations, respectively, all the possessions, rights, and privileges which they may have enjoyed or been entitled to in one thousand eight hundred and eleven, previous to such hostilities," proved hollow, since there was no clear map of native reserves.

For the most part, there has been harmony ever since between Canada and the United States. So in the end, both sides won the peace.

A Post Mortem on Prevost

> "If the art of war were nothing but the art of avoiding risks, glory would become the prey of mediocre minds."
>
> –*Napoleon*

Sir George Prevost was probably no Benedict Arnold, but this complicated man, this nephew of Aaron Burr, this grandson of a financier of the American Revolution, could be accused of, if not treason, at least betrayal of the British cause during the War of 1812.

Prevost's choice of himself to lead the Lake Champlain expedition was not a happy one. Either of his brigadiers could have routed the Americans, but not a self-important desk officer like Prevost. His conduct toward Yeo and de Salaberry showed he was a spotlight-hogger who hated to give credit where it was due. Not at all a leader, he was a classic narcissist. In the depths of his shallow psyche, he didn't really care about victory for his cause, but only about his role on the stage.

Provost would not share his intelligence with Wellington's brigadiers. He knew Downie's ships were not ready enough to give their best in battle but went ahead anyway. Downie's fleet was badly manned, with only a few professional sailors on board. Most were hastily recruited Lower Canadian militia. He forced Downie's fleet into action with untrained sailors. This, and his fixed vision of a combined land and lake operation, lost him the entire campaign. There was a part of Prevost that didn't really care, as long as he was making his enemy, Sir James Yeo, look bad, because Downie was Yeo's responsibility and under Yeo's command.

On the American side, Macdonough had manned his ships with well-trained seamen and gunners. Macdonough knew from experience that the wind died down on the lake at a certain time each day. He used that knowledge to trap the British, and did his duty well.

As with Sackets Harbor, Prevost adored the idea of taking advantage of the enemy's absence, and leading the charge, but when it came to execution, he made mistake after mistake in both battles. Prevost clearly loved the centre stage but resented the stagecraft of others that made it possible. Like a hardcore gambler, he cared not that he was losing, as long as he was in the game. He was devoid of empathy, unwilling to share the glory, and quite incapable of putting himself in the other's shoes.

Not only did he lack a fighting spirit, but Prevost was also an incompetent bumbler. As at Sackets, he had planned the attack on Plattsburgh overly quickly and rushed to execute. Perhaps terrified that he would be caught by the returning General Izard, he arrived at Plattsburgh too early. He fumbled the rapid crossing of the river due to lack of proper intelligence. When Robinson finally made it across the Saranac and was advancing on Macomb, Prevost recalled him.

Wellington's three brigadiers were quite rightly appalled and disgusted by Prevost's behaviour. Back in Montreal, Robinson wrote that he was "sick at heart. Everything I see and hear is discouraging. This is not a field for a military man above the rank of a Colonel of rifleman." William Smith, an enemy of Prevost, said that the officers were all "heartily tired of this Country, as every military man must be, who has any reputation to lose, under such a Goose as our little nincompoop."

Others whispered about Prevost's loyalty. Perhaps when it came to going for the jugular against the Americans, Prevost's heart was not in the fight, because this nephew of Thomas Jefferson's vice president Aaron Burr was American-born, and had many American cousins, with major land holdings in New York state.

The Iron Duke was furious when he heard the news from Manley Power that he, Brisbane, and Robinson had failed to overcome Sir George Prevost's timidity, and thereby never even engaged in a significant scrap. No doubt the veteran brigade leaders were right, but they were serving under Prevost, a commander who had gained his laurels in a couple of minor Caribbean skirmishes. But they were good soldiers, buttoned their lips, and had to obey his orders.

Wellington wisely declined an offer from Prime Minister Lord Liverpool to go to Montreal and take command, but on October 30, 1814, he wrote Bathurst,

It is very obvious to me that you must remove Sir George Prevost. I see he has gone to war about trifles with the general officers I sent him, which are certainly the best of their rank in the army; and his subsequent failure and distresses will be aggravated by that circumstance; and will probably with the usual fairness of the public be attributed to it.

Bathurst concurred, and Wellington sent his former quartermaster general, Sir George Murray, to Montreal, specifically to fire Prevost and order him to return to London to explain his conduct during the Plattsburg debacle.

News of the Treaty of Ghent reached Prevost in late February 1815, and he disbanded the militia and ordered the regulars to cease hostilities. George Murray arrived in Montreal on March 2, 1815, and delivered the order to Prevost to vacate his position. His replacement was to be Sir Edward Pakenham, Manley Power's previous commanding officer, and Wellington's brother-in-law.

On a last sour note, the Lower Canada Assembly voted to award Prevost £5,000 for a silver plate service, but the British majority on the council vetoed the testimonial. Prevost left Quebec on April 3, publicly humiliated by the news from Murray. Once in England, he smoothly deflected criticism of his conduct during the war, at least for a few months.

In the meantime, Sir James Yeo, saddened at the death of his friend Downie, wrote a lengthy report to the Admiralty on his experiences in the Canadas. He noted that British success mainly resulted from the "stupidity" of the enemy, in their failure to cut the vulnerable line of the St. Lawrence. He did not think that this error would be repeated in future. With great foresight, he urged the Army to transform Kingston into a major fortress and build an inland waterway along the Ottawa and Rideau river systems to link the lakes safely to Montreal.

In 1815, Yeo was invited to testify at the court martial of some of his officers who had survived the battle of Lake Champlain. All were honourably acquitted, and Prevost was held responsible for the disaster. Shortly afterward, the Admiralty published its official dispatch on the Battle of Plattsburgh, along with Yeo's complaints, both blaming Prevost.

To clear his name, Prevost requested a court martial, which was set for the following January 12, to give time for witnesses to travel from Canada. He died a week before it convened.

Prevost still has his supporters who argue that he successfully mounted a defensive war, following orders from the War Office. But the evidence shows that he was in general a slippery, self-serving character. He starved his troops on the frontier and hoarded most of the power and all of the intelligence in Quebec and Montreal, where it was not needed. In the two battles he led, at Sackets and Plattsburg, he let the enemy off the hook, enraging his inferior officers. I would argue that he threw both fights, scampering gratefully back to his office in Montreal to spin a yarn to his superiors in faraway England.

All through the War of 1812, Sir George Prevost's actions did far more to benefit the American enemy than his British and Canadian colleagues. Specifically:

- At the beginning of the war, his orders were to avoid provoking the Americans. Brock thought this a dangerous course of action and urged Prevost to "abandon our present inert and neutral policies toward the Indians."

- The cease-fire Prevost signed with Granny Dearborn in August of 1812 was either naive or cunning; it allowed the Americans to resupply their forces without danger and move ships out of a St. Lawrence blockade.

- If his orders to stand down had reached Brock in time, Detroit would never have been captured, Indian support would have melted away, and the capture of Upper Canada would have been "A mere matter of marching."

- Prevost never went west of Kingston, and Upper Canada was at no point a priority. While hoarding 4,500 troops in the impregnable fortress of Quebec, protected by the Royal Navy, he sent only 1,200 west.

- In 1813, his penny-pinching lost Lake Erie and Detroit, and if his troops had not disobeyed orders and captured Fort Niagara, Upper Canada would have been lost as well.

- Also against his orders, Red George MacDonell attacked Ogdensburg and drove Forsyth back to Sackets, to the great relief of people on both sides of the border. And yet Prevost turned around and made a private deal not to molest the interests of U.S. land dealer David Parrish in northern New York. Parrish, a former agent of the Rothschilds in Mexico, was building an iron foundry near Ogdensburg that could supply cannon balls to Isaac Chauncey at Sackets. Prevost gave him immunity from attack if he promised not to manufacture arms.

- Prevost's treatment of de Salaberry was appalling. After Chateauguay, protected by distance and a large ocean, Prevost sent Bathurst elaborate missives claiming glory for himself at the expense of his officers.

- In 1814, after Plattsburgh, Sir James Yeo had seen enough and called Prevost's bluff. To the relief of many in both services, Prevost was ignominiously booted back to England. Irony of ironies, the man died before he could be court martialled. It would not surprise me if he died by his own hand, although accounts suggest he suffered a heart attack.

Some historians gloss over or even romanticize Sir George Prevost as a capable wartime leader, almost Churchillian, a man doing the best he could under trying circumstances. Well, in my humble opinion, a better man could have done a far better job, and a slightly worse man would have lost it all.

I am left with a nagging suspicion. Was there something more to Sir George Prevost than just an inept, narcissistic desk officer? Was this New Jersey-born martinet Canada's Benedict Arnold, quietly damping down British and Canadian successes to benefit or protect the American cause, or his family's land holdings in New York State? That is a case that remains to be proven, but the evidence compels further study. I leave it to you, dear reader, to decide.

FIVE

BIRTH OF TWO NATIONS

NEW ORLEANS

THE WAR OF 1812 MIGHT HAVE BEEN OVER IN THE MINDS OF DIPLOMATS and politicians, but in the heart of Andrew Jackson, the fighting in the south continued until further notice.

OLD HICKORY COOLS HIS HEELS

> "As long as our Government is administered for the good of the people, and is regulated by their will; as long as it secures to us the rights of person and of property, liberty of conscience and of the press, it will be worth defending; a million of armed freemen, possessed of the means of war, can never be conquered by a foreign foe."
>
> *–Andrew Jackson*

William Henry Harrison's main goal in the northwest was to make the frontier safe for settlers, driving obstinate Indians out of lands eyed hungrily by speculators. By 1813, General Andrew Jackson of the Tennessee militia was pulling together a similar campaign in the south, mainly against the Creeks. With the half-hearted support of the government, he was also preparing a semi-secret war against the Spanish, to get them out of Florida.

Jackson represented the vigorous young cohort of a new western America that would someday split the country in two and foment a crisis leading to civil war. In 1813, most northerners were content to see themselves as New Englanders. Most Virginians shared the Republican ideals of Jefferson and Madison. But men like Andrew Jackson, not philosophical by nature, were unabashed expansionists, content to wage war against anybody who got in the way of their beloved country and its manifest destiny west.

Jackson hated the British and sported a boyhood sabre scar inflicted by a redcoat soldier when he tried to stand up for his rights. But he hated more the opponents who would not let him have his way. Tough and sentimental and proud, he was called Old Hickory by his soldiers, because he was a hard man and wouldn't be bent nor broken.

Where Virginia squires Jefferson and Madison happily devoured Latin and Greek, Andrew Jackson was a barbarian from the provinces who could barely scribble proper English.

Yet he could rouse the troops far better than the two Virginia squires:

> Who are we? And for what are we going to fight? Are we the titled slaves of George III? The military conscripts of Napoleon the Great? Or the frozen peasants of the Russian Czar? No. We are the free born sons of America. The citizens of the only republic now existing in the world. And the only people on earth who possess rights, liberties, and property which they dare call their own.

The pecksniffs in the U.S. Congress weren't sure what to do with Jackson the man of action, a man they found hard to control.

In 1813 Jackson wrote Secretary of War Armstrong that he had raised a force of 2,000 men and would "rejoice at the opportunity of placing the American eagle on the ramparts of Mobile, Pensacola, and Fort St. Augustine." Jackson's American eagle was the battle flag of Kentucky, the same that Isaac Shelby placed at Fort Malden after the Battle of the Thames.

How did Washington respond? President Madison fretted about Jackson, considering him a loose cannon. Congress agonized over the offer, finally approving only an expedition into that part of the gulf coast disputed by the U.S. and Spain.

Secretary of War Armstrong was jealous of anyone outside his control and could not bring himself to grant Jackson command. Instead, he left the furious Tennessean hanging in the wilderness, then cooling his heels in Natchez, waiting for his orders. Then he gave the expedition, the glory and the potential booty to the usual suspects, General James Wilkinson and his own brother-in-law, army Quartermaster General Morgan Lewis. After an easy two-week march through the countryside, Wilkinson's regulars occupied the disputed part of West Florida and the port of Mobile without meeting any Spanish resistance. The Spaniards were no doubt tipped off in advance, since Wilkinson was a paid agent of the Spanish crown, and had been for several years.

After this glorious feat of arms, Wilkinson and Lewis went north to lead Armstrong's disastrous campaign against Montreal.

Jackson Gets His War

Andrew Jackson had an existential need to get into battle. He found his reason for being in the summer of 1813 when the Red Sticks tribe of the Creek Indians, inspired by Tecumseh, went on the warpath with a series of outrages against white settlers and merchants.

On August 30, at Fort Mims, in that part of the Mississippi Territory soon to become Alabama, the Creeks massacred more than 500 men, women, and children huddling in the fort for protection. Jackson rose in a rage, put back together the army he had assembled for Florida, and moved to engage the Creeks. He was undone in this campaign by his primitive supply system, and he dangerously overextended his line of communications, nearly losing his army. His militia started deserting back to their farms, and Jackson had to retrench at Fort Strother until a regiment of regulars arrived.

In the cool of November, after the regulars helped him whip his mutinous militia back into shape, Jackson went after the Red Sticks and gave them no quarter. In a series of battles at Tallushatchee, Talladega, Autosse, Eccanachaca, Emuckfau Creek, Enotachopco Creek, and Calabee Creek, he whittled away at the Creek Nation.

Jackson finally cornered a force of about 900 Creek warriors and many women and children in a fortified camp at the Horseshoe Bend of the Tallapoosa River. He had nearly 600 regulars, 2,000 militia and volunteers, including western legend Davy Crockett, plus several hundred friendly Indians, and a few pieces of artillery. With a final bayonet charge, he conquered the Creeks and cleared the south for cotton. The remaining tribes fled west or into Spanish territory.

For all these victories, Armstrong was forced to swallow his pride and appoint Andrew Jackson a major general in the Regular United States Army.

THE BRITISH AT NEW ORLEANS

"Between a battle lost and a battle won, the distance is
immense, and there stand empires."

–Napoleon Bonaparte

Peace had already been declared, but the Treaty of Ghent not ratified by the U.S. Senate, when the British campaign against New Orleans began in December 1814. Its sole end seems to have been to take and hold the city for a time, using it as a bargaining chip in the peace talks. The British commanders were also interested in the rich booty reputedly held in the city.

This last real engagement of the war was a three-week-long affair, and one that the Duke of Wellington did not think advisable. New Orleans lay a hundred miles up the Mississippi in an unbeatable defensive position, built on a sandy outcrop and surrounded by mangrove swamps and alligator- and snake-infested bayous. Several forts protected the great river up its length. The only other way to New Orleans was by way of Lakes Borgne and Ponchartrain to the east, muddy inlets of the sea that were too shallow for Royal Navy frigates and transports.

New Orleans was an insane endeavour, and the British Army was not used to operating in these conditions. But the whole operation was eagerly promoted by Vice Admiral Sir Alexander Cochrane, who was given overall command. In London earlier in the year, Cockburn told the war office that his captains had scoped out the territory. He reckoned he could drive the Americans from Louisiana and Florida with a force of only 3,000 troops, backed by the local Choctaw Indians and a force of disaffected Spaniards and French. They gave him the go-ahead.

By December of 1814, the peace talks at Ghent were well under way, and Admiral Cochrane was in a hurry. After failing to take Baltimore, his mind was clearly focused on the prize money of New Orleans — an estimated four million pounds sterling, of which the commander could count on at least half a million pounds. In his fleet were several barges specially designed for one purpose only: to carry away the loot.

The British began to engage on December 12, 1814, when Cochrane's invasion fleet anchored outside the shallows of muddy Lake Borgne. On board were more than 10,000 soldiers, sailors, and Royal Marines. The army was led by General Edward Pakenham, Wellington's brother-in-law, replacing General Ross, killed at Baltimore.

Two days later, Cochrane ordered Captain Nicholas Lockyer with 2,200 British sailors and Royal Marines to clear a blockade of Lake Borgne mounted by U.S. Lieutenant Thomas Catesby and his flotilla of five gunboats. Lockyer's forty-two longboats, each armed with a small carronade, made violent work of Catesby's vessels in the Battle of Lake Borgne. But the little victory stung; seventeen British sailors were killed and seventy-seven wounded while the Americans lost ten killed, thirty-five wounded, and eighty-six captured.

Now free to navigate Lake Borgne, British General John Keane set up the attack garrison on Pea Island, about thirty miles (forty-eight kilometres) east of New Orleans, and British sailors began the backbreaking work of rowing back and forth from the transports and frigates, ferrying cannons and supplies and thousands of redcoats in shallow draft boats to and from the ships and the island. It was a round trip of three days. Each soldier had to haul his own gear, and many carried a heavy cannonball in their knapsack. On one trip in heavy waves, one of the boats was swamped and the entire boatload of men sank suddenly out of sight.

A week later, on the morning of December 23, General Keane led an advance body of 1,800 redcoats to the east bank of the Mississippi, nine miles (fourteen km) south of New Orleans. There he made a mistake that changed the whole outcome of the battle. Instead of boldly advancing up the River Road and taking the undefended city, Keane erred on the side of caution and decided to wait for reinforcements at Lacoste's Plantation. When Andrew Jackson's spies reported this, Jackson quipped, "By the Eternal they shall not sleep on our soil."

That evening, Jackson took over 2,000 men and mounted a sharp surprise attack on Keane's camp, inflicting over 200 quick casualties before pulling back behind the dry Rodriguez Canal, about four miles south of the city. A now very nervous General Keane fortified his position and stayed put for three days, while Jackson's men had time to do exactly what the defenders of Baltimore did and threw up a heavily fortified high earthen breastwork to defend the canal. Their line was a plain five-foot-high rampart of sugar barrels, logs, and rammed clay, faced by an eight-foot-deep trench, running between the river and an impassable swamp.

On Christmas Day, General Edward Pakenham arrived at the plantation. He too became infected with the spirit of caution and perhaps a premonition of doom. He simply did not have the intelligence he needed. Reports from local pirate Jean Lafitte suggested that Jackson had fortified New Orleans with 15,000 regulars. He simply did not know what to believe. In fact, Lafitte had already made a sharp bargain with Old Hickory for guns and ammunition and men.

Three days later, on December 28, Pakenham ordered a reconnaissance-in-force against the American earthworks. He did not like what he saw. That evening, Admiral Cochrane arrived, and the two commanders got into a fierce argument. Pakenham protested that the River Road was too dangerous. Jackson was dug in too deeply, and there would be heavy losses. Chef Menteur Road by Lake Pontchartrain was a far better invasion route. Cochrane, as senior commander, overruled Pakenham, insisting that his boats could provide enough firepower along the Mississippi to bombard Line Jackson from the river. If the British Army could not destroy a ramshackle American army, he scoffed, his sailors could do the job.

On December 28, Pakenham made some probing attacks against the Rodriguez Canal earthworks — now called Line Jackson by the defenders. Old Hickory reckoned they were getting ready for a frontal attack. He ordered his engineers to build artillery batteries to protect the earthworks. There were eight of them, with one big thirty-two-pound gun, three twenty-four-pounders, one eighteen-pounder, three twelve-pounders, three six-pounders, and a six-inch (150 mm) howitzer. Jackson also sent a detachment of men to the west bank of the Mississippi to man two twenty-four-pounders and two twelve-pounders from the grounded warship *Louisiana*.

Moral: Don't let your sailors boss around your soldiers.

JACKSON'S TRIUMPH

> "About sunrise the whole British army was in motion... And on they came as steady as on dress parade... Three times they recoiled and were rallied again by their officers, who led them up to our entrenchments...."
>
> *—U.S. Volunteer M.W. Trimble*

On New Year's Day, the main British army started to come ashore. An overeager Pakenham made the mistake of attacking the earthworks with artillery before all the British ships had unloaded. The British gunners knocked out Jackson's thirty-two-pounder and twenty-four-pounder, plus a twelve-pounder, but they ran out of ammunition after three hours, and Pakenham had to cancel the attack. He could have won the battle then and there; the Americans on the left of Line Jackson near the swamp had broken and run from their position.

By January 7, the British had landed enough artillery and ammo to begin the battle in earnest. In the early morning of January 8, Pakenham ordered his troops to begin a two-pronged assault. From the very start, the Gods of War began to pester the British, and everything that could go wrong did.

First, Colonel William Thornton of the 85th Regiment, who had crossed the river during the night, was to move rapidly upriver and storm the American batteries on the warship *Louisiana*, then fire on Jackson's rear with howitzers and rockets. But a diversionary canal dug by Cochrane's sailors collapsed, and Thornton's force had to drag boats through deep Mississippi mud, putting the men twelve hours behind schedule.

Second, when Pakenham began his main attack directly against Line Jackson under cover of night and a heavy fog, the soldiers of the 44th Regiment of Foot neglected to bring the siege ladders they needed to cross the Rodriguez Canal and scale the earthworks. Third, Pakenham hoped that the dense fog would

Jackson at New Orleans.

provide some protection, but just as the main British force neared Line Jackson, a light breeze came up, the morning sun burned off the fog, and thousands of soldiers were left completely, nakedly exposed to Jackson's Tennessee militia and Kentucky riflemen, secure behind their muddy berms.

Jackson ordered his cannons to start firing, and the slaughter began. As the red carpet of troops advanced over the flat green field, Jackson waited until they were within rifle range, and then ordered the cannons to stop until the smoke cleared. Then his officers told the sharp-eyed riflemen to aim just above the white cross belts of the British and pay particular attention to shooting the officers on horseback. Then the officers dropped their swords and shouted "FIRE!" The front ranks fired, and an orange sheet of flame rippled down the line. Then they stepped back to reload, and seconds later another accurate volley slammed into the British, and then a third and fourth.

The British officers were taken out easily. Pakenham had his horse shot out from under him, and when he mounted another one, he was quickly hit in the neck and stomach and fell over onto the turf to die.

It was pure military murder. Hundreds of highlanders and other British infantry were mowed down like stalks of cane, Generals Gibbs and Pakenham were dead, and Keane severely wounded. After only twenty minutes, the leaderless survivors were left huddling in shallow trenches to escape the murderous fire. When it was over, the British counted 2,042 casualties: 291 killed, 1,267 wounded, with 484 captured or missing. The Americans shrugged off their seventy-one casualties: thirteen dead, thirty-nine wounded, and nineteen missing.

Jackson did not molest the shattered remnant of Pakenham's army. As his engineer, LaTour, remembered:

> The bodies of all the British who had died on our side, were delivered to the enemy, on the advanced line of our posts and his; they were received by British officers and buried. On beholding the remains of the three officers killed on the redoubt, and particularly those of Colonel Renee, the British soldiers could not forbear to manifest strong emotions of admiration and grief....

For ten days the British recovered their dead, burying the corpses in a mass grave on the southern edge of the battleground. A Mississippi flood later disinterred most of those buried and floated their remains throughout the delta. The bodies of Generals Pakenham and Gibbs were gutted and packed in casks of rum for the journey home. They were both buried in St. Paul's Cathedral in London.

Cochrane's fleet kept sending up reinforcements and siege engines, but a shaken General Lambert ordered the campaign ended. For over a week, British tars rowed the surviving redcoats back to the troopships, then the admiral ordered the fleet to sail away to attack Mobile, Alabama, as a consolation prize. On February 5, a ship caught up to Cochrane's flagship as he was nearing Biloxi, Mississippi. The vessel carried news of the peace of Ghent, and orders to break off hostilities at once.

So ended the most lopsided beating ever inflicted on a British army in wartime and possibly the worst in the annals of military history.

We should not discount New Orleans as a senseless battle because the war was over. It showed that British that Wellington's Peninsular War veterans could be beaten, and beaten really very badly, by heavy artillery, a rag-tag band of riflemen from Kentucky, and the blinding greed of a naval commander, desperate for treasure.

THE JACKSON LEGEND

New Orleans was a small battle compared to massive European bloodbaths like Waterloo, but after the victory at Baltimore, news of Jackson's victory electrified the Americans, and gave them a cause for cheering after the shame of Washington.

The Jackson legend grew. The night before the battle, the Ursuline nuns gathered in their chapel before the statue of Our Lady of Prompt Succor, and prayed for the Virgin Mary to intercede and protect the city. On January 8, Vicar General William Dubourg held a morning Mass before the statue, and the prioress, Mère Ste. Marie Olivier de Vezin, made a vow to have a Mass of Thanksgiving sung every year if General Jackson delivered a victory. Just as the host was being raised during the communion, a courier arrived proclaiming that the British were defeated.

The general later visited the convent in person and thanked the nuns with these humble words: "By the blessing of heaven, directing the valor of the troops under my command, one of the most brilliant victories in the annals of war was obtained."

These and other legends would propel Andrew Jackson to the White House in 1829.

"The 8th of January," a traditional American fiddle tune, was used by Mountain View, Arkansas, schoolteacher Jimmie Driftwood to write the song "The Battle of New Orleans." The version by Johnny Horton topped the Billboard Hot 100 in 1959 and won the Grammy Award for Song of the Year:

> Well, in eighteen and fourteen we took a little trip,
> Along with Colonel Jackson down the mighty Mississip.
> We took a little bacon and we took a little beans,
> And we caught the bloody British near the town of New Orleans...
>
> Well, they ran through the briars and they ran through the brambles,
> And they ran through the bushes where a rabbit couldn't go.
> They ran so fast the hounds couldn't catch 'em,
> On down the Mississippi to the Gulf of Mexico.
>
> We fired our guns and the British kept a'comin,
> But there wasn't nigh as many as there was a while ago.
> We fired once more and they began to runnin',
> Down the Mississippi to the Gulf of Mexico.

Moral: Don't trifle with the meanest general in American history.

WATERLOO AND WAR WEARINESS

"My heart is broken by the terrible loss I have sustained in my
old friends and companions and my poor soldiers. Believe
me, nothing except a battle lost can be half so melancholy as
a battle won."

— *Wellington, from the field of Waterloo, June 1815*

A METICULOUS SOLDIER, WELLINGTON ALWAYS BELIEVED IN CONSERVING
his forces and avoiding battle unless it was necessary, and unless victory
was certain. That was the secret of his success. In forty-four engagements as
commander, from 1809 to 1815, he never lost a battle, though one or two
he admitted were draws. After receiving the news from New Orleans, he was
devastated. But his sufferings were not over yet.

On March 1, Napoleon escaped from Elba and landed in France, trig-
gering the Hundred Days. Bathurst ordered most of the British regiments in
Canada back to Europe immediately. On June 18, an Anglo–Allied army under
Wellington, and von Blücher met and finally crushed Napoleon's Old Guard at
the Battle of Waterloo.

Vice Admiral Cockburn was given the happy job of transporting the
emperor to his final cage and to serve for a time as his jailer, as governor of
the island of St. Helena, a speck in the South Atlantic, whence Bonaparte
would never return. It is the emperor's ashes that now are entombed in Les
Invalides in Paris.

THE REPUBLIC PRESERVED

In the end, Madison's worst nightmare did not come true. His beloved republic
was preserved, unity more or less cemented, and an empire rivaling Rome now
beckoned across a continent. Yet as Wellington said about Waterloo, "it was

a close run thing." In preliminary peace feelers, Britain forcefully demanded that the American states return to the Empire. And they would have been in a fine position to dictate such terms at the peace table if the Americans had not turned back Prevost at Lake Champlain and Ross at Baltimore.

But the British people were weary of ten years of war and were feeling the heavy burden of war taxes. Their merchants had been shut out of Europe and stung by American privateering. Adam Smith's free trade ideals were spreading,

The Duke of Wellington, 1812, by Francisco de Goya.

and wiser heads doing business with America preferred friendly competition and commerce to further fighting.

The Americans were also glad to get out of the war. Madison later admitted to a friend that the war had never been a necessity. He would not have let the War Hawks convince him to invade Canada if he had known that Napoleon was going to self-destruct.

Now with a broken treasury, burned up settlements along the Niagara frontier, and thousands of wounded to care for, the United States was chastened but still strong, even though the Jeffersonian value system took a beating.

The cost of three years of war was almost $160 million, excluding property damage and squandered economic opportunity. Ninety-three million went to the army and navy, $49 million to veterans' benefits, and $16 million for interest on the war loans. The U.S. national debt rose from $45 million in 1912 to $127 million by 1816. Albert Gallatin borrowed $80 million during the war, but the government got only $34 million in specie value, due to discounts offered to John Jacob Astor and friends. A very expensive little war for what was gained.

AFTER WATERLOO

After Waterloo, where the Iron Duke had lost most of his senior staff, Wellington was seen weeping. He was weary of further fighting. With Napoleon safely in St. Helena, he could afford to be benevolent.

He ruefully admired the Americans and their fighting spirit. They had shown a growing martial competence, killing some of his best officers, including Isaac Brock, and two of his best Peninsula generals, Robert Ross and his sweetheart Kitty's brother, Frank Pakenham.

Wellington knew very well that with his hundreds of thousands of battle-hardened soldiers, he could still take America back, making Madison's nightmare a reality.

Yet in a word to a friend he said that the Americans were probably unconquerable. Leave them alone.

But he would not let them have Canada.

TWIN DESTINIES

THE WAR OF 1812 PROVIDED BOTH THE UNITED STATES AND CANADA with useful national mythologies. And it forged the whole destiny of a continent for two hundred years to come.

EFFECTS ON THE UNITED STATES

Thomas Jefferson put his usual overwrought spin on the business of the past few years:

> I consider the war as 'made on good advice,' that is, for just causes, and its dispensation as providential, inasmuch as it has exercised our patriotism and submission to order, has planted and invigorated among us arts of urgent necessity, has manifested the strong and the weak parts of our republican institutions, and the excellence of a representative democracy compared with the misrule of kings, has rallied the opinions of mankind to the natural rights of expatriation, and of a common property in the ocean, and raised us to that grade in the scale of nations which the bravery and liberality of our citizen soldiers, by land and by sea, the wisdom of our institutions and their observance of justice, entitled us to in the eyes of the world.[1]

Yes, the War of 1812 did indeed shake up the American republic. It did play a crucial role in fixing the direction and identity of an adolescent nation. A young, half-formed people shook off many of its old British ties and grew into adulthood. And they turned an old drinking song, with new inspiring lyrics, into a national anthem.

The war tied up a lot of loose ends from the American Revolution. As the last breath of Jefferson, Madison, and the founding fathers, it made the U.S. feel it had a new standing and respect in the world.

Formerly a loose association of states scattered along the Appalachians, the Americans now looked west toward the setting sun. Beyond the mountains that once hemmed them in stretched a nearly limitless expanse of territory to explore.

They were now free to fulfill their "Manifest Destiny." From the end of the War of 1812 to the beginning of the American Civil War, the country pushed west to the Pacific Ocean — "from sea to shining sea" — defining its borders as they exist today.

By turning west, they also turned away from the temptation to capture or seduce Canada. Their bumbling invasions and cruel torching of the Canadian frontier turned people who should have been friends into wary enemies. They caused a new society to take root on the northern half of the continent, determined to forge its own version of democracy, one that did not include republicanism.

THE AMERICAN MILITARY

> "The primary causes of the humiliating failure of three American campaigns against Canada during the years 1812–14 were clear even to contemporaries."
>
> −C.P. Stacey

After the humiliating display at Washington, seeds were sown in the United States that that 100 years later made the country the most adept military power in the world.

The republican romanticism of the Jeffersonians gave way to a tough new realism. Jefferson's fabled citizen-soldier, the Cincinnatus who left his farm to do remarkable deeds to protect the republic, was no longer a sufficient role model to protect the republic and help it grow.

Cincinnatus was supposed to have no ambition. In fact, the War of 1812 turned the myth into farce. Cincinnatus after Cincinnatus was tried and found ridiculous: Dearborn, Hull, Winder, van Rensselaer, Wilkinson, Lewis,

Winchester, and Hampton, once Revolutionary War heroes, had become Falstaffian with time. Only Harrison made a creditable performance, and he was younger.

The U.S. Army's three campaigns to Canada ended in disaster or stalemate. Any minor victories gained were due to the Gods of War or the penny-pinching and punch-pulling of an inept British commander-in-chief, Sir George Prevost. It was only when charismatic young valiants like Winfield Scott and Andrew Jackson were given free rein in the last year of the war that American regulars were able to stand up to British redcoats, man on man. But by then it was too late. The arrival in Canada of British regiments freed from fighting Napoleon trumped any U.S. advantage in manpower or training.

And yet the Americans could be proud of one main fact. Their three most glorious victories occurred when they turned from playing offence (trying to invade Canada) to playing defence (fighting for their possessions). When they found they had to defend their own turf against the British, they performed magnificently, as citizens as much as soldiers. And they were rewarded for their performance, with land, positions, gold medals, and glory.

The Jeffersonians' dislike of a standing army and permanent navy also evaporated in 1815, as Congress voted a peacetime army of 10,000 men. Madison's new Secretary of War, William H. Crawford, had once begged Albert Gallatin, "For God's sake, endeavor to rid the army of old women and blockheads, at least on the general staff." Crawford soon weeded out most of the amateurs and added a competent quartermaster general to cut rampant corruption. He also created a permanent Corps of Engineers under General Simon Bernard, who had served under Napoleon.

Crawford also tuned the U.S. Military Academy to turn out more proficient soldiers. West Point began to use Winfield Scott's drill and deportment manuals as curriculum guides, and adopted the grey New York militia jersey worn by the regulars at Chippawa as its cadet uniform. The new veterans of the War of 1812 who had ousted the old Revolutionary War generals soon found themselves tested in more frontier battles. They fought the Creek and Seminole Wars, and in 1846 Scott's "lightning war" of conquest against Mexico added a vast new territory to the United States.

Effects on Great Britain

The War of 1812 gives us many chances to play the game of "What if?"

Its splendid little battles often hinged on the loss of a nail, an intercepted letter, a hidden path, a budding love affair, or a confusing order from a drunken general.

But in the larger picture, what if the British had decided to make Madison's nightmare come true? What if they had stuck to their program, captured Baltimore, taken Lake Champlain, and overthrown Jackson at New Orleans?

Would our world be a different place?

But they didn't. Britain had already moved on. With the defeat of Napoleon and the reopening of Europe to trade, Britain no longer had much interest in North American affairs, excepting Canada and its wheat and wood. Impressing sailors disappeared overnight, along with privateering. Trade was now booming between Britain and the continent of Europe, and American exports were less in demand. Only cotton would have growing importance to British mills as the steam engine ushered in the Industrial Revolution.

If you quizzed most Britons today about the War of 1812, some would mention Bonaparte's March on Moscow, or that famous overture by the composer of "The Nutcracker." It is as if the War of 1812 in North America never existed or was a mere footnote to the crusade against Napoleon. And yet it was one of the most important fronts in the whole campaign, and it briefly shook the Empire, handing its generals some of their most glorious victories, and worst defeats. It was a war that many Britons wanted to forget, and did.

Effects on Canada

With the coming of peace to British North America, a new national spirit began to jell among the loyalists, land dealers, army suppliers and even the "late loyalist settlers" who had been abused by their American cousins.

Many Canadians felt cocky about beating back their enemies. In his "Upper Canada Almanack for the Year 1815," John Cameron wrote that the war had been a useful medicine to purge the country of "Yankee" traitors: "The war might be called Madison's Patent–Nostrum. For to our House of Assembly it has been a timely emetic, to our Country, a gently sweating cathartic — one threw up two traitors, the other threw off some, and by the way of appendix, hung up some."

Others naively saw 1812 as a civil war. John Le Couteur of the 104th New Brunswick Regiment of Foot called it "a hot and unnatural war between kindred people." But the chief instigator, Thomas Jefferson, saw the war as a perfectly natural and wonderful thing, a tonic for the republic. Some Canadians would have said the same thing about their own emerging nation.

At first there was no unseemly hero-worshipping on the Canadian side. No official medals for victorious generals like Drummond or de Salaberry, although every town in Quebec seems to have a Rue Salaberry or a Rue Chateauguay. Brockville was named before the war, Drummondville after.

In 1816, some citizens produced a medal in memory of Isaac Brock, "The Hero of Upper Canada," which proclaimed "SUCCESS TO COMMERCE & PEACE TO THE WORLD."

One modest but charming medallion, called "Upper Canada Preserved," was given out "For Merit" by John Strachan's Loyal and Patriotic Society of Upper Canada, as a fundraising vehicle for charity.

Charity was indeed needed. Most farmers and settlers in Upper Canada were having a very hard time picking up the pieces of their shattered lives and were hardly feeling sentimental about their former kinfolk. Militia from Pennsylvania and New York had stolen their forage, butchered their farm animals, burned their houses, barns and mills, abused their wives and daughters, and taken as souvenirs even their most precious lockets and keepsakes.

One traveller between Niagara and Detroit said the whole district was a mass of charred ruins and starving people.

In Lower Canada, the American invaders did not get far across the border, but the Lower Canada Voltigeurs and militia suffered heavy losses in fighting back the attempt to capture Montreal, particularly at Crysler's Farm.

Some estimates say that about 1.5 percent of the total population of

The Upper Canada Preserved medal shows the Canadian view of the conflict.

Upper and Lower Canada died in the War of 1812, more per capita than in the First and Second World Wars.

As for the British military, they had learned hard lessons from the war, and the command now focused on correcting defects in Canadian and Maritime defence. With the Duke of Wellington firmly in charge, sometimes as prime minister, British taxpayers started to pour a fortune into Canadian fortifications from Halifax to Windsor.

From one of his officers, who had talked to James Monroe, Wellington learned that the Americans were bound not to make the same mistakes in the 1815 campaign. They would completely ignore Niagara and the west and do what he thought they would do in the first place, concentrate all their forces against Montreal.

Happily for Canada, the U.S. Treasury was empty, British regulars were now thick on the field in Canada, and the Gods of War were nowhere to be found.

In his 1814 report, Sir James Yeo had suggested building a canal from Kingston to the Ottawa River to bypass the St. Lawrence. Wellington soon put this in motion, sending the Duke of Richmond and then the Earl of Dalhousie to plan and execute this mammoth project. The Rideau Canal is one of the jewels of the Canadian countryside, and a World Heritage site.

Wellington's army also offered land grants to the officers and men of the regiments who had fought in the war. These grants were concentrated around forts and the Rideau Canal, where they provided a strong and loyal militia for years to come. Wellington's staff also developed a body of veterans, the Royal Canadian Rifle Regiment, to provide training and police services, and stationed these grizzled old regulars in forts as far away as Red River.

Future plans called for an Ottawa River-to-Georgian Bay canal, connecting Montreal to the Great Lakes, and the construction of a large fortress commanding the terminus of this northern route. But peace gradually spread over the North American continent. The Americans were distracted westward, and warships were banned on the Great Lakes. The site of this mighty fortress (now called Ottawa) was transferred to Canada, and the old barracks replaced by splendid new parliament buildings.

The British attachment became even stronger, in spite of some revolutionary flare-ups from Canadians who wanted the Yankee version of democracy or their rights as citizens of "Greater Britain."

Even Yankee-loving firebrand William Lyon Mackenzie, who fought in 1837 to have Upper and Lower Canada admitted as states of the union, returned from exile in New York in 1849 with this observation to a Toronto newspaper:

> American democracy as it presented itself in the form of political corruption, crass materialism and human slavery, filled his soul with righteous indignation. He was convinced that the vaunted liberty of the United States was merely a sham; that neither the grandiloquent principles of the Declaration of Independence, nor the unctuous guarantees of the American Constitution assured to the private citizen the same measure of civil and political freedom as was enjoyed by the humblest Canadian subject under the British Constitution.

During the U.S. Civil War, diplomacy and a few boatloads of British regulars prevented federal veterans from marching north after they had defeated the South. And in 1867 the British North Americans founded their own confederation of provinces, under their own constitution, which guaranteed not the "Liberty" of the American and French republics, but the more domestic Canadian virtues of "Peace, Order, and Good Government."

TECUMSEH'S DREAM

In war, it is said that both sides lose. But there was a third side to this war, and the greatest losers in the war were the Native Americans of the south. The battles leading up to Horseshoe Bend dealt them blows from which they never recovered. It broke their spirit and set the stage for the Trail of Tears, Winfield Scott's forcible removal of most members of the tribes of the "Five Civilized Nations" to the west beyond the Mississippi.

Sauk chief Black Hawk wept like a child when he heard the news from Ghent, and he vowed to keep Tecumseh's dream alive. Chief Sausamauee of the Winnebago told Lieutenant-Colonel McDouall at Mackinac that the British had betrayed his people and given them over to the Big Knives, exposing his nation to a lingering death. Indeed, his people, ravaged by conflict and European diseases, would have to move ever westward in advance of the settlers, eventually taking treaty and living on reservations in Minnesota and Nebraska. The border was now a real division, and the Native Americans south of this "medicine line" were not welcome in Canada.

For a time, the northwest Indians could still maintain hunting grounds and bring furs to Astor, as he and the Norwesters gradually extended their monopoly over the Great Lakes fur trade. But without the fiery inspiration of Tecumseh, and with the sure fixing of the frontier line between the United States and Canada, the heart went out of their movement to win a self-governing Indian state in America.

The fur trade changed as well, and the Montrealers, now shut out of Astor's territory by treaty, put all their energy into exploiting the Canadian northwest, through the lands of the Hudson's Bay Company. They fought their own war with the HBC, but the effort exhausted them, and in 1821, they sold out to their longtime rivals.

As for John Jacob Astor, he found the fur trade was going into decline. He got out of the business entirely, bought up half of Manhattan Island, and found new ways to skin his customers.

Only the Iroquois nations were victors among the Native Americans. If the Americans had captured Canada, the Iroquois would have undoubtedly lost their reserve lands in Upper and Lower Canada to settlers and land speculators.

PEACE

The Peace of Ghent and the end of the conflict produced some cathartic relief among those who survived the War of 1812. Indeed, both sides had successfully defended their home turf. They had driven away invading armies and learned how to fight for what they believed in. Now they could settle down to enjoy the fruits of peace — two shared centuries of peace — and for that we must all be thankful.

NOTES

1. Jimmy Driftwood, "The Battle of New Orleans," Video treatments. <*>
2. *The War of 1812: The Movie.* <*>
3. For example, note this Bill introduced in the U.S. House to protect Revolutionary and War of 1812 sites. <*>
4. See John Howison, *Sketches of Upper Canada.* <*>

CHAPTER ONE

1. Jefferson objected to many of Congress's revisions and deletions. During the summer of 1776, he circulated a copy of his original rough draft among his friends. For more on Jefferson's ideologies, see Conor Cruise O'Brien, "Thomas Jefferson: Radical and Racist." <*>
2. When one of his slaves, Jame Hubbard, escaped in September 1805, presumably in pursuit of life, liberty, and happiness, Jefferson had him hunted down and flogged in front of the others as an example.
3. June 20, 1797. John Adams to Uriah Forrest.
4. November 3, 1797. John Adams to John Quincy Adams.
5. George Washington's farewell address. <*>
6. Thomas Jefferson to William Short, January 3, 1793.
7. To justify the Louisiana Purchase, Jefferson even drafted a constitutional amendment authorizing Congress to exchange lands in the west for eastern lands occupied by Indians, so long as they pledged allegiance to the United States. It was never ratified, but future practice ensured that troublesome Native Americans east of the Mississippi would have to be resettled west of the river.

8.   January 16, 1804. John Adams to William Cunningham.

9.   See the Embargo Act of 1807. <*>

10. March 2, 1809. Jefferson to P.S. Dupont de Nemours.

11. In January of 1815, Jefferson was able to keep his creditors at bay for another few years by selling his entire library to the federal government for four dollars a copy, to replace the books lost when the British burned the Capitol in Washington the previous August. Congressman Cyrus King of Massachusetts meanly commented: "It might be inferred, from the character of the man who collected it, and France, where the collection was made, that the library contained irreligious and immoral books, works of the French philosophers, who caused and influenced the volcano of the French Revolution. The bill would put $23,999 into Jefferson's pocket for about 6,000 books, good, bad and indifferent, old, new and worthless, in languages which many cannot read and most ought not."

12. The whole Florida peninsula eventually became a full territory of the U.S. when Andrew Jackson waged the First Seminole War in 1818. Spain formally ceded all of its Florida territory under the Adams–Onís Treaty in 1819. After Waterloo, Joseph Bonaparte moved to the United States, where he lived for twenty years on the proceeds from the jewels of the Spanish crown he had taken away when he left Spain.

13. Here's Hegel, October 13, 1806: "I have seen the Emperor, the soul of the world. It is a marvellous feeling to see such a man, who, concentrated here, on a single point, sitting on his horse, extends himself over the world and dominates it all." And Schopenhauer: "Napoleon is the most beautiful manifestation of human will." And Nietzsche: "Napoleon represents the cult of the individual force, the super-hero of pure willpower."

14. This is the only true depiction of Tecumseh; from a drawing made by a fur trader who knew the Shawnee chief.

15. July 20, 1808. Isaac Brock to his brothers.

16. *Ibid.*

17. April 1812. Calhoun to a friend.

CHAPTER TWO

1. See *www.thehermitage.org/PeopleTOCBody.html*.

2. Five days later, Napoleon Bonaparte led 690,000 men of the Grande Armée across the river Neman towards Moscow.

3. See General Hull's "Proclamation to the People of Canada." <*>

4. Brock's purchased military rank was also an asset held by his brother in London, as Brock had to pledge his entire civil salary as governor to paying back the loan.

5. Tompkins will serve as James Monroe's vice president from 1816 to 1825.

6. One of the Canadian wounded was James Secord, of the 1st Lincoln Militia, whose wife, Laura Secord, will have an important role to play the following summer.

7. In 1828–29, Porter served as Secretary of War in the Cabinet of President John Quincy Adams and was a leading advocate of the removal of Eastern Indians beyond the Mississippi. Winfield Scott eventually carried out the removal.

8. Isaac Hull's "Report on the Battle with HMS *Guerriere*." <*>

CHAPTER THREE

1. Present day Monroe, Michigan.

2. The Society of the Cincinnati, founded in 1783 by Alexander Hamilton, was named after the Roman citizen general who was called upon to leave his farm and beat back invading tribes; he did so and went back to ploughing his fields. The order still has branches in the United States and France. Membership was limited to officers who had served at least three years in the Continental Army or Navy, and was passed down to the eldest son after the death of the original member or father.

3. They were later released unharmed.

4. The Civil War will shoot the U.S. into the stratosphere with a $3 billion debt. The First World War will push it to $25.5 billion.

5. Prevost would hear more from Macomb the following year at Plattsburgh.

6. See: Jacques Viger's "Account of Prevost's 1813 Attack on Sackets Harbor." <*>

7. See: Billy Green's "Account of the Battle of Stoney Creek." <*>

8. In 1852, Perry's brother led a fleet into Tokyo harbour to open American trade with Japan.

9. This was the first time in history that an entire British naval squadron surrendered.

10. Elliott and Perry were each honored with a Congressional Gold Medal. The two were embroiled in a thirty-year-long controversy over their respective conduct and fault in the battle — Perry claimed that Elliott failed to offer timely support; Elliott decried lack of communication and signals.

11. At his death in 1835, Hampton was the wealthiest planter in the United States, owning over 3,000 slaves.

12. In July 1813, de Salaberry learned that "Prevost had sent the British government a dispatch on the events making no mention of his name and congratulating the adjutant general, Edward Baynes, and Major-General Rottenburg, who had taken no part in the action." (*Dictionary of Canadian Biography*.) <*>

13. One of the Americans, a drummer, threw his drum, his canteen, and his musket and bayonet into the Chateauguay River, where they were very well preserved on the clay bottom for almost 200 years. The items, their original paint showing, are now on display at the battlefield museum.

14. See "Charles de Salaberry to his Father, on the Battle of Chateauguay." <*>

15. See the *Dictionary of Canadian Biography* article for more instances of Prevost's treachery. <*>

16. A captain in the Fencibles, Francis Cockburn, was a younger brother of Royal Navy Admiral Cockburn.

17. See "Thomas Ridout to his Father, on the Battle of Crysler's Farm." <*>

18. One of the young militiamen was fifteen-year-old Allan MacNab, later premier of the province and builder of Dundurn Castle.

19. To commemorate these terrible events against civilians, the Niagara communities of Fort Erie, Ontario, and Buffalo, New York, will be holding joint

bonfires in events called Flames Across Niagara. The village of Lewiston will be lighting ten fires along the middle of Centre Street to mark the burning of that community in 1813.

CHAPTER FOUR

1. The Pennsylvanians had refused to cross into Canada.

2. For an account of Scott at Buffalo, see "The Memoirs of Jarvis Hanks." <*>

3. See Amelia Ryerse's "Account of the American Raid on Port Dover." <*>

4. Chippawa is sometimes incorrectly spelled Chippewa. The name of the tribe is spelled "Chippewa."

5. "I'll try, sir" is now the motto of the 5th U.S. Infantry, a succeeding regiment.

6. See "Canadian Accounts from the Battle of Lundy's Lane." <*>

7. Willcocks is buried in Forest Lawn Cemetery, Buffalo, New York.

8. Cochrane will also lead the British force that wins the Battle of Lake Borgne in December 1814 and later is involved in the British defeat at the Battle of New Orleans in January 1815.

9. Cockburn's special instructions were to encourage the emigration of black American slaves and recruit a corps of black Colonial Marines. After the war, he was given the job of conveying Napoleon to Saint Helena, serving for a time as governor of the island and the Emperor's jailor. In his later career, he served as Commander-in-Chief on the North American Station, Napoleon's jailer, Admiral of the Fleet, a Tory MP, and First Sea Lord.

10. See Madison's Federalist Paper #10.<*>

11. A U.S. Army History neatly sums it up: "Brig. Gen. William H. Winder, was indecisive and exhausted from having to organize the defense of the capital without a staff. His subordinates were often uncooperative, while on the day of the battle he received the unwelcome 'help' of Secretary of State James Monroe. Without consulting anyone, Monroe redeployed the army in a most unfortunate manner. Even President Madison wandered onto the field, almost getting himself captured in the process. In the end, the troops could not overcome the disarray of their superiors."

12. *A Colored Man's Reminiscences of James Madison* by Paul Jennings, J.B.R. According to Jennings, Dolley Madison "was a remarkably fine woman. She was beloved by everybody in Washington, white and colored. Whenever soldiers marched by, during the war, she always sent out and invited them in to take wine and refreshments, giving them liberally of the best in the house. Madeira wine was better in those days than now, and more freely drank." For more details, read Dolley Madison, "Letter to Her Sister, on the Arrival of the British." <*>

13. The thick walls of the president's house survived. It's a myth that the modern name White House came from the rebuilt mansion being painted white to cover smoke damage. But the name was used before the war, and it was first whitewashed in 1798, to protect the sandstone from water and frost. For a detailed picture of the events, read George Gleig's "Account of the Burning of Washington." <*>

14. At war's end, Congress met in the Patent Office — now the National Museum of American Art — and debated moving the capital to more defensible territory. One congressman from New York wryly suggested it be moved closer to Wall Street, so government would be closer to its creditors. But caution ruled. As one Southern delegate declared, "If the seat of government is once set on wheels, there is no saying where it will stop." Reconstruction of the Capitol did not begin until 1815, and was not complete until 1830.

15. The song became even more popular during the World Series of Baseball in 1917, when it was sung in honour of the brave armed forces fighting in the Great War. Congress proclaimed it the U.S. National Anthem on March 3, 1931. The huge American flag that waved during the battle now hangs in the Smithsonian's American History Museum.

16. Ross's body was stored in a barrel of 129 gallons of Jamaican rum aboard HMS *Tonnant*. When she was diverted to New Orleans for the forthcoming battle, the body was later shipped on the British ship HMS *Royal Oak* to Halifax, Nova Scotia, where his body was interred on September 29, 1814 in the Old St. Paul Burying Ground.

17. Robinson was a Virginian and related to Upper Canada justice John Beverley Robinson.

18. The twenty-four-pound cannon that killed Downie is today displayed in front of Macdonough Hall at the United States Naval Academy in Annapolis, Maryland.

19. British naval historian William Laird Clowes later regarded Macdonough's victory as "a most notable feat, one which, on the whole, surpassed that of any other captain of either navy in this war."

20. Anne Prevost diary, September 12, 1814.<*>

21. July 5, 1814. Jefferson to John Adams.

CHAPTER FIVE

1.   Thomas Jefferson to P.H. Wendover, 1815.

INDEX

Adams, Abigail, 34

Adams, John, 34–35, 37, 39, 40, 44, 51, 56, 105, 113, 223

Adams, John Quincy, 35, 49, 50, 224, 226

Alexander I, Czar of Russia, 50

Amherstburg, 91, 143

Armistice, Prevost-Dearborn, 230

Armstrong, John, 119, 120, 153–54, 156–58, 160–62, 167, 170, 173–75, 184–87, 206, 208, 210, 217, 236–37

Army of the North, 184

Arnold, Benedict, 32, 154, 227, 231

Astor, John Jacob, 20, 24, 51, 60–64, 85–86, 119, 127, 184, 206, 226, 247, 255

Baby, Lieutenant-Colonel François, 89

Baltimore, Maryland, 14, 17, 22, 25, 41, 44, 60, 73, 75, 128–29, 137, 180, 200–04, 206, 207, 208, 209, 213–16, 224–26, 238–39, 243, 246, 251

Barclay, Captain Robert Heriot, 131, 136, 143–47, 153, 175

Barlow, Joel 34, 48, 110

Barney, Commodore Joshua, 23–24, 129, 201, 206, 210

Bass Islands, 144

Bathurst, Earl of, 82, 135, 160, 175, 196, 217, 222–25, 228–29, 231, 245

Baynes, Lieutenant-Colonel Edward, 133–34, 160, 260

Beaver Dams, Battle of, 15, 125, 137–41

Beckley, John, 35–36

Benedict, Maryland, 208–09, 227

Bermuda, 128, 180, 200, 216

Black Hawk, 254

Black Rock, New York, 80, 99, 142, 173, 185, 197

Bladensburg, Maryland, 23, 207–09, 210, 213

Blockade, British, 21, 37, 44, 49, 96, 107, 127, 182, 200, 226, 230, 239

Blucher, Field Marshal Gebhard, 23, 245

Blue Jacket, 57

Boerstler, Lieutenant-Colonel Charles, 140–41

Bonaparte, Napoleon, 16, 23, 27, 39, 40–44, 48–51, 54, 66, 71, 73, 79, 96, 126, 131, 153, 174, 175, 180, 198, 202, 217, 218, 223, 238, 245, 251, 259

Boyd, Brigadier-General John, 140, 162, 164, 166–67

Brant, John, 102

Brant, Joseph, 82

Brisbane, Major-General Thomas, 218, 221, 228

British Army, 10, 16, 73, 74, 80, 93, 97–98, 101, 102, 114, 121, 124–25, 137–38, 140–41, 149, 153, 156–57, 163, 165–67, 170, 186, 189–94, 198–99, 209, 217, 229, 253, 254

Brock, Major-General Isaac, 10, 15–16, 18, 24, 49, 65–69, 74, 81–82, 84–87, 90, 96–99, 114, 124, 140, 186, 226, 230, 247, 252
    Amherstburg defence, 91
    and Battle of Queenston Heights, 101
    and capture of Detroit, 23, 93–94
    death of, 101–03
    and Tecumseh, 91–92, 94

Brock, Savery, 97

Brown, Brigadier-General Jacob, 133–34, 136, 153, 162, 164, 174, 184–86, 187–95, 197–98, 212

Brownstown Creek, 90

Brush, Captain Henry, 90

Buffalo, New York, 21, 23, 56, 98, 120, 173–74, 185, 187, 190

Burlington, Heights, 125, 137–39, 141, 148, 150, 186–87, 189, 191, 199

Burlington, Vermont, 108, 156, 182

Burr, Aaron, 39, 40, 81, 154

Caledonia, 85, 99
Calhoun, John C., 52, 70, 71, 73
Canadian Fencible Regiment, 74, 157, 159, 164, 166, 260
Canadian Militia, 93, 116, 122, 125, 166, 172, 175, 192, 227
Castlereagh, Viscount, 179, 224–25
Caughnawaga Indians, 141
Chandler, Brigadier-General John, 137–39, 175, 208
Chateauguay River, 154, 156–58, 260
Chateauguay, Battle of, 17, 82, 153–67, 168–69, 184, 217, 231
Chatham, 149
Chauncey, Commodore Isaac, 24, 80, 105, 107–08, 132–34, 142, 161, 181–83, 185–86, 142, 161, 181–83, 185–86, 188–89, 191, 219, 231
    at Fort George, 124, 135, 139, 190,
    on the St. Lawrence, 184
    at York, 119–23
Chicago (*see* Fort Dearborn)
Chippawa, 68–69, 102, 169, 187–92, 195, 250
Chippawa, Battle of, 9, 189, 191
Chippawa Creek, 188, 190, 192
Chippewa Indians, 261
Chippawa, Upper Canada, 68, 102, 169, 187–88, 192–95, 250
Clark, George Rogers, 32, 154
Clay, Brigadier-General Green, 116, 117
Clay, Henry, 14, 48, 52–53, 64, 71, 224–25
Cochrane, Vice Admiral Alexander, 24, 200–01, 203–04, 206–07, 214, 216, 238–39, 240–41, 243, 261
Cockburn, Rear Admiral George, 51, 174, 200–02, 204, 206–07, 210–15, 238, 245, 260–61
Confiance, 219–21
Constitution vs. *Guerriere*, 105–07
Cornwallis, Edward, 29, 32
Covington, Brigadier General Leonard, 162, 166
Craig, Sir James, 55, 67–68, 82, 156
Crawford, William H., 250
Croghan, Major George, 82
Crysler's Farm, Battle of, 161, 165, 167, 168, 252
Cumberland Head, 220

De Rottenburg, Major-General Francis, 186, 218, 221
De Salaberry, Lieutenant-Colonel Charles-Michel d'Irumberry, 9, 15, 82, 109, 155–60, 175, 226–27, 231, 252, 260
De Watteville, Major-General A.L.C., 197
De Watteville Regiment, 160,
Dearborn, Major-General Henry (Granny), 73, 79–81, 94, 96–98, 110, 113, 119–20, 141, 154, 156, 175, 184, 230, 249
    and attack on Montreal, 108
    at Fort George, 123, 137
    at York, 120–23
Dennis, Captain James, 99, 101–02
Detroit, 15, 21, 24, 32, 57, 68, 73, 84, 86, 88–96, 97, 99, 102, 105, 113–14, 116, 140, 142, 148, 153, 171, 187, 198, 230, 252
Dickson, Robert, 61, 85–86
Dickson, Thomas, 85
Dickson, William, 171
Don River, 122
Downie, Captain George, 218–19, 220–22, 227, 229, 263
Drummond, Lieutenant-Colonel William, 134–35, 197
Drummond, Lieutenant-General Sir Gordon, 84, 169, 172, 183, 186, 190, 252
    at Fort Erie, 197–98
    at Fort Niagara, 173
    at Lundy Lane, 191–97
    at Sackets Harbor, 181–82
du Pont de Nemours, Pierre, 42
Ducharme, Captain François Dominique, 140
Dudley, Lieutentant-Colonel William, 117
Duke of Gloucester, 107, 120, 122
Dunlop, Dr. William Tiger, 196

Elliott, Lieutenant Jesse, 145, 260
Elliott, Matthew, 99, 117
Embargo Act of 1807, 46–47, 61–62, 82
Erie, Pennsylvania, 68, 116
Eustis, William, 73, 79, 98, 108, 113, 119

Federalists, 25, 37, 39, 40, 43, 47, 98, 105, 217
Finnis, Captain Robert, 131
FitzGibbon, Lieutenant James (later Captain), 15, 138, 140–41
Forsyth, Captain Benjamin, 121, 124, 163, 230

Fort Covington, New York (*see* French Mills)

Fort Dearborn, 73, 87, 90, 94–95

Fort Detroit, 16, 73, 79, 88–94, 116, 148

Fort Erie, siege of, 174, 189, 197–98, 217

Fort George, Upper Canada, 10, 63, 66, 84, 91, 97, 99–101, 103, 123–25, 133–34, 135, 137, 139, 140–41, 142, 169–70, 172, 185–86, 188–92, 208

Fort Malden, 68, 89, 91, 114–15, 116, 142, 143, 148–49, 151, 236

Fort McHenry, Maryland, 22, 204, 214–16

Fort Meigs, Ohio, 115–18, 142

Fort Miami, Ohio, 117

Fort Michilimackinac; see Michilimackinac

Fort Niagara, New York, 10, 73, 79, 84, 98, 101, 123–24, 137, 170, 173, 186, 191–92, 230

Fort Ontario (*see* Oswego)

Fort Schlosser, New York, 173

Fort Wayne, Indiana Territory, 90, 94

Forty Mile Creek, 139, 170

Foster, Augustus John, 71

France, 11, 12, 16, 19, 21, 22, 25, 29, 32, 33–34, 35, 38–40, 43–44, 46, 49–50, 65–66, 70, 74, 110, 119, 126, 128, 153, 179, 180, 218, 223, 245, 258, 259

Franklin, Benjamin, 29, 31–33, 81, 123

Fraser, Sergeant Alexander, 128, 139

French Mills, New York, 167

Frenchtown, Michigan Territory, 114

Gaines, Brigadier-General Edmund P., 167

Gallatin, Albert, 24, 46, 62–64, 126–27, 179, 206, 224–26, 247, 250

Gambier, Vice Admiral Baron James, 224

Genet, Edmond-Charles, 35

George III, 32, 33, 57, 236

Ghent, Treaty of, 63, 223–32, 238, 243, 254, 255

Glegg, Major J.B., 101

Glengarry Light Infantry (Fencibles), 74, 121, 124–25, 133, 194

Gordon, James, 172, 213–14

Gore, Francis, 67, 69

Goulburn, Henry, 224–25

Grand, Ferdinand, 33

Grand River Indians, 98, 188, 198

Grande Armée, 110, 259

Green, Billy, 137

Green Tigers (*see* 49th Regiment)

Guerriere, 105–06

Halifax, Nova Scotia, 52, 73, 108, 128, 129, 131, 141, 180, 253

Hamilton, Alexander, 35, 37–38, 40, 127, 207, 259

Hampton, Major-General Wade, 154, 155–60, 163, 167–68, 175, 250, 260

Hanks, Lieutenant Porter, 85-86, 93

Harrison, Brigadier-General William Henry, 19, 58–59, 113–15, 138, 142, 144, 147, 153, 175, 185, 204, 235, 250
and Battle of the Thames, 148–51
at siege of Fort Meigs, 116–18

Harvey, Lieutenant-Colonel John, 124, 137–38

Heald, Captain Nathan, 94–95

Hull, Isaac, 105–06, 108

Hull, William, 15–16, 23, 97, 99, 151, 249
and defence of Detroit, 88–90, 93–94
mental state of, 90–91, 93–94

Impressment, 37, 44, 46, 106, 128, 223, 224

Indiana Territory, 56–58

Iroquois Indians (*see* Caughnawaga, Mohawks, Senecas)

Izard, Brigadier-General George (later General), 158–59, 184, 197, 217, 218–19, 221, 228

Jackson, Andrew, 151, 184, 204, 235–37, 239–50, 251, 258

Jay, John, 21, 35, 37–38, 46, 61

Jefferson, Thomas, 12, 19, 20, 25, 27, 30–36, 37–39, 40–44, 46–48, 51–52, 54–55, 58, 60–65, 71, 73, 75, 79, 81, 82, 88, 108, 110, 119, 126–28, 154, 174–75, 204–07, 210, 212, 223, 228, 235–36, 248, 249, 252, 257, 258

Jesup, Major Thomas, 193, 194

Johnson, Richard M., 148, 150–51

Johnson, William, 82, 140

Kent, Duke of, 156, 161

Kentucky, 22, 24, 45, 52–53, 71, 73, 108, 114–15, 117–18, 144, 148, 149–51, 154, 236, 242–43

Kentucky Volunteers, 114–15, 149

Key, Francis Scott, 214–15

King's Regiment (*see* 8th Regiment)
Kingston, 67, 80, 91, 107–08, 119–20, 122, 131, 133, 135, 139, 154, 163, 170, 172, 181, 186, 187, 190, 229–30, 253
Kingston, Upper Canada, 67, 80, 91, 107–08, 119–20, 122, 131, 133, 135, 139, 154, 163, 170, 172, 181, 186–87, 190, 229, 230, 253

Lafayette, Marquis de, 33
Lake Champlain, 15, 18, 47, 55, 79, 80, 93, 154, 156, 169, 180, 184, 217–22, 225–27, 229, 246, 251
Lake Erie, 18, 67, 88, 90–91, 99, 122–23, 149, 174, 187, 199
Lake Erie, Battle of, 13, 15, 80, 113–14, 116, 118, 136, 142–47, 153, 214, 219, 230
Lake Ontario, 16, 67, 73, 80, 88, 97, 107, 113, 120–21, 123, 131, 135, 143, 150, 153, 161, 169, 181
Lawrence, James, 143, 145
Le Couteur, Lieutenant John, 134, 195, 252
Leopard, 46
Lewis, Major-General Morgan, 119, 123, 125, 161, 164–65, 175, 236–37, 249
Lewis, Meriwether, 43, 61
Lewiston, New York, 98, 100–03, 124, 173, 261
Livingston, Robert, 31–32, 42, 119
Long Sault, 164–65, 167
Loyal and Patriotic Society of Upper Canada, 252
Loyalists, 30, 54, 56, 67, 171, 251
Lundy's Lane, 9, 13, 21, 184–99

Macdonell, Lieutenant-Colonel Red George, 230
Macdonough, Commodore Thomas, 155–56, 219–22, 227
Mackinac Island (*see* Michilimackinac Island)
MacNab, Allan, 260
Macomb, Brigadier-General Alexander, 133, 184, 218–22, 228, 260
Madison, Dolley, 19, 22–24, 48, 64, 204–06, 210–11, 262
Madison, President James, 12, 14, 23, 25, 27, 32, 34–35, 37, 47, 48–53, 54–55, 58–64, 70–75, 79, 80–81, 84, 88, 94, 96–97, 108, 110, 113, 118–19, 121, 126–27, 137, 153–54, 179–80, 184, 201, 203–08, 213, 217, 223–24, 226, 235–36, 245, 247, 249–51, 261
Markle, Abraham, 187
Mascotopah (*see* Dickson, Robert)
Maumee River, 113–16
McArthur, Brigadier-General Duncan, 198–99
McClure, Brigadier-General George, 141, 170, 173–74
McDouall, Captain Robert, 254
McKee, Thomas, 117
Menominee Indians, 85
Merritt, William Hamilton, 138–39, 170–72, 193
Michilimackinac, 84–87, 91, 171
Michilimackinac Island, 62, 85
Miller, Colonel James, 194, 196
Mississippi, 41–43, 61–62, 180, 237, 238–44, 254, 257, 259
Mohawk Indians, 10, 16, 82, 102–03, 137–38, 140–41, 156–57, 165–66, 170, 173, 189, 192
Monroe, James, 23, 46, 91, 81, 119, 127, 206, 208–09, 253, 259, 261
Montreal, 16, 30, 51, 54–55, 60–63, 69, 71, 74, 79, 82, 85, 88–89, 96–97, 108, 131, 135, 140–41, 148, 151, 153–54, 156, 158, 160–61, 163–64, 167–68, 172, 180, 201–02, 218, 222, 228–30, 237, 252–53, 255
Moraviantown, Battle of, 149
Morrison, Lieutenant-Colonel Joseph, 163–64, 166–67
Moscow, Russia, 110, 251, 259
Mulcaster, Captain William, 143, 163–64, 166, 181
Murray, Colonel John, 169–72, 229
Myers, Lieutenant-Colonel Christopher, 124

Napoleon (*see* Bonaparte, Napoleon)
National Intelligencer, 213
Necker, Jacques, 33, 174
Nelson, Lord Horatio, 43, 44, 65, 80, 200, 221
New Brunswick Regiment (*see* 104th Regiment)
New England states, 25, 31, 40, 47, 50, 52, 55, 75, 127, 179, 200, 217, 235
New Orleans, Battle of, 9, 10, 15, 22–25, 42, 154, 180, 217, 224, 235–45, 251, 261, 262

New York City, 32, 60, 61, 68, 74, 80–81, 98, 119, 123, 129, 163, 202, 211, 254, 262

New York State, 23, 25, 31, 35, 40–41, 45, 52, 53, 55, 63, 80, 97, 103, 104, 107, 133, 141, 157, 160, 168–71, 185, 187, 189, 206, 217–18, 222, 228, 231, 250, 252, 260

Niagara Frontier, 21, 91, 141, 169, 184, 196, 247

Niagara River, 10, 67, 98–99, 120, 124, 139, 192

Niagara, 145–46, 151

North West Company, 55, 60, 61, 63, 85

Norton, John, 98, 102, 137, 141, 188, 193, 198

Norwesters, 60–63, 255

Odelltown, Lower Canada, 109, 156

Ogdensburg, New York, 111, 163, 230, 231

Ohio River, 30, 38, 57

Ohio Volunteers, 88

Old Ironsides, 12, 105–09, 144

Oswego, New York, 97, 133, 181–84, 188

Pacific Fur Company, 60, 63

Paine, Tom, 34

Pakenham, Sir Edward, 229, 239, 240–43

Perry, Commodore Oliver Hazard, 80, 116, 124, 136, 142, 175, 214

Pike, Brigadier-General Zebulon M., 121, 122

Pinckney, Charles, 39, 42

Plattsburgh, New York, Battle of, 120, 141, 154, 156, 160, 167, 197, 217–19, 220–22, 228–29, 231, 260

Plenderleath, Major Charles, 137–39, 166

Port Dover, Upper Canada, 21, 91, 143, 174, 187, 198, 199, 202

Port Talbot, Upper Canada, 187

Porter, Colonel Moses, 208

Porter, Peter B., 52–53, 97, 103–04, 185, 188–89, 194, 259

Potawatomi Indians, 88

Power, Major-General Manley, 218, 221, 228, 229

Prescott, Upper Canada, 162–64

Presque Isle, Pennsylvania, 116, 142–43, 145

Prevost, Sir George, 19, 24, 68–69, 81–85, 88–89, 92, 96–99, 120, 131, 133–37, 143, 148, 153, 156, 160, 163, 170, 173, 175, 180, 186–87, 197–98, 201, 217–19, 220–22, 227–31, 246, 250, 260

Prince Regent, 107, 110, 120, 122, 132, 151, 181

Procter, Lieutenant-Colonel Henry, 15, 18, 91, 142, 145, 150, 151
    and Battle of Frenchtown, 114–15
    and Battle of the Thames, 148, 149
    and massacre at Fort Meigs, 142–44

Purdy, Colonel Robert, 157–59

Put-in Bay, Ohio, 144–45

Quebec, 11, 43, 48–50, 52, 55, 65, 73, 75, 81–82, 85, 94, 107, 103, 115, 120, 131, 154, 160, 167, 169, 180, 229–30, 252

Queenston Heights, Battle of, 10, 15, 18, 23, 96–105, 113, 121, 140, 185

Queenston, Upper Canada, 98, 125, 140, 169, 190, 192

Randolph, Jane, 30

Red-haired Man (*see* Dickson, Robert)

Riall, Major-General Phineas, 172–73
    at Chippawa, 188–93, 198
    at Lundy's Lane, 185

Richardson, John, 114

Ridout, George, 100

Ripley, Lieutenant-Colonel Eleazar W. (later Brigadier-General),
    at Crysler's Farm, 166, 168
    at Chippawa, 188
    at Lundy's Lane, 191, 194–95

River Raisin, Battle of (*see* also Frenchtown), 113, 114–15, 117, 150

Roberts, Captain Charles, 85–87

Robinson, Major-General Frederick Philipse, 218, 220–21, 228

Rolette, Lieutenant Frederic, 90

Ross, Major-General Robert, 202, 206, 247,

Rottenburg, Baron Francis de, 160, 186, 218, 221, 260

Royal George, 107, 132

Royal Navy, 25, 44–45, 49–50, 54, 63, 73, 119–120, 128–29, 131, 143, 182, 187, 202, 216, 224, 230, 238

Royal Newfoundland Fencibles, 69, 74, 114, 116, 124, 157, 159, 164, 166–67

Royal Scots,
    at Chippawa, 188
    at Fort Niagara, 173

Russia, 19, 23, 48–50, 55, 71, 126, 131

Sackets Harbor, Battle of, 131–36, 228, 230,
Sackets Harbor, New York, 80, 83, 107, 119–121, 141,153, 161, 170, 181, 183, 185, 188,
Sandwich, Upper Canada, 89–90
Saranac River, 219–20, 228
Sauk Indians, 254
Sausamauee, 254
Scott, Lieutenant-Colonel Hercules, 192, 194
Scott, Winfield, 102, 124–25, 153, 164, 175, 185, 187–92, 194–95, 198, 250, 254, 259
Secord, Laura, 15, 40, 226, 259
Seneca Indians, 188
Shawnee Indians, 57, 90, 151, 258
Sheaffe, Major-General Roger Hale, 67–68, 91, 97, 131, 143
    at Queenston Heights, 101–03
    at York, 121–22
Shelby, Governor Isaac, 116, 151, 236
Sherman, Roger, 32
Sioux Indians, 85
Smith, Adam, 246
Smith, Samuel, 209, 215
Smith, William, 228
Smuggling, 47, 185
Smyth, Brigadier General Alexander, 23, 98, 100, 102–03
South West Company, 60, 63
St. Davids, Upper Canada, 140, 192
St. George, Lieutenant-Colonel Thomas, 89, 91
St. Joseph's Island, 62, 85
St. Lawrence River, 9, 60–61, 79, 97, 120, 131, 153–54, 161–63, 167–68, 186, 229–30, 253
St. Petersburg, Russia, 50
St. Regis, New York, 167
Staël, Madame de, 33, 174–75
Stoney Creek, Battle of, 137–39, 141, 208
Strachan, Reverend John, 122–23, 180, 252
Superior, 181–82

Talbot, Thomas, 187
Talleyrand, Marquis de, 40
Tecumseh, 15–16, 23, 56–59, 90–92, 94, 96, 113–14, 142, 149–51, 226, 237, 254, 255, 258
    at capture of Detroit, 92–94
    death of, 150

    at Fort Meigs, 116–18
    Indian confederacy movement, 24
Ten-squát-a-way (Tenskwatawa), 56
Thames, Battle of the, 148–49, 236
Thames River, 153
Thompson, David, 63
Thornton, Colonel William, 209
Tippecanoe, Battle of, 58–59,113, 116
Tompkins, New York Governor Daniel, 97–98, 113
Tonawanda Creek, 173
Towson, Nathaniel, 189–90
Tucker, Lieutenant-Colonel J.G.P., 192
Tweeddale, Marquis of, 189
Twelve Mile Creek, 140–141, 170

U.S. Army, 53, 80, 103, 133, 250
U.S. Army (regulars), 79–80, 85, 88, 94, 97–98, 109, 117, 121, 124, 133–34, 140, 157, 169, 189–92, 218, 236–37, 240, 250
U.S. Militia, 10, 22, 32, 71, 86, 91, 98–99, 101–03, 109, 116–17, 123, 134, 191, 175, 185, 191, 194, 198, 207, 211, 215–16, 235, 242, 252
U.S. Navy, 48, 73, 107
United States, 30, 32, 36, 39–40, 42–44, 52, 55, 58, 61, 72–75, 89, 96, 110, 127–28, 151, 201, 226–27, 248–50,
Upper Canada, 67, 69, 74, 98, 113, 120, 141, 151, 170, 172, 175, 187, 226, 230, 252

Van Horne, Major Thomas, 90–91
Van Rensselaer, General Stephen, 98, 249
    and attack on Queenston, 23, 98–100, 102–03
Van Rensselaer, Lieutenant-Colonel Solomon, 97–98
Vincennes, Indiana Territory, 116
Vincent, Brigadier-General John, 67, 91, 124–25, 133, 137–39, 142, 170, 175, 200
Vrooman's Point, 99

War Hawks, 14, 48, 51–52, 60, 70–71, 73, 75, 88, 96, 180, 184, 247
Washington, D.C., 17–18, 21, 23, 40, 43, 47, 62–64, 90, 98, 147, 160, 174, 180, 200–11, 213–14, 243, 249
Washington, George, 24–25, 32, 35–36, 38, 81,113, 119, 208, 210–11

Wellesley, Arthur (*see* Wellington, Duke of)

Wellington, Duke of, 9, 22–23, 48, 84, 129, 153, 175, 180, 186, 198, 202, 218, 224–25, 227–29, 238–39, 243, 245–47, 253

Western Battery (York), 121

Wilkinson, Major-General James, 154, 157–58, 161–68, 175, 236–37, 249

Willcocks, Joseph, 141, 169–74, 187, 197

Williams, Captain John, 99, 101–02

Winchester, James, 114–15, 250

Winder, Brigadier-General William, 137–39, 208–10, 249

Winnebago Indians, 85, 254

Wool, Major John E., 101–02, 133

Wright, Philemon, 55

Wyandot Indians, 88, 90, 114

Yeo, Commodore Sir James Lucas, 19, 80, 84, 120, 131, 130–37, 139, 163, 181–82, 190, 218–19, 227, 229, 231, 253

York, Upper Canada, 21, 67, 69, 85, 90–91, 96, 119–23, 143, 172, 175, 186, 190, 192, 202, 207

York Volunteers, 97

10th Royal Veteran Battalion, 69, 74, 85

100th Regiment (British), 74, 133, 189,
    at Fort Niagara, 173

103rd Regiment (British), 74, 189

104th Regiment (New Brunswick Regiment), 74, 120, 133–34, 141, 195, 252

41st Regiment (British), 89, 91, 114, 116, 173, 197

49th Regiment (Green Tigers) (British), 65, 67, 74, 91, 99, 124–25, 137, 140, 163–64, 166

85th Regiment, 209, 241

8th Regiment (King's), 74, 133, 137, 170
    at Chippawa, 193
    at Fort Erie, 124–25
    at York, 121

89th Regiment, 163, 166